2
CRACKED
WHEAT

Coteau Books

Edited by Gary Hyland, Barbara Sapergia, and
Geoffrey Ursell.

Cover and text illustrations by Bill Johnson.
Cover and book design by Shelley Sopher.
Typeset by Val Jakubowski.
Printed and bound in Canada.

The publisher gratefully acknowledges the financial
assistance of the Saskatchewan Arts Board, the Canada
Council, and the Department of Communications.

Canadian Cataloguing in Publication Data

Main entry under title:

200% cracked wheat

ISBN 1-55050-038-4

1. Canadian literature (English) - Prairie Provinces.*
2. Canadian literature (English) - Canada, Northern.*
3. Canadian wit and humor (English) - Prairie Provinces.*
4. Canadian wit and humor (English) - Canada, Northern.*
5. Canadian literature (English) - 20th century.*
I. Hyland, Gary, 1940-   II. Sapergia, Barbara, 1943-
III. Ursell, Geoffrey.

PS8255.P7T96 1992   C810.8'09712   C92-098131-3
PR9198.2.P72T96 1992

COTEAU BOOKS
401 - 2206 Dewdney Avenue
Regina, Saskatchewan
Canada S4R 1H3

Contents

viii   Preface: A Totally Fictitious
        Dramatic Interlude

I   *When I Grow Up, I Wanna Be a Station Wagon*

2   Baby Seeds   *Wendy Agnew*
3   The Frog and the Spider   *Wendy Agnew*
4   God's Tonsils   *Wendy Agnew*
5   Move Over Lassie   *Bonnie Ryan-Fisher*
7   A Sliver of Liver   *Lois Simmie*
8   How to Tell What You're Eating
     Lois Simmie
9   The Plan   *Patricia Coulter*
13   Beasties   *S. A. Crooks*
15   Mr. Kroski   *Gary Hyland*
16   Allowances   *Aritha van Herk*
19   Unsuitable Suits   *R. P. MacIntyre*
20   The First Moon of Moose Jaw
     Gary Hyland
22   Tricks   *Robert Currie*
23   Exam Time   *Rob Bryanton*
25   How Teachers Relax   *Bruce Rice*
26   Fools   *Ron Welgan*
27   Cavitation   *Edwin Hall*

II   *If You're This Close, We Should Be in Bed*

30   Getting Pregnant   *Lorna Crozier*
31   *Heista Kopp* in Love   *Armin Wiebe*
45   Down the Ice-road   *Katherine Piper*
46   Janvier Makes a Picnic   *Joe Welsh*
47   how there in the plaid light . . . .
     Dennis Cooley
49   The First Time   *Judith Krause*
50   Call Me   *Judy McCrosky*

54	Tickle	*Mick Mallon*
55	Man of My Dreams	*Brenda Baker*
58	Go Like Sixty	*Gertrude Story*

III *Honk If You're Horny!*

66	Sex in a Pan	*Roberta Nichol*
67	Test Your Hardness, Moh?	*Edwin Hall*
68	News Flash from the Fashion Magazines *Lorna Crozier*	
70	How to Talk to Boys	*Kim Morrissey*
78	Turning Forty	*Roberta Nichol*
80	Bill's Sperm Count	*Fred Stenson*
96	Contraceptives	*Melanie Misanchuk*
97	Crucial Quiz	*Sharon MacFarlane*
99	Undergarment Trilogy	*Myrna Garanis*
100	Indecent Exposure	*Marlis Wesseler*

IV *Caution: I'm Looking at the Crops*

106	A City Woman's Guide to a Country Man's Farm	*Karen Morrison*
110	George said about the speaker *Marilyn Cay*	
111	Where in the Hell Are We?	*Mick Burrs*
113	Living in Small Towns: A Guide for Decentralized Civil Servants *Lorianna Gundersdatter*	
115	Getting Even	*Carol Anderson*
118	Dad and the Maz	*Brett Balon*
127	Knowing the Game	*Lorne Kulak*
128	Old Jack	*Lorne Kulak*
129	The Mask	*Lorne Kulak*
130	Mother and the Bull	*Audrey Johannesson*
134	In the Beer-Parlour	*Robert Currie*
136	The Winter of '49	*Doug Nelson*
146	Outside/In	*Paul Wilson*
147	Argument Over Snow	*Andy Suknaski*

V   *Give Me Space Pizza Face!*

152   Local News   *Gary Hyland*

153   Getting the Hang of Privatization
          Hazel Jardine

155   dog's revenge   *Ed Upward*

157   We Wait Around the Gallows
          Neal Davis Anderson

162   help   *Lois Simmie*

163   Blood and Guts   *Birk Sproxton*

164   Bomb Threats   *Birk Sproxton*

165   The Hockey Fan As Professor
          Birk Sproxton

166   After the Revolution   *William Robertson*

168   Angel with a Full House   *Sheldon Oberman*

VI   *If I Stop, Wake Me Up*

180   God Lives in Saskatchewan   *Cathy Jewison*

181   Lobsters of the Air   *Eugene Stickland*

186   Cruising   *Bruce Finlayson*

187   Standing By   *Judith Krause*

188   Sunday Afternoon At De Keulse Pot
          Glen Sorestad

190   canoe trips   *Marilyn Cay*

191   the well-equipped carman   *Jim McLean*

192   I'm sure the C.P.R. invented Spring
          Jim McLean

194   the interpreter   *Jim McLean*

195   The Day We Burned the Iglu Down
          Erik Watt

197   Wailing   *Brian Lewis*

198   Going to Cuba   *Lee Gowan*

224   to the man who didn't wave . . . .
          Marilyn Cay

225   visits   *Steven Smith*

VII   *Support Wild Life—Throw a Party*

228	The Rabbit *Rod MacIntyre*
230	Celestial Orinthology *Bruce Rice*
232	There Ain't Nobody Here But Us Chickens *Geoffrey Ursell*
250	Gulls *Rick Hillis*
252	Fubar *Richard Stevenson*
253	The Land of the Lizards *Judith Wright*
254	The Prince and the Pelicans *David Carpenter*
257	The Politics of Moose *Tony Penikett*
261	The Bannister Boys *Jon Whyte*
263	Norris *Jake MacDonald*
278	Why Is It That We Do Not See Tyrannosaurus Rex Any More? *Christian Stuhr*

VIII   *Till Debt Do Us Part*

280	On the Seventh Day *Lorna Crozier*
282	Joni Went to Market *Don Kerr*
288	A Cotton Flannelette Man *Barbara Sapergia*
299	Another Life to Live at the Edge of the Young and Restless Days of Our Lives *Rhona McAdam*
301	Black and White *Myrna Garanis*
302	Incident in Thunder Bay *Glen Sorestad*
303	After Twenty-Five Years, Still Working It Out *Byrna Barclay*
304	the post-macho man after mating *Kim Morrissey*
305	His Bowels *Donna Caruso*

IX   *Baby, I'm Bored*

312	the meaning of my time with you *Rhona McAdam*

313 Sweetie Pie   *Lois Simmie*

324 Gator   *Shelley A. Leedahl*

327 City in Pain   *Bev Ross*

329 Star Bright   *Pat Krause*

X ***This Vehicle Stops for all Metaphors***

348 My Muse is a Tramp   *Barbara Mulgahy*

349 A Girl's Story   *David Arnason*

357 Karamazov   *Ravi Jeyachandran*

358 Writing Romances   *Hazel Jardine*

360 Insomniacs' Guide to TV Movies
        Mick Burrs

362 How I Became a Poet   *Robert Currie*

380 Gag!   *Dave Margoshes*

402 My Muse is Tired of Literature
        Barbara Mulcahy

404 Acknowledgements

The Preface:
A Totally Fictitious Dramatic Interlude

Barbara and Gary, one female, the other male and middle-aged (as men reckon time, i.e., post-baseball bat and hockey stick and pre-cane and walker), lounge around a tastefully-furnished (i.e. post-Depression) Saskatoon living-room. Geoffrey—tall, or relatively tall, long of hair and slightly ragged of beard, enters carrying mugs of strong tea. Concealing his disgust at the offering of yet more tea, Gary unobtrusively presses a button on a small sleek machine on the end table. As all available spaces are littered with books and thick manuscripts, Geoff balances a mug of tea on Gary's balding (as men reckon hair loss) head.

GARY: (*Hiding tea behind couch*) I don't see why we need one.

BARBARA: (*Holds up large book, pronounces—with emphasis on each word*) It . . . is . . . traditional.

GARY: Since when?

BARBARA: (*Drops large book on Gary's foot*) Since *100% Cracked Wheat*—circa 1983.

GARY: Oh, oh, a tome on the toe. That smarts.

BARBARA: You say tome on the toe, I say book on the foot.

GARY: Let's call the whole thing off.

GEOFFREY: The point is, Barbara and I want it—two-to-one vote, democracy, etc. How soon can you have a draft?

GARY: I'm tied up worse than a first ministers' meeting. Just super busy.

BARBARA: (*Approaching Gary with an even larger book*) We're all busy, but *our* busyness is so much more—how can I phrase it diplomatically—so much more *busy* than your busyness. Don't you agree?

GARY: (*Covering toes*) I see what you mean.

GEOFFREY: Of course, we'll give you a few ideas to start you off. (*Gary whips out a notebook and pencil*) I think it would be useful to look at some of the differences between this new book and *100% Cracked Wheat*. For instance, how in the intervening years, more writers have been writing comic pieces, giving us more to choose from.

GARY: I had to get heavy-duty shocks on my car to carry the manuscripts.

BARBARA: Let's not forget geographic scope. *100%* featured only writers from Saskatchewan. *200% Cracked Wheat* includes writers from Alberta, Saskatchewan, Manitoba, the Yukon, and the Northwest Territories.

GARY: Good point. We picked up Fred Stenson, Aritha van Herk, Dave Arnason, Rhona McAdam, Cathy Jewison, Armin Wiebe, Birk Sproxton, Karen Morrison, Tony Penikett (a funny premier, for Pete's sake), and Sheldon Oberman, and Barbara Mulcahy, and—

GEOFFREY: The greater reach shouldn't hurt sales, either, but I don't think we should mention that.

GARY: (*Nodding*) Too crass, no class.

BARBARA: I wish we'd had even more submissions from outside Saskatchewan. I noticed in-province submissions exceeded the others by almost eight to one.

GARY: We've probably had more to laugh about in the last few years—drought, deficits, and Devine government. Adversity fosters humour, they say.

BARBARA: I think we should avoid philosophizing about humour.

GEOFFREY: Maybe we had more submissions from Saskatchewan because we're better known here and the success of *100% Cracked Wheat* is better known. After all, how many people outside the province know *100% Cracked Wheat* sold over ten thousand copies, went through three printings, and is still going strong?

GARY: Damn few, I suppose.

BARBARA: We've done some analysis you could probably use. Over sixty per cent of the contributors to *200% Cracked Wheat* weren't in the first book.

GEOFFREY: There are also more writers in this one—seventy-seven, compared to forty-nine in the first one.

GARY: Should I go onto the old business of how difficult it was to select from so many good pieces?

GEOFFREY: No, it's a cliché.

BARBARA: But it's true.

GEOFFREY: But it always sounds trite. Nor should we discuss our criteria. I mean, could you articulate them?

GARY: Well . . .

GEOFFREY: You see?

BARBARA: I wonder, does anyone actually read introductions?

GARY: I do. Irving Layton has some fine ones. Quite profound and stimulating in a belligerent sort of way.

BARBARA: Let's not be too profound, unless we can do it in a silly way. I mean, all that stuff about comedy as medicine. Discovering the pain and beauty inside the laughter.

GARY: Huh?

GEOFFREY: Don't forget all those absolutely true clichés—humour as serious business and hard work; humour as wonderful therapy and good exercise; or as disguised aggression; and of course, humour has to offend someone, humour—

GARY: You said no philosophizing. Anyway, we've got it all here—serious business, first-rate writing, something to offend every faction of the politically correct, side-splitting therapeutic stuff, and apparently frothy material with a hidden knife blade.

BARBARA: You could talk about regional identity. Many of the pieces reflect place in one way or another.

GARY: Except that many of them reflect no place in particular, except the human condition.

BARBARA: Isn't that what I've been saying?

GEOFFREY: So just write a nice clean introduction without any of that claptrap.

GARY: How long do I have to write this thing?

GEOFFREY: Shelley needs it tomorrow morning. I realize we're putting you on the spot, but as you know, Barbara and I are off to Banff today. (*Rising*) In fact, we have to do a few last-minute things downtown.

BARBARA: (*Rising*) We won't be more than an hour or two.

GEOFFREY: (*As they leave*) You're being a real sport, Gary. We'll bring you back a trinket from Banff. See you shortly.

GARY: (*Laughs*) I'll do the best I can. See you later.

BARBARA & GEOFFREY: See you. (*They leave*)

GARY: (*Goes to small sleek machine, pushes button, waits a moment. We hear the first four lines of* The Preface, *he removes cassette, goes to phone, dials, waits.*) Hello, Shelley? It's Hyland. About the preface for 200%—(*Listens*) No, no don't worry. I think I've got it. (*Looking at cassette*) Can one of your people transcribe a sound cassette? (*Listens*) Great. You'll have it by courier tomorrow. (*Listens*) No problem, no. You see, Geoff and Barb have left for Banff and they've delegated the whole thing to me. No, they don't need to see it at all. (*Snickers*) At least not until the book comes out.

WENDY AGNEW

Baby Seeds

Yes Lillian
When it's dark
that's when the
baby seeds fly
around—that's
why when you're
afraid you should
cover your head
in bed because
the baby seeds can
smell your fear and
where do they go
when they smell it?
—Thru your eyeballs
but we're too young to
have babies so they
just make you crazy
and you flunk math.

WENDY AGNEW

The Frog and the Spider

OK Lillian Pillian Rillian
listen to this

    Mothers and fathers have
    a deal with the devil
When they decide not to become
nuns but to get married
and have sex because *that's*
where we get babies
The devil makes the man
swallow a frog on
their wedding night
that's why your father
burps sometimes and
the woman has to swallow
a spider. Then the
frog and the spider crawl out
and look at them when they're
sleeping and see what they
look like and then the frog
spits on some dust and
the spider weaves the
dust and spit into a baby that
looks sorta like your mom and dad and
then the spider drags it back inside
the mommie's tummy.
That's how you got born
pretty neat eh
Now the baby grows inside
there cause your
mom catches flies and
eats them at night
when nobody can see

her OK that's why
mothers are always swatting
flies in the daytime—to
build up a supply so
the spider keeps weaving
the baby and when the
baby comes out there's
this cord on it from
the web and when they
cut the cord the
poor spider dies

When I have a
baby I'm going to keep
eating lots of flies after the
baby's born so my spider can
still live

WENDY AGNEW

God's Tonsils

When a baby's born there's
a cord stuck onto its
thing and the cord goes
thru the mother and is
hooked onto God's
tonsil and when
the baby comes out and
the cord breaks
then God's tonsil
goes awigglin and
awigglin and
he makes a song
and that's the wind.

4

BONNIE RYAN-FISHER

Move Over Lassie

There's a story told by a comedian about the old Lassie series. "What I hated," he says, "is how smart that show made adults look." Then he goes on to relate a typical tale. Dad is sitting on the porch smoking his pipe, when Lassie appears. She is panting from a run. She runs up to the feet of her master and barks excitedly.

"Woof, woof," she says. "Grruff, woof!"

Dad leaps to his feet with a shout. "What?" he cries. "The sheriff is tied up and the jail is on fire?"

"Woof!" Lassie answers with relief. Presumably she means "You got it!"

Masters of smart dogs like Lassie are especially smart themselves, it seems.

There's another group of smart adults out there that hasn't been properly recognized. They're called parents. Specifically, parents of toddlers.

The neighbour's child rang my doorbell the other day. His mom was standing apologetically behind him when I opened the door and she explained quickly that she hadn't been able to catch him in time to stop him. I assured her there was no harm done, and now that they had my attention, I stopped to chat for awhile. The little boy pulled eagerly at my pant leg.

"Yamma tunga porp," he said, pulling at his shirt and waving one chubby hand. "Thith ging glova nik." He smiled with satisfaction and stooped to pick up a toy truck at his feet and wave it in my direction.

I smiled uncertainly and nodded, raising my eyes to his mother who was beaming proudly.

"He says that I took him shopping for new

clothes," she explained patiently, "and he got that new truck at the store too."

How about that! "It's a very nice truck," I assured the child who was gazing affectionately at his mother now. "Thank goodness," I'm sure he was thinking. "If Mom weren't around this dumb lady would have missed the whole story."

I'm wondering just when we dumb parents of infants are transformed into such clever parents of toddlers. So far, I can't make out a single phrase in my son's language. He repeats things carefully and watches me with an encouraging gleam in his eye but I'm just a slow learner, I guess. The spark of hope I'm able to hold onto is that my own mother hasn't lost the ability. She can translate her grandson's words with ease.

"Nyang gop," he said with conviction one morning while she was visiting.

"Listen to that," Grandma exclaimed with awe. "He said Mommy."

Oh well, I shouldn't be surprised really. My mom has never lost the knack of understanding what I had to say, no matter how poorly it was expressed. "But Mom," I said one day seeking to express a profound opinion on a serious matter, "well, you know, umm, gee, it's just, uh."

She nodded thoughtfully. "You know," she said finally, "I've always thought that myself."

LOIS SIMMIE

A Sliver of Liver

Just a sliver of liver they want me to eat,
It's good for my blood, they all say;
They want me to eat just the tiniest sliver
Of yukky old slimy old slithery liver
I'm saying no thanks, not today.

No, I'll pass for tonight but tomorrow I might
Simply *beg* for a sliver of liver;
"Give me liver!" I'll cry. "I'll have liver or die!
Oh *please* cook me a sliver of liver!"
One piece might not do, I'll need two or a few,
I'll want tons of the wobbly stuff;
Of that quivery shivery livery pile
There may not be nearly enough.

Just a sliver, you say? No thanks, not today.
Tomorrow, I really can't say . . .
But today I would sooner eat slivers of glass,
Eat the tail of a skunk washed down with gas,
Slivers of sidewalks and slivers of swings,
Slivers and slivers of any old thing
Than a sliver of slimy old quivery shivery
Livery liver today.

LOIS SIMMIE

How to Tell What You're Eating

Apples snap between your teeth
With juicy, squirty zest;
Bananas loll upon your tongue
All soggy and depressed.

A salad made of spinach leaves
Will make your tongue feel furry;
If fire glows from teeth to toes
You're likely eating curry.

If your face all shrivels up
The berry's goose. Or boysen.
And if your toes are pointing up
You'll know you've eaten poison.

PATRICIA COULTER

The Plan

Cripes, I think the little buggers have done it! They've finally worn me down. I am so mad at myself that I let this happen. It isn't working out at all like I'd planned.

The plan, you see, is that even though I am the mother of these three little stress factors, I wasn't going to let myself love them. Once you let yourself open for love, you only get hurt. I was not going to let that happen. The only reason I had the little twerps was so I'd have plenty of help in my old age.

Somewhere along the way they developed a plan of their own. How they communicated this to each other, I don't know. I never came upon them talking about it amongst themselves or ever caught them giving each other a signal or anything like that, but right from the start, they definitely had a plan. And I bet as scientists find out more and more about babies in the womb, that someday they're going to discover that these little guys start working on the plan then.

My little monsters looked the way all babies usually do when they're born, you know, all red and wrinkled up like an old man! I think everybody looks at a newborn and thinks, "My God! Is this what a baby looks like! Yuck!" Of course the parents never say this out loud. They are far too embarrassed to say anything. And almost always, the nurses say "Oh, she's just beautiful" or "He looks just like you!" I think they teach nurses to say those things at nursing school. Along with all those other outright lies they teach them to say like, "This won't hurt a bit" and "In no time at all, you'll be up and moving around." I'm sure in nursing classes all over the country, they have to recite these lines fifty time a day. And their teachers make them do it with that phoney, half-baked smile they all use, too!

They say these things because if you are a first-time parent, you just plain don't know any better. You might be thinking, "This can't be any relation to me!" but when the nurse puts that tiny, shrivelled-up looking thing in your arms and says "There, isn't he darling?" you are too stunned to argue. Besides, if they say the baby looks just like you, you feel so sorry for the thing, you take it home anyway.

Soon after, my little stress factors started turning into these darn cute little tykes. Almost anyone would fall for those big innocent eyes, those gurgling smiles, but not me. I was tough. I knew they were on to something. They might try and win some people over with those cute ways, but not me. Like peeking out at you from under a blanket and smiling when they see you come into the room—oh, they're out to get your heart, all right.

Even when they were at the ankle-biting stage, they didn't turn into whirling dervishes like some of them do. Once, when a friend of mine was over for coffee one afternoon her little rug rat did his tornado imitation, leaping off the coffee table, pulling the knobs off the TV and stomping cookies into the carpet. She commented on how well behaved my little rug rat was who was happily colouring at the coffee table.

"Look at that!" she said. "Why, she's not even eating the crayons! And she's colouring on the paper. Not on the coffee table like my little genius does!"

She turned to me, "How do you do it? How come she's so good?"

I tried to tell her that it was all part of a plan.

"A plan?" she said, looking at me strangely.

10

"Yes, a plan," I confided, "you know, to make me love them. Of course, it's not going to work on me but they're giving it their best shot."

She looked at me in a puzzled way. "What do you mean, make you love them? Isn't that the whole idea of being a parent?"

"Oh no!" I stated. "You must remember the only reason you are a parent is so you have someone to care for you in your old age." She looked confused, but I went on, "You can't let yourself be open for love. It is such a powerful emotion. Why, you let yourself open for love, you'll only get hurt. Then they have that power over you, you see. So it's a plan they have. They start on the plan, right away, right after they're born or maybe they even start before."

But I trailed off for she was grabbing her kid who'd been busy yanking on the drapes and she got him cleared out of the house—pronto.

Later that night, she phoned to tell me about a microwave cooking class that was held in the evenings when my husband could babysit and if he couldn't babysit, why she offered to come over herself. I realized that she'd been thinking about what I'd said and thought I needed to get out more. I never told anyone about the plan again.

If they'd been whiny kids with stringy hair and runny noses and high-pitched nasal voices that grate on your nerves like chalk screeching on a blackboard, it would have been easier to intensely dislike them. But for some fluky reason, they turned out to be not bad looking and reasonably intelligent. Their teachers said they had lots of friends and did well at school. It was all quite disgusting.

The first little monster we had turned out to be a likable kid. She was fairly well-behaved, too. I don't know where we went wrong. But when the second one seemed to be turning out like the first, I really got

11

worried. What was I doing wrong? After the third one, I knew we had to quit. Besides, they were starting to outnumber us!

And now, after all these years, I see they've worn me down. Finally after years of tough resistance, I've given in. For the first time in years, I had the chance to go away by myself for a few weeks with a friend on a holiday. Everyone said how much I'd miss the kids, but secretly all I could think about was how it was going to be so neat to be away by myself. Everybody thinks a little bit better when they can put some distance on a relationship, right?

And now here I am away by myself and all I can do is think of the little monsters. I went shopping twice and both times all I came back with was stuff I'd bought for them. Oh, so-and-so would love this and this is perfect for the middle one and on it went. Man, it made me sick when I saw what I'd done.

And when we went out touring, I just thought of how the little twerps would like to see these places too.

And now here I am enjoying all this peace and quiet and all I can think about is how much I miss them. My eyes are doing their old waterworks routine and the whole time I'm thinking about how much I want to go back home. Somewhere along the way something has gone wrong!

S. A. CROOKS

Beasties

When bogles an' beasties
are lyin' in wait,
they aye seem tae ken
jist whaur a puir wee lad or lass
is gaun tae be.

They hing aroon'
at the bottom o' the yaird
whaur the dust bins are,
an' when their mither says,
"Jist tak thae fish heids
doon tae the midden, Tom.
They're stinkin' oot the hoose,"
the puir wee chiel has got tae go,
whether he wants tae or no'.

He canna say tae his maw,
"There's beasties oot there, Mammy.
They'll get me when Ah lift the lid
tae pit the fish heids in.
They're there inside,
waitin' tae pu' me in an' a'!"

Oh no! He's got tae go
if he's a man at a',
even if he's jist eleeven or twelve.

But he rins,
an' wi' a fine brave clatter o'dust bin lid,
as though it were King Robert's shield,
he chucks the rubbish in
an' turnin'
bolts for the back door.

He staun's quite nonchalantly
on the step
an' draws his braith
in ane or twa deep puffs
that still the jumpin'
in his breist.

An' in he goes,
whistlin' jauntily
a fine auld tune
like "Scots Wha Ha'e,"
imaginin' he's led the clansmen
intae battle
an' slain the ancient enemy.

GARY HYLAND

Mr. Kroski

Mr. Kroski had this funny way he used to speak
(He was the old guy on Maple Street
who had the spud and corn patches by the creek)

Spoke of "muzdos" and "naffer-gonna-gatter"
run-together flurries roared in a blur
and tumbled at us down his pipe stem's quaver

"Muzdo-zumzin-bout-dat-der-cafe-in-fence-all-bent
Lomber-gattin-hard-ta-get Got-troublez-nuff-to-no-
    can-count
Yewz-boyz-go-zum-udder-where Go-and-make-
    zumwherez-an-axzadent"

We swiped his corn whenever it was politic
"Yewz-boyz-ban-rusalin-diz-corn?" he'd yell across
    the creek
"No sir, Mr. Kroski." "Goot-coz-I-sprayed-her-all-wiz-
    arzanic."

Allowances

What you weren't. Allowed.

:to go uptown at noon. Either to the store, the post office, the café, someone's house. All potential trouble. Candy and chips in the store, loitering in the post office, the basement in someone else's house, the jukebox in the café, cigarettes everywhere, not to mention make-up and sex. All potential trouble. You were supposed/expected to stay in school, play on the swings, in the gym, read a book, do homework. Between the desks an illusory safety, the classroom aisles had just as many initiations and bloodlettings as the streets uptown. At noon you trembled with energy, needing to turn Del Shannon up loud in the café, drink Coke, suck cigarettes from each other's fingers. You read it as strangely tame now. But the miracle of danger rotates from its source, not itself. As dangerous for you to sneak uptown as for a kid now to rob a bank.

:to play ball after school. Base/ball diamonds were suspect, between the catcher's mitt and the pitcher's mound anything could flash past/get loose/be taken. After school the teachers dribbled home, what did they care what game you played. Basket/ball winter's game, the court echoed with repeats, the stage in the gym had curtains that closed. And there were tumbling mats, beautifully stacked to soften floors, the space under the stage a dark warren of chairs. Foot/ball required taking the bus or a car somewhere else, and that was for boys, the girls only along for the ride/cheerleaders/providers of liniment. Curling bonspiels just used rocks instead of balls, and they went on all night, later and later as the

16

winners won. Ball /games were time bombs.

    :to ride in a car with anyone other than an adult older than thirty. Which may explain why you were forbidden to play ball/or your being forbidden to play ball may explain why you were not allowed to ride in cars with anyone other than an adult older than thirty. Or drive yourself. Which is what incited you to make up for this loss, your white Porsche a double driving: flaunting and denial, although it would take some genuine contortions to do anything in those snug bucket seats. Besides, you are older and your knees do not bend so easily as they might have then. (Still, you hiked up your skirts to show them, your knees. They were damn good knees.) But cars were sites for potential danger: where you were killed, or where you got knocked up, or where you got drunk: transportable sites of sin and transgression with doors that could lock, engines, heaters, back seats.

    :to go do dances. A multiple grief of denyings. You wanted to dance: you still love dancing, you are and will always be a passionate dancer. Danced to the radio as far back as you can remember, danced when you should have been pretending not to, danced while you were reading, read while you were dancing. But dances were not dangerous for dancing: they were dangerous because they were in the Elks Hall and because people went to them in cars with back seats and in the middle of the dances went outside for a drink, and bang, you were knocked up. You were not allowed to go to dances because it was a sure thing that you would be instantly knocked up. Who would do the knocking and whether you would permit yourself to be a knockee was irrelevant. Going to dances had only one outcome. Can you refuse to dance? can you fall in love dancing? can you dance your way out of love? You went to a dance in the Elks

17

Hall in Edberg only a few years ago and you were surprised at how staid it decanted itself, how careful, how cautiously polite, when you had been led to expect such wild revelry/such drunken staggerings/such furtive gropings of instant hands and bodies in the long grass beside the building, all of your fiction etched to a never readable page. Saved from your own story.

:to smoke, drink, or screw (in any guise under any circumstances); swear too (although that could always be done under your breath). You deliberately tried them all. Not screwing, nobody you wanted to do it with badly enough, figured it was smart to wait until you hit the big city and found somebody with experience, a likely potential for improvement, a trained professional. The furtive gropings of Edberg boys were dangerously innocent. Boyfriends came from Heisler or New Norway; if you were really lucky, Camrose or Bashaw. Seduction from a distance, the unknown stranger, not the cow-licked grin sitting across from you since grade two, no way to make romantic those gangly arms, those bitten fingernails.

:to fail. This was the only easy interdiction. You couldn't have failed if your life depended on it, school was too easy and you had figured out the mechanics/rituals of giving the right answers to assignments/tests/questions so early you could have composed them all (assignments/tests/questions). Just never let on you knew more than the teachers did: it pissed them truly off, these smart-ass immigrant kids reading more than they were supposed to know how to read.

Unsuitable Suits

Not only is everyone getting ready for Christmas, but for the great vacation as well. Five days to departure. You'd think they were going to the moon. Maybe they are.

Mom has bought herself a new bathing suit. She even showed it to me, on. Personally I think there should be more to it in the way of cloth. The top comes down kind of low. I mean, for a mother, because she jogs and everything, she's got legs that come all the way up to her waist. There's not enough cloth there either. And she's as white as a snowbank, of which there's plenty outside.

"Mom, aren't you embarrassed?"

"About what?"

"About showing all that skin."

"No." She says. Very cool.

I mean really, normally she wears sweaters that come up to her earlobes and skirts that scrape the floor. I never knew she had so much skin.

"Guys are going to whistle at you, Mom."

"No, they won't. Your father will be with me." She's got a point there.

"They'll probably laugh then."

"They can whistle or laugh whatever they like," she says.

"You'll burn," I say.

"No I won't. I got this." And she pulls these plastic bottles of suntan lotion out of a drugstore bag. There's about five of them, with different numbers on them. "Sunscreens," she says.

"You wouldn't need them if you had more cloth on your bathing suit," I say.

19

All she does is laugh. Very funny.

Dad's bought a new bathing suit too. He's got the opposite problem. His doesn't show enough skin. Where he found it I don't know, but it looks like one of those things you see in old photographs. The trunks come down to his knees with a matching top—that's got sleeves. If you throw in a scarf, he could be dressed for a football game in Regina, in October.

"Very flashy, Dad," I say.

"Don't you like it?"

"I think you should trade with Mom."

GARY HYLAND

The First Moon of Moose Jaw

We stash our clothes in Scrawny's car
and go bare-ballin down by the dam
me, Scrawny, Zip and Magoo
After, we dress in the back seat
Magoo, as usual, still in the creek
and the sun meltin the upholstery
A few horn blasts and he waddles up
sloshes over Zip and starts dryin
hunched-up like a pregnant walrus
Zip takes exception to being drowned
and they start shovin back and forth

Before long Zip pins Magoo's head
and somehow pushes the poor bugger
so his rump's jammed outa the window
till the bulgin flesh spills out
and sizzles on the hot chrome trim
Magoo screams and squirms first-rate
but Zip's got him pretzeled real snug
Scrawny he never misses a good chance
so he starts the Dodge and we light out
with a windowful of Magoo's pink cheeks
bouncin like a coupala baby pigs

Right away I see where we're headed
cause there's a mess of Holy Rollers
havin a prayer orgy down the road
There musta been maybe three hundred
fryin in their shiny Sunday outfits
around some thumper on an oil-drum stage
Then we roars up like Judgement Day
and Scrawny leans out and hollers
Behold, brothers, the face of Lucifer
He cuts through the field to give em
a close-up wide-angle view so to speak
then floors her and we dust outa there
horn ablastin and Magoo ascreamin
and us three roarin like all royal hell

ROBERT CURRIE

Tricks

So the town cop put a scare in Yarrow
That's all Doesn't mean a thing
In the ol days on Hallowe'en
we used to have some *real* fun

There was this bachelor
lived just north of Magpie
name of Bill Tackaberry
He'd built himself a shack on skids
Well one year me and Luke
we took both teams down there after dark
We waited till we was damn sure
then crept up close and listened
Bill was sawin logs all right
so we wired the door shut
hitched up the teams
dragged his whole house
clear into the middle of the slough
water up to his knees I'll bet
He couldn't do a thing cept yell
and he was mighty good at that
him being an auctioneer and all
Still it was broad daylight
before anybody let him out
Never did find out who to blame

Hell woman Yarrow's okay
That cop'll never charge him
for tippin over a backhouse
no matter what happened to Fulton
Besides Fulton shoulda known
not to take a dump on Hallowe'en

ROB BRYANTON

Exam Time

Now I've done it, I'm really in a jam
We write tomorrow morning, haven't even started
    studying for the big exam
I'll get some Old Dutch ripple chips, some dill
    pickle dip and some ice cold Gatorade
I'll get my stereo cookin' loud to help me concentrate

Cause it's exam time
Stay up and cram time
Do all you can time
To get yourself a passin' grade

Some people like stayin' up late—crammin' the night
    before
Some people get up way before breakfast and cram
    till they walk out the door
Some people actually study one hour a night for
    three weeks before and that's all
My only hope now is it's multiple choice or maybe
    even true or false

Cause it's exam time
Stay up and cram time
Do all you can time
To get yourself a passin' grade

Some people's studyin' consists of makin' these tiny
  little notes
To hide in their shoes or the lid of their Bic pen or
  the pocket of their coat
Some people wait for sneakin' peeks when no teachers
  are around
Some people stay up prayin'—that the whole school
  might burn down

Cause it's exam time
Stay up and cram time
Do all you can time
To get yourself a passin' grade

Some people prefer it solitary—never quit till the
  whole thing's done
Some people throw study parties—they sure have a
  lot of fun
Some people memorize textbooks till they can reel
  off every line
Some people do nothing—and get a hundred per
  cent every time.

BRUCE RICE

How Teachers Relax

From over the river Castlegar teachers come to our
house, safe from the eyes of the tip-toeing school
board. Mother bakes through the day, helped out by
Ivy, who cooked for Vincent Massey once—now she
only wants to escape from the meatless, no-spice
kitchen of the man she married.

Studebakers and Mercs straddle our driveway
like that's where the drivers passed out. Our house
fills with teachers—Socreds and Reds, all sporting
crewcuts flattened on top as if they'd been run
through the sawmill at varying lengths. They talk too
loud, too much, and the air gets worldly, smoke
billowing. Pipes for the men, cigarettes for the ladies.
And when I sneak out to pee on the lawn, I see all our
windows glowing like the furnace in Trail.

Joyce, the grade two teacher, whips up a batch of
Purple Passion. She clears the table of gin, vodka,
grape juice, soda and wine, as the VP cries *Waste,
whotta waste*! then my father gets out the 78s and puts
on Paul Robeson's transatlantic concert; the Reds
break into "The Internationale," "Mademoiselle
d'Armetières," "I've Got Sixpence," and "White Cliffs
of Dover," then everyone shouts and stomps their
feet until Bill gets out his trombone and starts a
parade that files out the front door and disappears
into the void: "Saints Come Marching In" down
through the cherry orchard, John Philip Souza up
through the barn and into the kitchen. They roll
back the rug, dance to one Glen Miller tune after
another as the mountain of cast-off shoes spreads like
Vesuvius. It creeps toward our sleeping dog whose
shaggy belly sags under the weight of all those

nanaimo bars.

I wake up early. Mother is still in the kitchen serving coffee and strangled eggs. Nothing to do so us kids go to the lane where the cars are. We find two feet jutting out of a window, tie them to the door handle, bang on the hood and take off. *Judas priest!* screams the voice, as father's bony forehead lashes the ceiling light.

RON WELGAN

Fools

Impatient youth pushed through the crowd
"I do not yield to fools," he vowed.
His neighbour said, "I always do."
and stepped aside and waved him through.

EDWIN HALL

Cavitation

Now listen, son,
I've told you before that
schist is not a nice word.
I don't care if those podzols
at the university speak that way,
you're not going to,
at least not as long as
I'm paying the bills around here.
And I'll thank you
to keep your varves to yourself,
young man.
When I was your age
I showed a little respect for my elders,
not like the kids today,
not like those creeps and gullies
you hang around with,
those moholes you call friends.
If you want my opinion
it's all because of those smelly foreigners
they hire for professors,
like that weirdo Chernozemic
and his buddy Solonetzic.
I heard they been excommunicated
for preaching isostasy.
I wouldn't doubt it,
them and their commie ideas about pluvial love.

They're nothing but
a couple of homoclines
and don't try to tell me they're not.
I know all about the sort of thing
they encourage up there—
chalcedony in the washrooms,
pumice under the elms,
and shameless flocculation.
And wipe that smirk off your face,
mister man.
If you want to get clastic and
show off your fumaroles,
you'd better do it someplace else.
And don't interrupt me when I'm . . .
What's that?
What did you call me?
A drumlin?
A washed-out moraine?
Why you young scarp, that does it!
You haul your butte out of here
before I lose my lustre and
belt you in the dripstones.
Bloody kids,
think they know everything.
I'm warning you,
if you slam that door . . .

LORNA CROZIER

Getting Pregnant

You can't get pregnant
if it's your first time.

You can't get pregnant
if you do it standing up,
if you don't French kiss,
if you pretend
you won't let him
but just can't stop.

You can't get pregnant
if you go to the bathroom
right after,
if you ride a horse
bareback, if you jump
up and down on one leg,
if you lie in the snow
till your bum feels numb,
if you do it in the shower,
if you eat garlic,
if you wear a girdle,
if you hold your breath,
if it's only your second time.

You can't get pregnant
if he keeps his socks on,
if he's captain of the football team,
if he says he loves you,
if he comes quickly,
if you don't come at all,
if it's only your third time.

You can't get pregnant
if he tells you
you won't.

ARMIN WIEBE

Heista Kopp in Love

The year they built the TV tower I was *heista kopp* in
love with Shaftich Shreeda's daughter, Fleeda. I was
only almost sixteen and Fleeda was almost sixteen,
too, and I had been in love with her all the way since
we were only almost fourteen when she looked at me
in her little pocket mirror from where she was sitting
in the next row in school and I just went *heista kopp* in
love. And now we were both almost sixteen and
everything should have fit together real nice, only
when you are almost sixteen the whole world seems
to get in the way of things that you want because when
you are only almost sixteen you don't have a driver's
licence. That's where the puzzle doesn't fit. That's
how come the weeds grow in the garden.

I mean, me and Fleeda were going pretty good.
Like I walked with her home from choir practice
three times, and one Sunday after dinner when I
knew that her brothers weren't at home I went to visit
her and we went for a walk down to the big ditch that
cuts us off from the States. The new TV tower was
there on the States side and we talked about how
scary it would be to have to climb all the way to the top
to screw in a new light bulb and we talked about some
of the funny things people said when they were first
building the tower. Like some said you wouldn't even
have to buy a TV because the tower was so close that
all you would need would be rabbit ears with a white
cloth hanging over it and you would be able to see the
picture. Others said that they were going to put a big
ball at the top of the tower with a helicopter, and
some said no, they would put big mirrors on the top
because with TV you had to have mirrors because of

31

the picture. And so some right away said that if you wanted to watch the TV you would just need to line a mirror up with the tower and you would be able to see it.

Fleeda and me laughered ourselves over these stories and I was feeling pretty good and was sneaking my hand close to Fleeda's so that I could maybe hold it a little bit because when you are *heista kopp* in love you should hold hands with a girl. But when my finger touched her hand just a little bit she said she would have to go back home because her mom and dad were going to visit some cousins and she wanted to go with. So we walked back to her place and I didn't try to take her hand but I was still feeling okay and I was thinking that I would come back the next Sunday in the evening because it is maybe easier to do such things in the evening. But when I did the next Sunday, Fleeda was not home and then after I found out that she had gone to the Neche show with some *shluhdenz* from Altbergthal and I mean I was *fee-maesich* mad over that, but what can you do when you are only almost sixteen?

Then the next Sunday in Sunday School, Shtemm Gaufel Friesen had the nerve to say that girls mature faster than boys and the girls all sat there with their noses just a little bit higher and I thought, that's just what we need for girls to hear and they will all be going out with grandfathers like that *shluhdenz* from Altbergthal who is seventeen or eighteen or nineteen even. Something must be wrong with such old *fortzes* that they can't pick up girls their own age. Mature faster! Shtemm Gaufel must think that girls are like grain or something that he talks about maturing faster. It's just something else against you when you are only almost sixteen. Why can't the world do nothing right and let people hang around with their own age?

Well, even when you are *heista kopp* in love and floating in a sea of heartbreak your Muttachi still makes you stand up in the morning and go to weed beets by Yut Yut Leeven's place. And on the beetfield I make the time seem not so long by pointing my eyes all the time to Shtramel Stoezs's long legs that are sticking out from her blue jeans that are cut off quite high from the knee and are getting burned in nice and brown from the sun, and it seems like if I let myself I could fall into love with her quite easy, even if she is sixteen already. But come to me baby I'm a one-woman man. Still it's nice to have Shtramel weeding in front of me in the next row and if I don't look at Shtramel I can look at her sister Shups, who is fourteen only and her legs are shorter but they are so nice and smooth and have more curve than Shtramel's and if I was a cradle robber I could let myself fall into love with her, too. But I say to myself that I'm only practicing looking for Fleeda, and that even if the Stoezs girls have nice legs, for sure they couldn't be so nice as Fleeda's even if I have only seen Fleeda's up to her knees when she has a dress on in church. A man needs a woman his own age and that is Fleeda Shreeda. But the Stoezs girls are nice to have on a beetfield.

So anyways on Sundays after dinner Hova Jake usually picks me up. Hova Jake is only almost sixteen, too, but he has this grandfather that's ninety years old and can't drive his own car any more, so Hova Jake drives it for him and they come to pick me up and we go looking at the crops, me in the back seat and Hova behind the steer and the grandfather sitting on the woman's side looking out the window and knacking sunflower seeds or sucking on his cigarette holder. And it sure is exciting riding around in the back seat with Hova Jake singing while he drives because the old Plymouth doesn't even have a

33

radio and the old grandfather is singing his own song in Flat German or Russian and qwauleming smoke from his cigarette. It is a terrible thrill to ride around like that but it is better than staying home and playing catch with yourself.

Then one Sunday Hova Jake comes on Sunday evening to pick me up and his grandfather isn't with and Hova says, "C'mon Yasch, let's take some girls along." My heart starts to clapper real fast and I think maybe I should go to the beckhouse but I creep in the car and as we drive along I ask Hova, "Well, which girls do you want to take with?" and he says, "Let's see if Fleeda Shreeda is at home." And my heart clappering speeds up so much I think it will bounce right through my ribs but I say, "Well for sure." I start to wonder right away whose she will be if she comes along and I wish I had smeared on some of Futtachi's green Rawleigh shaving lotion after I did the chores, but it's too late now because I can see Shaftich Shreeda's place already. And I am hoping that Fleeda is at home and I am hoping that Fleeda isn't at home and I am terribly scared that if she is at home she will say no and I am terribly scared that she will say yes to Hova Jake and I am scared too that she will say yes to me. And I wonder if Hova Jake is scared, too, but I sure can't say what he feels because he is humming "Just as I am without one plea" and I wish there was a radio in the car because listening is easier than talking.

"Are you going to talk?" Hova asks when he slows down by Shaftich Shreeda's driveway, and before I know what I'm saying my mouth says, "Sure, okay" and then my heart clappers a hundred miles an hour. Then there is Fleeda sitting on the porch steps playing with a cat and she has her hair in rollers and she is wearing short pants with no shoes. Hova honks his horn. Fleeda looks at us but she doesn't stand up.

And I wonder me a little how come she would have her hair in curlers on a Sunday evening. "Hello Fleeda," I say, almost steady. "Want to . . . "

"Joe isn't home," she calls. "He went to Mouse Lake." Joe is her brother and I don't even like him so what the *dukkat* is she talking about him for? I am quiet for a minute, then I say, "Want to go for a ride?" Fleeda looks at us, then she looks to the barn. She stands up, starts to walk to the car, the cat in her arms, but she is wiggling her whole body just a little as she walks and for an eyeblink it almost seems like her legs are a bit lumpy and bowlegged and for sure far whiter than the Stoezs sisters' but that's only for an eyeblink and then she is perfect again, even with rollers in her hair, and I wish she would put the cat down so I could see everything when she walks and she is all the time looking to the barn like she is watching out for something. Then Hova Jake sticks his head past me and says, "Want to go for a ride?" Fleeda tilts her head sideways a bit and she looks us on with her eyes almost closed. She chews her gum a bit.

"Can't," she says.

"How come not?" I ask.

"Grounded."

"How come?" Hova says.

"Came home too late last night."

"Fleeda, get back in the house!"

Fleeda jerks around like a bee bit her and she runs in the house. We turn and see Shaftich Shreeda walking from the barn with two pails of milk but even then his overalls are wiggling back and forth like when a dog is wagging his tail. But it is easy to see that Shreeda isn't shaftich today. Hova starts to drive away and he says "Shit" under his breath but I am thinking in my head that maybe it's not so bad because if Fleeda is grounded she can't go with that shluhdenz from Altbergthal neither and I am thinking that it

35

would have been maybe a good time to go visiting on foot and I could have sat on the step with Fleeda and played with the cat. But it's too late for that now and I am wondering if Fleeda is grounded for a long time. And I am wondering so much to myself that I don't notice that Hova has held the car still again.

"Get in the back." Hova is opening the door for Shtramel Stoezs. Her sister Shups is there, too, and I know that Jake wants me to get in the back with her. Well, it's not like I'm scared of Shups or nothing like that because we weed beets together. It's just that I'm a one-woman man and what will Fleeda think about this and for an eyeblink I think maybe she wouldn't give a damn, but I wipe that away real fast. I open the door for Shups and she slides in the back seat and I slide in after her and everybody is talking real easy and I am thinking that maybe riding with Shups in the back seat will be good practice so I know what to do when I get my driver's licence and I take Shaftich Shreeda's daughter Fleeda along.

The time goes quite quickly. We have so many things to talk about because we weed beets on the same field and the smell from the clover fields is nice and I can smell some perfume from Shups even if she is sitting almost on the other side of the car. It gets a little darker and we are driving slowly through a lot of field roads because we can't go to town without a driver's licence. Shtramel just has her learner's even if she is already sixteen. Hova Jake sings lots of songs because the car doesn't have a radio. Soon we are driving through some trees and there are no farmers for some miles around and it is getting a little bit darker and I see that Shtramel is slipping herself closer to Hova Jake and I look at Shups and she smiles at me. The moon is coming up and I move a little bit closer to Shups and then Hova is driving along the road beside the ditch that cuts us off from the States.

36

He holds still there for a while and we can see the lights on the TV tower blinking on and off. I think about the talk I had with Fleeda about it and I look at Shups and she has slipped a little bit closer to me. I carefully reach out my hand to hers and I wish my hand wasn't so wet and I wish I had some shaving lotion on because it seems like I can smell the barn a little bit but Shups is holding my hand and then I only smell her perfume and I almost forget about Fleeda Shreeda there in the moonshine in the car where we can see the TV lights blinking off and on. In the front seat Hova Jake is sitting real close to Shtramel but he doesn't do much neither. They just talk and laugh a lot and then all of a sudden Shtramel says that it's time to go home. We drive home slowly and I hold Shup's hand all the way and think this is sure good practice.

Next day on the beetfield Shups and Shtramel are real friendly, only not so friendly that the Leeven boys have anything to tease me with. Most of the time I can be quiet and look at the sisters' legs and think about Fleeda Shreeda. Then in the evening when it is almost dark and all the chores are finished I go walking down the road to Fleeda's place, just dreaming that maybe she will be walking alone, too. It would be nice to walk to the boundary ditch and stand there in the dark while the TV tower lights blink on and off and I forget that before I can get all the way to Fleeda's place I have to go past Shtramel and Shups's place, and really I am walking in my head more than on the road when all of a sudden I hear somebody say, "Who's that bum?" and I turn to look and there are Shtramel and Shups standing by their driveway. "Hallelujah, I'm a bum," I say. They laugh and come walk beside me.

We walk along the road to the States, past Fleeda's place, and I try to look at the window in the house that I think is Fleeda's without letting the girls notice it. When we are past about a quarter mile we see somebody walking toward us and soon I can see that it is Fleeda, alone. In my head I am swearing at the Stoezs girls and why did they have to come with tonight when here would have been my big chance, but I mean, two's company and three's a crowd. What can I do now except try not to let my eyes fall out while the girls stop to talk to Fleeda. Fleeda wants to know if they are walking their dog. Shtramel laughs and says "Yes" and Fleeda wants to know where they found such a mutt. Then Fleeda says she better go home and tells the Stoezs girls not to fight over who will play with the dog. We all laugh again and I am sure glad that it's night-time because for sure my face must be real red.

So I walk farther with Shtramel and Shups when all of a sudden Shtramel says, "Oh, I have to ask Fleeda something," and she turns and runs back and I am left with Shups and we walk alone a little while and don't say anything, but it feels real nice because it is warm and there is a little bit of wind, just enough to blow the mosquitoes away. The TV tower is blinking off and on and there is a slice of moon in the sky. I ask Shups if she ever went all the way to the tower and she says no and I can feel she has moved a little closer to me, so I tell her about the time me and Hingst Heinrichs went across the boundary all the way to the tower and there was a guy working there, just sitting in the little shack under the tower, watching a TV that was built right into a workbench and there were lots of knobs and things. We talked with him a little bit and he said we should watch out for the border patrol and we thought it was pretty funny how the States people are always so full of police stuff and everything, but we didn't stay long because he was finished his shift and he wanted to go home to Pembina where

38

he lived. And while I am telling Shups all this, she is listening quietly and her hand touches mine, sometimes accidentally on purpose, and after she has done this three times I catch it in mine and we walk along the boundary ditch.

We stop walking when we're even with the tower and I almost say, "Let's go all the way to the tower," but I think well maybe it's too late already and Shups is only fourteen and besides I should maybe save going to the tower for sometime when I'm with Fleeda. I mean, this walking around with Shups is just practice I figure.

"Let's sit down a little bit," I say and we do. I let the tower blink five times, then I put my arm around her and she leans her head on my shoulder and we watch the tower blink, talk about the beetfield and things that happened in school last year, and she laughs when I say a joke and she smells like clover and earth and Camay soap and I am trying to gribble out if I should kiss her or not. I mean how is a guy to know exactly how to do it, like the Danny Orlis books for sure don't say how and the Sunday School leaflets talked about fondling breasts one time, but they sure didn't say how to get from here to there and then Shups says she'll have to go home now. So I say, "Okay, but maybe next time we can go earlier so we would have time to go all the way to the tower," and Shups just giggles and says, "Maybe the border patrol will get us." I walk with my arm around her waist and it feels good and I forget to take my arm back when we walk past Fleeda Shreeda's place, but lucky nobody is looking.

When we stop by her driveway we don't want to say goodnight yet and I figure I should get all the practice I can so I whisper, "Shups," and she turns to me and I quickly lean over and give her a kiss on the lips. She doesn't slap me or nothing like they do on

39

TV. She just stands there, then I say "Goodnight" and Shups runs to her house.

So I feel pretty good when I walk home, thinking I got lots of good practice. I turn around a few times, looking at the tower blinking behind me, and I think next time we'll go all the way to the tower. Then I stop dead in my tracks. I am thinking that I would go next time with Shups to the tower when I should be thinking I would go next time with Fleeda. I get a funny feeling that maybe Fleeda, now that she has gone riding around in cars with all those grandfathers from Puggefeld and Prachadarp, she maybe won't want to do stuff like go walking to the tower. I mean on Sunday when me and Hova Jake tried to pick her up it was like she was talking down her nose at us. And when she said she was grounded, I don't know, she sure didn't seem like the same girl that went for a walk with me that time on a Sunday afternoon.

I have to help Futtachi get a few loads of hay the next day so I don't see Shups and Shtramel on the beetfield, and they finish the field that day so I don't see the girls till Sunday after church when the Stoezs girls and Fleeda are standing on the church steps and Shups and Shtramel have on brand new white high heels and Fleeda is wearing brown open toes with a flat heel and it seems like the real Fleeda doesn't match up the Fleeda that I have in my head and I get all mixed up inside. Shups sees me and gives me a wink and I think, "Well, okay Fleeda if you want to go with grandfathers from those other darps well it's your own funeral." Then Fleeda holds her head a certain way and she is laughing about something and I fall *heista kopp* in love with her all over again.

The whole afternoon I lie on my bed listening to country songs on my red plastic radio and I'm dreaming about Fleeda Shreeda and thinking I should have

40

won that red convertible by the Morris Stampede and how it would be driving Fleeda around all over the country with a red convertible and all the farmers with their half-tons would be jealous. I wonder if she is still grounded yet and I fall asleep and dream that I am parked with Fleeda in the red convertible under the TV tower with the red lights blinking, only the red convertible has bucket seats and I think I can't have Fleeda sitting on the gear shift with her white dress and then Shups Stoezs climbs in between us and it doesn't bother her to sit on the gear shift. Then Fortz Funk from Puggefeld honks his horn on that old half-ton truck he has and Fleeda climbs out of the red convertible in her white dress and she doesn't even open the door, she just climbs over the side and creeps into Fortz Funk's truck and I see she gets some grease on her white dress and Muttachi calls me to come and eat faspa.

Hova Jake comes to pick me up again in the evening. His grandfather isn't along and Hova says he isn't feeling so good anymore, but he doesn't seem to worry himself over it. Hova doesn't even ask where we will go. He just drives straight to Stoezs's place to pick up the girls. From the way the girls are ready, it seems like Hova must have phoned them up to say he was coming. Well, Shups doesn't wait for it to get dark to slide closer to me on the seat. Hova drives on the field roads for a while, Shtramel sitting close to him and Shups close to me, and we sing some songs because there is no radio and we laugh a lot and by the time Hova stops the car by the big ditch and the tower is blinking there a half-mile over the border, I am holding Shups's hand in my wet palm and her leg inside her stretchy slacks is pressed against mine. Hova puts his arm around Shtramel and rubs his cheek against hers and Shups is leaning against me and I am a little nervous. So I whisper in her ear, "Let's go to the tower," and she says in my ear, "Okay." We crawl out of the car and Hova and Shtramel don't even notice when we leave.

The sunset is beautiful and we walk down into the ditch through the pepper bushes that grow there and up the other side and we are in the States. There is a strip of grass, then an alfalfa field with stacks of bales all over the field and then alfalfa smell mixes with Shups's perfume as we walk together holding hands. We look at the tower with two lights blinking and two lights on steady all the time and the light second from the top is burned out. The tower gets higher and higher as we come closer and we can see the white sections and the red sections even if it is starting to get dark. Then Shups trips on a clump of dirt and I reach for her with both arms so that she doesn't fall down and she is pressed against me and I feel her breasts through my shirt and her blouse. My heart pounds real fast and I hold her like that till she says, "We're not by the tower yet," so we walk closer with our arms around each other till we have to lean our heads back to see the top.

Shups slips away from me and runs to the bottom of the tower and it's not quite dark yet and I follow her and we can see the ladder that goes up the tower that they use to put new light bulbs in. And there is a sign that I can still read in the dark: DANGER DO NOT CLIMB. I look straight up the tower and from so close I can't even see the top lights blinking. The wind is shaking the tower just a little and I step closer to Shups and reach for her to give her a kiss and she wriggles away. "Catch me if you want to kiss me!" she yells and starts to climb the ladder.

"Hey, what are you doing? You're not supposed to climb up there."

"C'mon. Catch me and give me a kiss."

Shups is already ten rungs up the ladder. Well,

shit, I figure, if she can climb up I can too. So I climb after her, looking all the time at the seat of her pants, thinking that that is maybe the only place I can kiss because there is hardly any room on the ladder. She climbs higher and higher quite fast and I follow, never looking down but I can't get closer to her. She is climbing as fast as I can, not slowing down at all, and the wind shakes the tower a little. I look down for the first time and it seems like I am just as high as a hydro pole already and Shups is ten rungs still higher. The sun going under is covered with clouds and it's getting pretty dark and when I look up again I can hardly see Shups above me. I climb higher even though now I feel like I need to piss, but I have to climb just as high as she does so I call, "How high are you going to go?" She answers, "To the first light or the second!"

I look past her to where the first light is blinking and it sure seems like a *hartsoft* long way yet. I climb up five more rungs and I can't see Shups anymore, it's too dark, and then I can't see the ground, just dark. All I can see is the red blinking light and some yardlights back in Canada and one car going along a road. I keep climbing. My arms are starting to get tired and the tower seems to shake each time I climb another rung and when I call to Shups again she doesn't say nothing and I get scared and think that maybe she fell off only I think if she fell off she would have screamed but maybe she was so scared that she couldn't even scream. So I call for her again and still she doesn't say nothing so I keep climbing and climbing and climbing and it is getting so dark I can hardly see my hands holding on the ladder in front of me and I'm feeling along the cold iron for each rung. I call for Shups again and listen and all I can hear is the wind and the wind seems terribly strong.

"Five steps more," I say to myself. And I pull

myself up one, then two, three, then four and there is something just darker than dark and something lighter and I reach up and touch rubber and it is Shups's runner.

Shups giggles. "Boy, you are sure slow. I thought you'd want a kiss more than that."

I laugh a little and say, "I thought you were going up till the first light."

"Naw, who wants to kiss with a red light on!"

"So do I get my kiss now?"

"Okay, if you want to kiss my foot."

"Climb all the way up here just to kiss a foot? No way. I want more than that."

"Well then, you'll have to wait till we get down."

"Okay." I start down one rung.

"Yasch, wait."

"Okay, what?" Shups's shoes come down past my nose and I have to lean back a little to let her legs down between me and the ladder, then the seat of her pants is in front of my face and she says, "Yasch, hug me just a little bit." So I do it the best way I can, my head leaning into the seat of her pants and my arms around her legs and the ladder and I hold on as tight as I can and it feels good and starts to feel warm. "That's good, Yasch. Now I can climb down." Then I know that she is scared, too.

So we talk all the way down and it seems to take forever and when we stop to rest I put my hand on her leg or on her ankle that's bare between her shoe and her pantleg until she says, "Okay, now I can go again."

Some clouds move away from the half moon and when I look down I can see the tin roof of the little shack beside the tower, and it doesn't seem so terribly high any more and we climb down faster. But when our feet touch the ground our knees just bend like rubber and we fall down on the ground. I hear Shups's breathing beside me.

44

I raise myself up on my elbow and look at her lying there in the moonlight. Her eyes blink and they look wet. Shups sits up.

"You didn't kiss me yet," she says.

"I was just waiting for you to stop panting." I reach for her and I kiss her on the lips and squeeze her body to mine and she kisses me back and I don't think about it being practice for something else. I just do it because it is good to do right now and I think that it's good that when you are almost sixteen you don't have to climb all the way to the top of the tower. Then Shups says, "We better go back before the border patrol catches us." And I say, "Yeah, Shtramel and Hova Jake have probably smeared lipstick all over the car already." Shups gives me a poke. "Shtramel didn't have any lipstick on." So we walk back and when we can see the car already we turn and look at the tower blinking.

"How far do you think we climbed up?"

"Far enough," Shups says and she squeezes my hand.

KATHERINE PIPER

Down the Ice-road

My sweetheart lives over in Dettah.
He seldom has time for a lettah.
So he waits for the cold
and comes down the ice-road.
He says "Passion, in person, is bettah."

JOE WELSH

Janvier Makes a Picnic

Ever'time Janvier make a picnic
Wit Rosalie Boyer
He take Fodder Beaulieu dog wit dem
So one day I tell him
How come you take Fodder Beaulieu dog
When you make a picnic
Wit Rosalie Boyer

So he tell me
Flies
Dey use to bodder me lots
So one day I tink
I like to borrow dat ugly dog
En duh priest he tink I like duh dog
En Rosalie she don' mind
She let him ride in her car

When we get to duh picnic place
I let duh dog out
En he run aroun' fer a while
Pretty soon he have a shit
Den we move duh picnic up out duh wind
En duh flies
Dey don' bodder us no more

Sometime when dey get real bad
I borrow Gilbert LaRoque dog too

DENNIS COOLEY

how there in the plaid light in broad
daylight she played
with his affections plied them spikes from
his heart
she stood by pliers in hand
he has his pride

lady lady how you play
with me & my tennis ball heart
the pleas i let loose plop them prop them at your
feet
please i say please

how petty it all seems how paltry
you sitting pretty & partly it is
my putty heart flaps
the way poultry flap when a skunk shows up

when i go courting your affections
you lob them archly achingly
back to the back of courtesy
right to the very edge of cow pastures
smash my overtures when timidly
they approach the net hope for some small return
gentle return is what i go for

& yet you volley my hopefulness
boom it back in thunder
it's lumber you're stacking
not that i mind my hesitant serves you slash cross
court your loud & curt returns your backhand
compliments

but
do you really think i deserve this
the passing shots you serve me ill madam
the way you take shots at me
stroke after vicious stroke
boy oh boy i don't mind saying i find it hard
to go in for this courting
feel i am somehow
courting disaster
plain & simple

though you stand constant as Thor
at the net you have strung
between us my heart slams
when you slam your racket
when you shout love
at the top of your lungs

JUDITH KRAUSE

The First Time

there isn't enough room in the bed
for all the people who want to join us—
my three-year-old with her stuffed toys
bedtime books and dog,
your teenaged children and their friends,
my ex-husband slouched in the corner of the room
making snide comments.

You keep your socks on
while my mother sits downstairs
at the kitchen table sipping tea,
hoping it won't last.

Eventually, their interest fades.
The three-year-old turns four,
wants to sleep in her own bed.
The dog returns to his basket.
Your children decide they'd rather go out
and my mother's tea grows cold.

Even the bed is bigger.

JUDY MCCROSKY

Call Me

(A penthouse high above the Big City. The living room is spacious, and contains a white modular sofa with matching chairs and three glass-and-chrome tables. The room is dark and shadowed. On one table stands a telephone and an answering machine. A red light on the answering machine is on. The only other light in the room washes in from the city, through the glass double doors along the back wall. The phone rings.)

Hello. This is telephone answering machine XB 1700. *I am currently on my coffee break. If you wish to speak with me, you must make an appointment. Leave a message after the tone, and I'll have my human contact you to set one up.*

Shawna, it's George. Sorry I missed your call. Listen, I have a free evening next week. Let's get together. Call me.

(A young woman enters. She wears a square-shouldered black jacket and a calf-length skirt and carries a briefcase. She places the briefcase on the floor beside the glass doors. She lifts her arms above her head and stretches, her body a dark silhouette against the shimmering lights of the City below.)

Hi. You have reached George Lipincott's line. This evening I'm at the office for a couple of hours finishing up an account, and then it's off to the ballet. Please leave a message after the beep and I'll get back to you as soon as I can.

George. Shawna here. Sorry, next week is fully booked. I do have Thursday the 26th free. How about a movie?

50

Sorry, I can't come to the phone right now. I'm watching all seventy-nine episodes of Star Trek, non-stop. Leave a message after the tone and I'll call you when I beam back to earth.

Ha ha, great greeting, Shawna. Love it. You Trekkie, you. It's George. The 26th sounds fine. I've marked it in my calendar, and I'll see you then. 8:30?

(The young woman is sitting on a chair. Her briefcase is open on a low table in front of her. It is early evening, and the orange and pink of a magnificent sunset can be seen through the glass doors. The young woman appears to be satisfied with the contents of the briefcase. She nods once and snaps it shut. Standing, she takes a navy blue blazer from where it lies across the sofa, puts it on, and leaves. The phone rings.)

Hello. (There are sounds of children laughing.) *As you can hear, I'm a little busy right now.* (The sounds intensify.) *Leave a message after the tone and I'll get back to you as soon as the kids untie me.*

Hi, it's George. Just wanted to tell you how much I enjoyed the other evening. The movie was good, and sharing it with you made it special. You sitting there in the dark beside me, well, I'll only tell you I had a hard time concentrating on the movie. Your silk-clad leg, so close to mine. Our arms, brushing as they shared the arm rest. I'd better stop right here. If I say more it might shock those kids I heard. Say, where'd those kids come from, anyway?

You have reached George Lipincott's line. I'm out all day today, no time even to come home to change before the dinner tonight. John Crosbie is the speaker. Leave a message after the beep and I'll call you first thing tomorrow.

I borrowed the kids from my sister. I enjoyed the other evening too. Sorry I had to rush off right after the movie, but the presentation the next day was a success, so I'm glad I put in those extra hours that night. Let's get together again. No movies, though. Let's go somewhere we can talk. I'd like to get to know you, George.

I can't come to the phone right now. Please leave a message after the tone and I'll get back to you as soon as I can. Thank you. This has been a generic, no-name brand message.

Shawna, Shawna, how do you think of them? And do you think of what your last message did to me? That husky undertone in your voice when you said you want to get to know me. Well. I'll tell you, my heart rate shot up even higher than it does during my aerobics class. By all means, let's go somewhere we can talk. How about we meet for a drink on the 6th? 9:30?

(The apartment is dark. A shaft of light slides across the floor. There is the sound of a door closing. The light disappears abruptly. The young woman enters. She drops her briefcase and walks slowly across the floor. She falls into a seat and takes off her shoes. She rubs one foot. After a while she stands up and exits. The apartment is quiet. Then there is the sound of a shower running. The phone rings.)

I can't come to the phone right now. Please leave a message after the tone and I'll get back to you as soon as I can. Thank you. This has been a generic, no-name brand message.

Shawna darling, you must be working too hard. The same greeting again on your machine? Still, I mustn't chide you. Your dedication is one of the things I admire most about you. Thank you for the other night. I've never had a watermelon daiquiri before. Deee-lish. And the band was good too. I liked

52

watching you move to the music. In the dark your red dress shimmered enticingly and your hair was like a pale silver cloud. I liked it even better when the music turned slow and you stepped into my arms. The scent of your hair had my senses reeling. What kind of shampoo do you use? And when can I see you again?

Hi. You have reached George Lipincott's line. I've gone sailing today. George is a lucky devil, you must be thinking. Don't worry, it's business. A new client to entertain. And, lest we forget, it's deductible! Leave a message after the beep and I'll call you the moment I come in, my hair smelling of salt spray, and my eyes filled with sea and sky.

Hi George. It's me. (Sounds of heavy breathing.) That's from the thought of you with your hair ruffled by the wind, smelling of the sea. I enjoyed the other night too. Dancing was fun. Still, it's a shame the music was so loud. We weren't really able to talk. And it was dark in there, wasn't it. What colour are your eyes? If they are filled with sea and sky, does that mean they're blue?

No brilliant witty scintillating greeting today. It's your turn. Leave your message after you hear the tone.

Sorry about the mixup last night. It's George, by the way. The boss came in just as I was leaving and asked me to go through an account with him. He depends on me, I couldn't let him down. By the time I got to the restaurant, you'd left. Can you ever forgive me?

I want to tell you something funny that just happened. I was in my car driving home. I was alone. No more car pools for me. I value that time to unwind on my own from my day. Anyway, I got stopped at the 52nd and 8th traffic light, and I happened to glance at the car next to me. The driver was you! I picked up my car phone to call you. But then I didn't. I was struck by a sudden doubt. What if it wasn't really you?

It's always been so dark when we've been together. Is your car a black BMW?

Sorry if this message isn't witty or scintillating enough.

(The apartment is dark. A full moon hangs in the night sky outside the glass double doors. Silver light bathes the modular sofa but the rest of the room is in heavy shadow. Off to one side, the red light of the telephone answering machine glows, a beacon in the dark.)

MICK MALLON

Tickle

There was a young lady from Clyde
who swam out at the top of the tide.
On arrival at Pond,
she'd become rather fond
of a walrus who'd tickled her hide.

BRENDA BAKER

Man of My Dreams

So I'm supposed to be meeting the man of my dreams
for lunch and my hair just won't go right so I wet it
down starting all over again and when it's passable
but not perfect I scurry to my car wondering all the
while if this will be The Day, start the engine and just
then I hear this loud thump on the car floor so I look
over to the passenger side and there, rolling around
on the mat is my head which doesn't entirely surprise
me but does make me think "Oh no, now I really am
going to be late" because this isn't one of those nifty
tricks your mother teaches you like scotchtaping a
hem or dabbing a stocking run with nail polish since
reattaching a head requires stitches and stitches re-
quire a doctor and I have to get my priorities straight:
do I want to see the man of my dreams right now or
do I want to see a doctor, and of course I go for the
former figuring no big deal, I'll just fix this up temporarily and go to the doctor after lunch, so locking my
head in the car and with my coat over my neck to
avoid drawing attention to myself I run back to my
apartment where no one's waiting for the elevator
which is a stroke of luck but just as the door's about
to close my mind's eye sees old Mrs. Capino running
through the lobby and I have little choice but to shut
the door in her face and I will never hear the end of
it but what's important right now is fixing this head
problem so in my apartment I rifle through the
storage closet to find this old styrofoam wig stand
from my theatre days and it's a little small but nicely
formed so I stretch a nylon stocking over it, draw on
the eyes, nose, and lips with make-up, blush the
cheeks, and poke earrings into the sides making it

passable, even pretty close to perfect, and when it's pinned to my neck and tied with a scarf I whiz back to the car, cover my real head with an army blanket and meet up with the man of my dreams who greets me with a passionate kiss that makes me numb from the neck down so I suggest that maybe we should skip lunch and go to his place for dessert but he says that he's hungry and besides he just wants to look at me for awhile which makes me feel very romantic so I agree and we sit very close in the restaurant making goo-goo eyes, letting our hands and feet make love and he tells me that I am a devastatingly beautiful woman and kisses me on the neck which wasn't a good idea because one of the pins pokes him in the lip making it bleed and I apologize feeling badly for having to lie about how I must have left the price tag on the scarf but he says not to worry, it's just a scratch, as our food arrives so we eat and when we finish he orders more wine and brings out a little blue box saying "Darling, I've been carrying this around with me for some time now, but I had to wait for what seemed like the perfect moment to do this, will you marry me and make me the happiest man in the world?" and I feel a tear welling up in my mind's eye and I can hardly believe it so I embrace the man of my dreams saying, "Yes my love, yes" and then I begin to laugh thinking "Wouldn't you know it, the day my head falls off the man of my dreams proposes" and when he sees me giggling away like that he wants to know what's so funny so I decide since he's in love with me I can share my innermost secrets and he will still go on loving me so I tell him "That pin that poked your lip, it's holding my head on" and he acts like I'm joking but when I pull off my scarf and show him the row of pins around my neck he goes white as a sheet and starts to stutter and shake and I say "Y'know, it's no big thing 'cause I'm gonna get it fixed right after lunch and you did say I was a devastatingly beautiful woman" but the man of my dreams looks like he's gonna throw up any second as he puts the little blue box back in his pocket, throws a fifty on the table, and clutching his stomach runs out of the restaurant without so much as a goodbye kiss so by the time I gather my wits and go after him he's long-gone forever, at which point it dawns on me that everything mother told me about true love and the man of my dreams could not possibly be correct.

Go Like Sixty

"She wanders in the halls all hours of the day and night. She knocks on doors and asks what time it is twenty times a day. It's not the interruptions," said Kurt, "though heaven knows I can ill afford the time away from my research to conduct a senile old woman back to her room repeatedly in one morning. I'm sure she has family. Relatives of some sort. Why don't they put her away somewhere?"

"Where?"

"Well, you know. Somewhere. Nursing home. Care home. I don't know what they're called. Government places. Manitoba is supposed to be the epitome of socialized medicine, everybody here keeps bragging that England and Sweden and you name it come here to study the system, so surely there's a place for an old woman to be taken care of by people who are paid for it."

It was all-you-can-eat spaghetti night at the pizza place at the local mall. I was new; Kurt knew all the angles. He'd invited me for supper "any Monday" I liked. Now I knew why: Monday was Two Eat for One Price night. Which was okay with me. I was six years away from "The Pension" and had learned to appreciate economy.

I'd learned also to insist on dutch treat years ago. It kept things cleaner somehow; it's surprising how many guys edging into their seventies are still interested in the come-up-to-my-place stuff after they've bought you so much as a hamburger at the Woolco lunch counter. Real elegance. If they only wanted you to sew buttons on a favourite shirt, its last contact with the inside of a washing machine patently long in the past, it was McDonald's they offered.

The spaghetti wasn't too bad, just not very to-mato-ey, and I was hungry. At the age of fifty-nine I was belatedly doing my artist-in-a-garret phase and was allowing myself only two meals a day. Not as much for the heady replay of Hemingway *et al.* starving in a Paris attic or its equivalent in some other exotic milieu, but because the roly-poly genes that had come to me undiluted via seven generations of Bavarian peasant women had begun to do their dirty work and I was beginning to huff after the first set of stairs at the Lady Duchess Apartments.

No duchess would have set foot in the place. No charwoman who could afford anything better either. Not Kurt, not me, not Miss Burney, I'm sure—if we had the price of anything better.

"How many times did she bother *you* today?" said Kurt. "This spaghetti is like rubber, even my last wife could do it better, how many times did she bother *you* today?"

"You mean Miss Burney?"

"Of course I mean Miss Burney, weren't you listening at all? Women never listen. I thought you'd be different, but women never listen."

I was beginning to see why the laundry room gossip had Kurt pegged as impossible. He looked gorgeous; he could speak intelligently (and very quickly) on twenty subjects in as many minutes. That he was poor was nothing—we all were in that place. But he had the personality of a nutmeg grater; I'd simply been pretending it didn't bother me.

"I am listening," I said. "The spaghetti tastes pretty good to me."

"I've heard of people whose taste is all in the mouth," said Kurt, "but that opinion certainly could not be levelled at you, my dear, now could it?"

Kurt loved the conundrum of backhanded compliments which, upon consideration, had nothing whatever complimentary about them. Rather than figure this one out I opted for home. I laid my four dollars and a quarter beside his water glass and got up.

"But you haven't had the second helping," said Kurt.

"It was so good I don't need a second go-round," I said. If he got up and followed me I might punch him one in the mouth. As it was, I had decided not to tell him about the red smear of spaghetti sauce that dribbled like Count Dracula's supper at one corner of his mouth. Let someone else tell him. Let Miss Burney tell him when she came for the "twentieth" time in one hour to ask him what time it is. Or to ask where she lived. Or what her name was. Or whatever the hell she supposedly asked Kurt twenty times in any hour of his precious day. Since flinging myself into my garret phase I had trained myself to say *hell* a lot in the inner dialogue.

I huffed up the five flights to my floor, hefted open the stubborn door to the fifth floor hall and thanked my stars my "fully accoutred bachelor suite" was just around the corner. I turned the corner. And there stood this little white-haired biddy with her nose scrunched to the numbers on my door. "Hello," I said.

She turned towards me. "Hello there," she said, stepping towards me and peering. "Who are you then? Do I know you?"

"I'm Vanessa, Miss Burney," I said. "I live here now. I'm new. I'm from Saskatchewan." Who cares?

"Oh yes," she said, "how very nice. Will you tell me, dear, do I live in this place?"

"Yes, Miss Burney. Just down the hall, I believe."

"Not right here? Not behind the numbers on this door?"

"No, Miss Burney. See? There's a name on the mailbox: V. Shaftbury. That's me. Now let's go down the hall and look for *your* name, shall we?"

"Oh yes, dear heavenly father," she said, "let us go like sixty, for I have a pressing call to nature that will not be denied."

She had about her an air that suggested nature had already taken matters into its own hands, but I offered my arm and she groped for any part of me she could clutch and we went like sixty, or at least as fast as her slippery-sloppery orange and purple string slippers would permit.

"Here is your door, Miss Burney," I said. "Shall I help you in?"

She was groping for the whereabouts of the mail-box. She found it and opened it and ran her hand around inside it. "Oh no, dear heavenly father," she said, "no mail again, oh dear, oh dear, oh dearie little me." I tried to open the door to speed things up. It was locked.

"Have you your key then, Miss Burney?" Oh please, dear heavenly father and all the angels, let her have her key.

"Yes, yes, yes," she piped, "we must always carry our key." And she felt about under the grey-white dressing gown, buttoned askew but tightly at the throat, and pulled out a key on a greyed old-fashioned store string. With the forefinger of her left hand she found the key hole and traced its pattern. She bent towards it and with her right hand fitted the key, turned it. "Oh now, dear heavenly father but that's a blessing," she said, "it turns. Did you see that?"

Get in, get in there, 'cause I'm back down that hall like sixty the minute you close the door.

"I said," she said. "'Did you see that?' It tu-u-urns." Not only had it turned, it had released the door. The key

61

was in the door, the string to the key was about Miss Burney's thin little neck. She gave the door a surprising heft with one small orange and purple foot and was drawn into the room along with the swinging door in the manner of a reluctant calf being drawn into the pen on a taut halter rope.

"Oh dear heavenly father," she sang now, "take me home for I have had enough of this durance vile! Please take me home, dear father, for I am weary for you, for you, for you." Her nose was snubbed against the door. I had the devil's own time to disconnect and reconnect all the appropriate items. Then I pointed her towards the bathroom and ran. When I was a kid we used to go to the city sometimes on a Saturday, to the west side market where all the farmers went, and nearby was what everybody called The Comfort Station. Miss Burney's abode had about it something of the do-not-tarry essence of The Comfort Station of long ago.

I hated myself. Or the one of me that still had feelings did. That'll be you someday, you know, that Other One said. You'll wish for someone to lead you home and set you on the pottie and cook a little something for you too, I expect. Who cooks for her? Who does for her?

Aw come on, this is no Dickens storybook, I said, there are government agencies to look after people like that.

Who has told them she even exists? said that Other One. I hate it when She is so logical. It means I won't sleep much that night.

By next morning I had decided I'd call Social Aid. Or some seniors' agency. They must have them here in Manitoba, else what are all those Brits and Swedes studying when they come over? But my phone had been disconnected due to an altercation with Man-Tel and I was trying to get by without one as long as I could. Social Aid didn't know about it yet and I had better things to do with ten dollars a month. Like springing for an extra jar or two of peanut butter.

There was a dinky little room on the ground floor that was respectfully referred to as the solarium. No sunlight ever reached it, but it was hot as the heart of Old Sol himself all summer. I chugged down the five flights and was just passing the solarium to go out and find a phone when from the dim confines of the room someone called, "Who goes there? Come in here, please. At once, mind you!"

Oh God. In I went. "Good morning, Miss Burney."

"Ah, good morning, my dear. And who might *you* be? I'm afraid I don't see as well as once I used to. It's a dreadful handicap, if I may say so, but one must bear up. Play up, play up, and play the game, am I right? am I right?"

"Now. Your name, please."

"It's Vanessa, Miss Burney. Vanessa Shaftbury. *You* know . . . the fifth floor . . . "

"Indeedy do, I most certainly do know the fifth floor, for haven't I lived on it for these thirty-seven years? Oh yes, longer than anyone else in the building. Indeedy do. And you, my dear? You are just moving in? Is someone helping you with the baggage? You mustn't try to carry things up those five flights by yourself; we'll ask Miss Evans when she comes to find you someone to help. She's very good, Miss Evans; she's ever so organized. I admire that in a woman so much, don't you?" Her face seemed animated; her eyes, had there been light enough to check them out, might have been sparkling.

It was like being caught in a time shift. Or at least what I think it must be like to be caught in a time shift. Or an Alfred Hitchcock movie. *This* was the addlepated little old lady who had got her nose snubbed to her own door last night? I was just as glad Miss

Burney's eyesight lacked a little something because I'm sure I was gaping like a fish out of water.

Then this very smart young woman came in the door. "Oh my goodness," she said, "let's have a little light on the subject, shall we?" She went about, flicking on lights. I didn't even ask if she was Miss Evans; I turned tail and laboured up the stairs again, swearing if I met Kurt on the way I'd spit in his eye just for the pure hell of it.

There was a note under my door when I got there. It was on pale pink notepaper and had computered hearts spun out all over it. Kurt had brought home my seconds from the spaghetti place and wanted me to come for lunch. He wondered if I could bring half a loaf of buttered bread to eke out the pasta. I tossed the note's pinkness with appropriate disdain into the waste basket.

Then, *Hemingway!* said the Other One into my mind, very, very clearly. I grabbed the pinked hearts up again like sixty and started to plan what to wear.

HONK IF YOU'RE HORNY!

ROBERTA NICHOL

Sex in a Pan

I love to eat,
There's just no denying
Feed me baby till my tastebuds start flyin'
Culinary bliss
That's the ecstasy that's second to none
Well, maybe one.

Bring on the food
Make it spicy or mellow
Down right decadent and not diet Jello
Make it something nice
Starchy, salty, sweet and fatt'ning in one.

Passions wake with carrot cake
And pasta fulfills my desire
Fevers rise with apple pies
And nachos set my soul on fire.

I don't want sex
Give me sex in a pan
Thick and creamy and as fast as you can
I'm weak in the knees
Don't just stand there honey
Quiche me you fool.

I go limp, for curried shrimp
Milk chocolate, cheesecake and fries
Häagen-Dasz wins my applause
Applied directly to my thighs.

So, go ahead, we'll both fry it or bake it
Make a bunch so you can roll in it naked
A glutton you say,
I prefer to think a lover of art,
So have a heart.

66

Let's bake a trip somewhere I've never been to
Give me something I can sink my teeth into
Slap on that apron and I just might fall in love.

EDWIN HALL

Test Your Hardness, Moh?

I have a knob and kettle topography.
My lustre, streak and cleavage are something else.
I know the Laws of Horizontality and
    Superposition.
I can put ripples in your bedding-plane.
I can make your hornblende or your greywacke.
If you're interested in a little horst and graben,
Or dip and strike;
If you don't lack a lopolith,

Come feel my magma push.

LORNA CROZIER

News Flash from the Fashion Magazines

Breasts are back!
You can see them everywhere.
On movie screens, in restaurants,
at baseball games. You can feel them
bump against you in the subway
like friendly spaniels.
Big as melons they bob
behind grocery carts,
they pout under denim.
Breasts are back!
They won't stay locked up.
They shrink the space
in elevators, they leap
out of jogging bras,
find their own way
down the road, running
hand in hand. They wave
at you from buses,
swaying around corners
and swinging back. Oh,
how they move! Graceful
ballerinas, a *pas de deux.*
They rise and fall
under your grandmother's floral apron,
they flutter under your daughter's
T-shirt, small shy sparrows
learning to fly.
Breasts are back. On the beach
nipples peek from bikinis
as if they were eyes, wide open,
wanting to watch the sea.
Sailors rise from the Atlantic,
clutching their Mae Wests
for breasts are back.

But wait! Not just any breasts.
A breast should not be able to support
a pencil underneath it.
A breast must fit into a champagne glass,
not the beer mug you raise
to your mouth on a hot summer day.
A breast must have nipples
no bigger than a dime.
A breast must be hairless,
not even one or two small hairs
for your lover to remove
with his teeth. A breast must bear
no stretch marks, must be smooth
as alabaster, luminous as pearls.

Enough of that!
Let's stand up for breasts
any size, any colour,
breasts shaped like kiwi fruit,
like mandolins, like pouter pigeons,
breasts playful and shameless as puppies.
Breasts that pop buttons,
breasts with rose tatoos.
Let's give them the vote,
let's make them mayor for the day.
Let's remember our old secret
loyalties, the first words
they placed in our mouths,
the sweet warm vowels
of our mother's milk
urging us toward our lives
before we even knew our names.
Breasts are back, let's shout it,
and they're here to stay!

How to Talk to Boys

"Wanna fuck?"

I couldn't believe I'd said that. That's the problem with having a rich inner life—you lose your grasp of reality sometimes, and say things you shouldn't even have been thinking. The problem was: once something's been said, there's not much you can do about it. Except maybe laugh it off.

Stevie didn't look like he was laughing.

"It's a joke," I said.

He started to relax a little.

"Really." he said.

"One of Jimmy Bodell's. It isn't very funny, really." Maybe cool sophistication was what I needed.

"What's the rest of it?"

"No, really."

"Really." He seemed genuinely interested, Goddamn him.

"Well," I said, thinking quickly, "There are these two guys . . . . " My back was starting to ache with the strain of holding myself up. I decided to waft gracefully to the floor. "And they're identical . . . . "

Stevie was still looking deep into my eyes, which meant that somehow *he* was on the floor too.

"Go on," he said seductively.

I took a deep breath. Helen Gurley Brown says to breathe from the diaphragm, so that you get the heaving breasts effect that all real men secretly desire. I wasn't sure Stevie was a breast man though. He seemed to be sinking into my eyes (or staring at my mouth, maybe he reads lips).

And was it? Yes it was! The smell of Old Spice, and an arm, not attached to my body, attached to my body! I looked deeply into his dark, dark eyes, as I felt the arm that wasn't mine touch the small of my back, and I saw the eyes come closer, closer, closer, too close to stay in focus, and I'm near-sighted, so I knew it was *very* close, and the eyelids started to flicker and close, and the lips . . . and o my God . . . .

I started coughing.

While Stevie was getting me water, I did a lot of thinking, and by the time he'd come back, I'd made up my mind to tell him everything.

"Stevie . . . I want to tell you everything."

"Yes? . . . "

"Stevie." I licked my lips. "See, there was this guy, and he and his friend go to the Beaver Hotel —"

Actually, the choice of Jimmy Bodell's joke was only partly accidental. Masters and Johnson and the Happy Hooker agree that the more titillation there is, and the more use of well-placed obscenities, the more erotic the situation. And if it's supposed to work on women, who have a really strong moral and biological responsibility if they succumb to the titillation, then it ought to work even faster on males, who don't. Right? That was the way I saw it, anyway.

I watched Stevie, to see how he saw it. He could go along with the whole thing, and carry on with a slightly more ribald train of conversation, or he could say "how gross" and my entire life would be ruined.

"—so his friend says, Well, I just used Ancient Masonic Love Charm Number One.

Number One, says his friend, What's that?

Well, that's where you go up to a girl and say, 'Wanna fuck?'"

Stevie stared at me, a little tight-mouthed, I thought, rubbed his nose, which, as you know, is a sign of aggression, and paused.

"O God o God o God," I prayed.

"Stephanie . . . . " he said, in exactly the same tone my father used the day I spit in his milk.

O God.

"Do you know why roosters don't have hands?"

I didn't even try to guess. This could still turn into a biblical proverb. "I don't know, Stevie. Why?"

"Because hens don't have tits!"

It was going to be all right. I could feel it. Right on the brink, and almost over. All I had to do was sit back and enjoy, enjoy, enjoy.

And flatter, flatter, flatter.

"That's a great joke," I said.

"Not as good as yours."

"Sure it was."

"No, it wasn't."

"Sure it was."

"Not at all."

All the titillation was disappearing fast. Why did I have to pick such a *polite* person to have sex with? I had to think defensively.

"Gee, Stevie, do you know any more?"

While he was telling his jokes, I stared into his eyes and started to review everything I'd dreamed, or seen, or heard, or read about sex. I wasn't quite sure what I should do. Should I throw myself on his mercy and admit I'd never kissed anyone before? Helen Gurley Brown and *Playboy* and *Modern Sex and Hygiene* all seemed to suggest the virginity angle would work best, but of course, they weren't written for high school audiences. I mean, let's face it, if you're as old as I am, and you still have all your teeth, and you wash fairly frequently, then you must be a real turkey if you haven't even managed to be *kissed* by anyone. You must be a complete social misfit. Which I admit I am, being a teacher's daughter, but I didn't want Stevie to know. Besides, it really wasn't fair. The *reason* I hadn't been kissed was partly because I didn't want to be kissed by just anybody, I wanted to be kissed by Stevie Brown My Own True Love. So if there was anything I didn't know (and there was probably a lot) it was just as much his fault as mine.

On the other hand, I didn't know what he'd do if I did as some of those old novels suggested, and cast myself at his feet, weeping, "Kind Sir! Take that which no man can give me back."

It didn't look like I was going to have to worry. It was only quarter after ten, and we were already rolling around on Stevie Brown's bed, having a really nice time. I mean, it was a lot better than just playing footsie when you're playing cards. A lot better. And I didn't feel seriously out of my depth, either, until Stevie started running his left hand up and down my spine, pressing really hard with his fingers, which gave me tingles the first couple of times, and then didn't, because it hurt. Finally, I couldn't stand it any more. "What's wrong?" I whispered.

"Nothing." he whispered back, but he kept pressing down on my spinal column, right at the back of my ribs, digging his fingers right at the small of my back, like he was searching for something. I could tell he was worried.

So was I. I had no idea what kind of sexual lunatic Stevie Brown might be. I mean, how well did I know him? Actually *know* him. Forty-five minutes a week in the weight room, and two and a half seconds between classes for a couple of years is no guarantee of up-rightness of character. Of course, he was with me right now, which might be some kind of character reference by association, but on the other hand probably only a lunatic would be caught dead in bed with the algebra teacher's daughter when he still had a year and a half to go before graduation.

It suddenly occurred to me that if I took off my lumberjacket, whatever Stevie was looking for might be more apparent, and everything would start happening a lot faster. Under it I was wearing my hot pink Danskin (which my mother doesn't allow me to wear by itself, because she says it makes me look like a French hooker). But of course I want to look like a French hooker, which is why I bought the thing in the first place. I don't know why parents always try to give you a hard time about the way you look, when that's exactly the look you were trying to achieve. I don't tell Momsy she looks like a dowdy, over-weight housewife. (Well, if I do, it's for her own good. Some-times it's embarrassing to walk down the street with her).

Once I took my lumberjacket off, Stevie seemed to cheer up.

"Oh . . . you're not *wearing* a bra," he said, and sounded relieved.

"Neither are you," I said, and deftly undid his shirt-buttons.

Everything was going as planned, but it was way behind schedule. For one thing, I'm never going to listen to anyone complain about Wham Bang Thank You Ma'am again, because I think those kind of seductions would be probably very refreshing if you have any commitments at all—other than emotional. I mean, when I went into Stevie's room at *ten*, I never expected to still be rolling around on the bed, fully clothed except for the article which I had myself removed at 2:31.

I was beginning to see how my English teacher Mrs. Beebee could take sex for granted. I'd be cranky too if I had to stay up all night every night.

The thing I was dreading was that in the morning, Stevie Brown would walk me back to my hotel room, shake my hand, and tell me how much he respected me for letting him go as far as he did, and how much he respected me for not letting him go any farther, and maybe we could go for coffee sometime, and that would be it: my big chance to get pregnant and live happily ever after with the Man I Adore would be lost forever.

Actually, he didn't look like he was going to last until morning. He kept tugging here, and making furtive little forays, but he never really managed to displace anything for very long. It wasn't just the lack of a bra that had confused him. He didn't seem to know anything at all about Danskins. You can't pull *up* on a Danskin. You have to pull it all down at once, with one swift tug, and Stevie just couldn't seem to screw his courage to the sticking point long enough to do any good. "I think Mrs. MacBeth was right about one thing," I said. "If twere done when done, Twere well it twere done quickly." But he didn't seem to take the hint.

By 2:45 (I still had my watch on) even I had lost interest.

"Look, what's the problem," I asked briskly. "Don't you like me?" If it was my fault, and it probably was, I wanted to know, whether it hurt or not.

He didn't say anything.

"Well, don't you?"

"How can you say that?"

"Just answer the question."

"Of course I like you. I wouldn't be here if—I mean, you wouldn't be here if I . . . I mean . . . . "

"But you don't love me, is that it?"

He didn't answer.

"That's it, isn't it?" Whether it hurt or not, I had to know.

He started to huddle into himself, and his voice started to shake. Actually shake.

"Look," he said, "I'm sorry if . . . I know you think I'm . . . I just . . . I just don't . . . I just didn't . . . I never dreamed . . . I . . . I've never done this before."

And then he started to cry, at 2:48 in the morning.

I didn't know what to do. None of my sources had prepared me for emotional outbursts on the part of the male. I mean, I knew, theoretically, that they were human, but I'd never had to deal with them as such. Secretly, to tell you the truth, I felt a little embarrassed.

Not that it made me feel any differently about Stevie. I mean, I loved him, right? That doesn't just disappear overnight, or I'd be a pretty shallow person. And I'm not. But honestly, you didn't see Stephanie H. Nickel breaking down because she was in an impossible situation, did you? No, I went home, I did my research, I considered my options, I got into a compromising situation, and I tried to compromise. I accepted the challenge. Now, I agree there's a little more pressure on Stevie Brown in this situation, because he has to be actively interested in the sexual pursuit (by which I mean, erect) before anything can happen, but that shouldn't be too difficult, should it?

I did up his shirt buttons for him, and put my lumberjacket back on.

"Look, Stevie," I said. "It doesn't really matter."

"No?" he said, his chin trembling a little.

"Of course not. I think you're great."

And to tell the truth, it really didn't matter. I mean, I figured it had been a learning experience, even if we hadn't gone all the way. Up to ten o'clock last night, I knew zippo first hand about making out, and now I knew how to kiss (rather nicely, if I do say so myself). More importantly, I knew what it was like to be alone with a boy. Really *alone*, without him, or me, showing off or having to pretend we were something we weren't, which I wouldn't do anyway because I'm not a shallow person, but I have to admit that sometimes people who don't know me think my naturalness is occasionally a bit forced.

"And don't worry," I said, "I had a really nice time."

76

"Really?"

"Really."

I know it sounds sick, but I sort of like a guy in tears. It picks up the colours of their eyes. Besides, now we didn't have to actually *do* anything, I started to notice—again—how attractive Stevie Brown was, even at 2:52 in the morning with his eyes all blood-shot and puffy.

"Look, I'm really sorry if I put any pressure on you . . . I just wanted to show you how much I cared."

"That's all right," he said, "I understand."

"No, I really am sorry if—" and I guess I was tired or something, because my chin started to tremble, and I had to put my hands over my face so he wouldn't notice, but it didn't do any good.

"I'm really sorry if . . . I just . . . well . . . I've never done this before either." And all of a sudden, I'm bawling, twice as hard as Stevie Brown, and he's bawling with me, and we're both bawling together, if you can believe it, and then suddenly, nobody's bawl-ing, we're just holding each other tight, like the world was flat and we're standing in a strong wind at the edge.

Nothing happened, of course. But it was a really good nothing. I'm ready for Greek tragedy next semester, because now when Mrs. Beebee talks about catharsis, I'm not going to be confused at all.

Catharsis is getting really seriously involved with someone, and getting seriously close to them, and when you're really involved and really close, you go through some sort of tremendous emotional up-heaval—like your father being made a senator and moving you to Ottawa, or something—and then you get together, and you stay up all night, and you exhaust each other completely, and you have a good, knock-down bawl.

And the point that Mrs. Beebee misses is this: it

feels *good*. Even if at the end you find out that you have to run at nine in the morning, and the man you adore can't date you because he's already going steady with some convent girl, because he thinks they're not as fast as the girls who go to Thomas Hardy High.

He's wrong of course.

ROBERTA NICHOL

Turning Forty

You're not getting older, you are getting better
This is what we often hear.
Proud we embrace this knowledge to our bosom
Which has sagged with one more year.
Maturity has made us wise
Good sense has slapped us in the head
Worldly attractive and sophisticated
Then why is this a fact of life that we all dread
Why is this a fact of life that we all dread

What's this you say
You're fast approaching forty?
At your peak you lucky girl!
Now salute that powerful libido
Which they say starts to unfurl
Doctor says you're A-okay
You're healthy, here's your bill, goodbye
Sexy, vital, perfect working order
But what's that fat deposit doing on your thigh?
What's that fat deposit doing on your thigh?

In so many ways you won't feel any different
Than you did ten years ago
Your saddle bags and haunting little crow's feet
Poise you for that crushing blow
Like your mother and her mother
Something you have always feared
Go and behold you look into the mirror
And voilá you've grown a beard
And voilá you've grown a beard.

No you're not getting older you are getting better
Gained respect as well as weight
Courtesy is simply automatic
People call you man, it's great
You just reached another plane
Embrace this time with all your might
Cap those teeth and focus on the future
Don't you dare give up without a damn good fight
Don't you dare give up without a damn good fight.

Bill's Sperm Count

Alice clattered into the house about an hour later than usual. Clatter was the right word because the heels of her boots on the parquet floor made a sound like bungled flamenco dancing.

It was this sound that caught Bill's attention. He left his desk and went to the head of the stairs. From there he could see what the feet were doing. They weren't dancing but they were taking small quick steps around the entry, as if trying to condense a long hike into a five minute exercise.

Bill started down the stairs. He noticed other disturbing things about Alice the closer he got. Her fists were clenched, her knuckles white dots. Her arms were so stiff at her sides that each fist-forearm combination looked like a shock absorber. Her neck above the peach scarf was red as if she'd been rubbing it. And she was crying.

This last detail brought Bill to a stop. In nine years of living together, four years of marriage, he had only seen Alice cry twice before: once when their dog escaped the yard and was hit by a car and, more recently, when they received the letter telling them that their Peruvian foster child's home had been buried by a mudslide. Bill knew that something terrible had happened.

He reached her and turned her gently around. The clattering stopped.

"Alice, what is it?"

The wet, red eyes met his.

"We're infertile," she said.

Before this announcement Bill's mind had been full of dark possibilities. His first reaction to her words was relief. No-one had been run over by a bus. No lump had been found in anyone's breast. The United States had not invaded Cuba. When this relief showed on his face, something like hate appeared on Alice's. She pushed him away and ran for the stairs.

Bill hurried after and caught her on the top step.

"I don't see how you figured this out all of a sudden. Yesterday we were fertile, today we aren't?"

"One year of trying, Bill," she said. "That's the rule they use at infertility clinics. It's over a year since that time in Mexico. We're infertile."

The argument that followed had a predictable and fruitless quality. In the bedroom, Bill started attacking the infertility principle on the grounds that they had been pretty clueless back when they first set aside the armament of birth control devices. Like most couples who had spent a lot of time fearing pregnancy, they assumed that all you had to do was take your hands off the handle-bars and the bike would crash, all on its own. It was months before they regarded pregnancy as a problem to be approached with basal thermometers and special positions. So maybe, Bill argued, they had quite a lot of time left in their year.

Alice had by this time got out of her work clothes. Jerking the rope on her bathrobe tight, she explained that the one year principle was based on a random sample composed of many people, most of whom had probably never heard of a basal thermometer.

In the kitchen, Bill slid into an attack against the arbitrariness of this notion that the flipping over of a calender year could demarcate the fertile from the infertile. Whose pointy-headed idea was that?

"Look, Bill, take a stats course. Of course they aren't saying that one day you're fertile and the next day you're not. What they are saying is that every month of the previous year has slipped us into a lower category of probability. After a year that probability is so low that we fall into a probably—not absolutely— but probably infertile class."

"Probably!" Bill seized the tiny corner of field left to him. "There's hope in other words."

"Oh, hell, yes! But not much. And *that's* the point."

On those occasions when Bill and Alice felt the need to compliment themselves, they often pointed to their ability to talk. So many of their friends had spun out into silence in their marriages; the silence so often led to divorce. Faced with this new problem, Bill and Alice quieted themselves with a glass of wine: a standard preparation for a long talk that would tell them what to do.

They didn't have to go into why they wanted children; those conversations were history. Suffice to say that Alice was thirty-two and felt that statistics of all kinds were closing in on her. Bill was not so keen, but that was okay. Clearly the human race got where it is through the mothering instinct of women and the protective instinct of men. Bill could only assume that he would feel fiercely protective and proud of his offspring whenever it arrived.

They skipped all that and went straight to the infertility problem. Every time either of them mentioned the word, tears started up in Alice's eyes and a needle of hurt poked Bill. To see her so vulnerable; he wasn't used to it. More in character, Alice had already been in touch with the city's infertility clinic and had made an appointment for them, if Bill would consent to go.

"Of course, honey. Why wouldn't I go?"

Alice gave him a run down on what would happen at the first appointment. The doctor would ask them for a medical history of their sexual relations—to see if they were making any obvious tactical errors. Then they would give Alice a check-up, take a blood sample and analyze it for hormonal imbalances, things like that. Oh yes, and they would also like to have a sperm sample from Bill, preferably in advance of the first appointment. A great many of these problems owed to faulty sperm so it made sense to check that before going to any further trouble and public expense. Suddenly Bill felt uneasy.

"How would we go about doing that?" he asked.

Alice brightened a little, even managed a giggle. "You've never had a problem before."

Bill tried a little laugh of his own. "We just sort of do it then? And you race down to the clinic?"

Alice laughed more boisterously. "Uh-uh, boyo. You go there yourself and jerk off into a bottle."

Bill made no attempt to laugh.

"You come with me though, right?"

"Bill, for God's sake, both of us should take time off work so you can give a sperm sample?"

When Alice had that rhetorical tone, Bill knew better than to argue.

The appointment was made. One week before it, Bill made a desperation call to his own doctor, Dr. Ed, and begged for an immediate consultation.

Dr. Ed had become a friend. Bill had gone to him for the last two years and it was the first time in his life that he had a doctor who didn't make him feel like a fool. Dr. Ed told jokes and had sixties music playing on his office stereo. There were copies of *Rolling Stone* and *Playboy* in his waiting room. But most important, Dr. Ed did not make light of Bill's ailments. When Bill had gone in with chest pains, fearing they were angina, Dr. Ed sheduled a number of tests. Even though it turned out to be some small stress thing, nerves getting caught between ribs or something, Dr. Ed was careful to tell Bill that he had done the right thing by coming in.

This time, when Dr. Ed popped into the examining room, he was wearing a loose-fitting flowered shirt instead of a white coat. He asked how Bill was hanging and Bill gave it to him straight. Infertility. Infertility clinic. Sperm count.

"Is there any way I can get out of going there and jerking off into this bottle?"

"No sweat, Billy boy," said Dr. Ed and Bill could feel the tension in his neck dissolving. "Tell you what we'll do. I'll give you the same damn bottle right now. Just make love to your lady wife in the morning, pull out (if you remember how), get it in the bottle and bring it down here before you go to work. Those fertility guys are fanatics."

Bill woke Alice out of a deep sleep. Her breath was bad. His own mouth felt terrible. Ordinarily they didn't even face each other mornings until both had brushed their teeth and gargled. He enclosed her in an embrace.

"What's with you?" she asked, her voice muzzy.

"Just, you know, a little horny."

She pulled back and got up on one elbow. She smiled, one set of eyelashes glued together.

"This is a new one."

"Maybe I was having a dream."

"Was it about me?"

"Yes."

"Liar."

But she got up and went to the bathroom. He could hear her brushing her teeth. Still, when she came back in, she looked suspicious.

"You hate making love in the mornings."

"Exception to every rule, I guess."

It lasted about five minutes and was awful for both of them. He thought about saying something that would prepare her for the end but decided on a mute approach. He bounded off the bed and into the bathroom without a word. He whipped the bottle out of its hiding place and prayed. Please, please. And he came.

"What's with you?" Alice asked from the bed when he came back in.

"Sorry, honey. I just saw the clock and remembered I have a breakfast meeting with Blasket. Shit."

Did she believe him? He suspected not. He didn't have time to think about it. He put the bottle in its envelope, the envelope in his briefcase. He raced it down to Dr. Ed's, cursing at every snag in traffic. He imagined his sperm dying in droves against the cold glass.

Two days later, Bill phoned Dr. Ed from the office.

"Ed. It's Bill. What's the score?"

"Score? Man, you are a phenom!"

"What do you mean, Ed?"

"You could fertilize the entire Pacific Northwest and have enough left over for Montana."

"The results are okay then."

"Are you listening to me here, Bill? They are great. Look, I'll give it to you in numbers. You had over a hundred million fast swimmers going for you. All alive, all moving. The average is fifty-sixty. They were motile little suckers too."

Bill thanked Dr. Ed effusively, as if Ed had somehow coached him to this success.

Bill was in a good mood for the rest of the day at work. It was only in the car going home that he was struck by guilt. It was Alice. Alice had the problem. What a selfish bastard he'd been, rejoicing when

Alice had this problem.

Bill arrived home with roses and said nothing about the test. He took Alice out for dinner even though she had a small headache and wanted to stay home. When the religious guy came around with the basket of flowers, Bill bought her another two blooms.

It was two days later, with three days left before the appointment at the infertility clinic, that Bill mentioned the test at Dr. Ed's. He mentioned it only because Alice wanted to know what he'd done about giving a sperm sample.

"I hope you don't mind, Alice, but I went over to Dr. Ed's and did it there. I know it's stupid but I just felt a little more comfortable that way. I got him to write out all the numbers and what not."

"Aren't you going to tell me what the results were?"

"Well, they were okay. Pretty good, actually. Above average. You're not mad, are you?"

"Why would I be? I mean it's great that the results were good— Obviously. I guess I don't really see why you had to do it this way, that's all."

She looked at him oddly, as if he were a stranger.

The appointment at the infertility clinic had a very adult tension about it. No-one was at ease but everybody pretended to be at ease. The questions and answers were frank, all except when the doctor asked them how many times a week they made love and Bill said three and Alice said once. There was an embarrassing lull and then Alice said, "I guess what Bill means is that in the key part of the month it's about three times but the average overall is once a week."

The doctor took Alice into another room and examined her. Then got around to the sperm count.

"You didn't come in earlier, Bill? I don't see a

86

count on your chart anywhere."

Bill produced his piece of paper.

The doctor looked at it and frowned.

"Pretty amazing numbers."

Bill tried not to smile. He tried to keep his face from doing anything.

"Too amazing by far, frankly."

The doctor set the piece of paper down and Bill picked it up. He was wishing the numbers were typed and not handwritten.

"What I'm saying is, these numbers are so high I have to suspect there's been an error. This is the reason that we insist on having the counts done here."

"Counts?"

"Yes. We like to have three. Spaced out over a period of about three weeks. These things can vary a lot and the more counts we do the more accurate the picture."

Bill felt confused. Hot and a bit angry. What was this anyway? Some damn competition between doctors he was caught in? I can count sperm better than you can?

"The nurse will tell you what you have to do."

The nurse, when they talked to her, said Bill could come in any time. She stressed the importance of doing it soon. She expressed special venom for husbands who were reluctant. "Imagine it, " she said. "Here they are getting enormously subsidized assistance toward having a child, and some of these damn, pardon my English, damn husbands won't even give a sperm sample." Everyone agreed this was about as low as you could go.

A week later, Bill returned. He was strangely nervous, almost faint. Grow up, he told himself. He approached the counter. A small man, a very dirty small man in a T-shirt, with an unattractive tattoo of a bull's head on his strong bicep, was ahead of him. Bill hung back trying to look like a doctor or a medical supply salesman. He couldn't decide which.

The small man was getting instruction from a brisk and slightly hostile nurse. Bill tried not to listen, which wasn't hard as far as the small man was concerned; he was whispering so low the nurse kept asking him to repeat. But the nurse was loud.

"Do you want me to show you where to go?" she shouted at one point. The small man's entire body said no and his hand flew to the cigarette pack he had tucked up into the short sleeve of his T-shirt.

Finally the nurse did lead the small man across the hall. They disappeared around a corner, the cleats of the man's work boots giving up mud all the way. Bill read a poster on the wall, or pretended to until he realized it was about infertility. He dodged away then and looked at a corkboard covered in baby pictures. The successes. In the space of a second he felt both elated and depressed. Then the loud nurse was back and he went to her.

"Name, please," she shouted.

"Bill Armstrong."

"Say again."

"Bill Armstrong."

"Bill Armstrong?" she shouted. "Are you here to give a sperm sample?"

"Yes." Bill looked around. Two young women in white coats were passing. One had her hand over her mouth.

"Someone's in there right now, but it shouldn't be long. It usually takes only a minute. You can wait right here if you like."

"Where is the place?"

"Over there, across the hall." She pointed down the trail of boot mud.

The nearest place to hide was the bookstore. The infertility clinic was in the medical school and the bookstore was for the students. Bill tried to look like a student and then like a publishing rep. He looked at a book about infertility, furtively. It could have been a nudie magazine. He looked for a simple answer. A position, or some hint about the exact instant to let go so a sperm would go positively zinging at the egg. But all there was in the book was a list of potential horrors. Ways that the various tubes can get blocked. Ways that weird chemical agents in your body can wipe out the whole army of sperm the second it's launched.

Bill was sweating. His suit was damp and he made a mental note to have it dry-cleaned. Don't think about it, he commanded himself. Grow up. But still he had in his mind a perfect image of the dirty, small man with the tattoo and the cigarette pack sitting in the room. The small man was having a smoke, butting the ash in the mud his boots were leaving all over the floor. He was doing some creepy thing to himself. His body was touching all the surfaces Bill's body would soon be touching.

Shaking and sweating, Bill returned to the counter. The loud nurse was doing paperwork. She looked up and grinned.

"It's okay by now," she said after checking her watch. "Do you know the way?"

Bill made a sign to her, a nonchalant sign, and turned away. He followed the mud trail around the corner and up to a closed door. He grabbed the handle and turned. It was locked. He cursed aloud and was about to start back to the stupid, loud nurse who obviously must have the key when a frightened voice, small even for a small man, came from inside.

"Just a minute! Hold on! I'll be done in a minute!"

Bill walked quickly away. Down the mud trail to the intersection of hallways. He peeked around at the counter and, seeing that the nurse's chair was empty, he ran. On his way into the elevator, he was sure he heard his name being shouted.

Two weeks passed. Alice's first set of tests, some involving grisly invasions of her person, showed fallopian tubes that were clear and navigable. The blood analysis pointed up a slight deficiency in progesterone. She was given progesterone suppositories to be vaginally inserted before bed. It was suggested that Bill not make love to her after insertion lest he start exhibiting feminine characteristics. Bill gave Alice a version of what had happened at the clinic. Their lab wasn't working the day he went so there was no sense giving a sample. He prayed that she would not double-check.

Another week passed and Alice began to ask regularly what he was doing about the samples. "The only day I could get away from work was Thursday and we'd made love the night before. You're supposed to leave seventy-two hours after intercourse, you'll recall." That was the first excuse. The next several had to do with unexpected meetings. He'd never known the office to be so busy at this time of year.

Another week passed and Alice acquired a special tone in her voice when she spoke of it.

"Are you deliberately avoiding this, Bill? To see if the progesterone will work?"

"No. Hell no, Alice."

"Because, if you are, you're wasting tremendously valuable time. I'm going to be thirty-three in a month and I want to get pregnant while my body can still snap back, to say nothing of having a kid who's normal. Do you understand?"

When Bill arrived at the clinic, no-one was in the room. The loud nurse did not talk about last time and neither did Bill. She did lead him right to the door even though he told her twice that he knew the way. She told him he would find a plastic glass on the counter inside, also a pencil and a form to fill out.

"Magazines are in the corner."

Bill walked the room's perimeter several times. The floor was checkered linoleum. The small man's mud had been cleaned up. Still, Bill felt his presence. Many skin magazines were scattered on a vinyl couch in one corner, some open, some closed. The walls were bare. There was a sink and the fluorescent lights were very bright.

Bill, who had never really had any attitudes about pornography, suddenly felt disgusted. Why not dirty movies, he asked himself? Why not have nurses come in half-naked to beat you off? Why not a big rubber glove on the wall that the loud nurse could put her arm in from the other side to help you do the dirty deed? Bill was amazed to find himself with an erection.

But by the time he sat down with the skin magazines, fumbled with his fly and got himself out in the open, his erection had died. He looked at every single skin magazine—at maybe a thousand women staring up at him in sultry ways from between their own knees—but it only made him feel sad. He held onto himself like he might have at night when he was a child; hanging on for dear life. He tried thinking about the half-naked nurses again, about the loud nurse with her arm in a rubber glove, but it was no use.

He sat and his back was round. He stared at the floor waiting for the inevitable. The loud nurse shouting, "Come on, come on! We don't have all day!" Or the small man whispering, "Hey, buddy,

could you hurry it up? My truck's double-parked."
And as he thought of the small man, a tenderness
overtook him. Much of his sadness now went to the
small, grimy man. How could he have been such an
elitist pig, he wondered? Not to have recognized his
brother? Brothers in infertility. Fellow jerkers off into
bottles. But, as he thought it, he knew somehow that
the small man had succeeded in doing what Bill
could not do.

There was no escaping this time. Bill walked up to
the counter, to the loud nurse who looked at him
with a not unfriendly expression, and he said, "I
couldn't do it. Please don't say anything because your
voice is very loud, but I just couldn't, okay? I'll be
back."

But as Bill walked to the elevator, what he was
really thinking was that he would never be back.

The loud nurse betrayed him. The next time that
Alice phoned the infertility clinic the loud nurse told
her outright that Bill had not given a sperm sample.
She had better get on his back about it. Before they
contemplated surgery for Alice (some awful thing
called a laparoscopy involving the insertion of a fibre
optic tube through the abdomen) they had to know
if Bill's sperm was good.

There was a fight.

"What in hell is with you, Bill?"

"I don't know. It's just . . . I'm sensitive about
something here."

"Well get goddamn unsensitive fast! It's *my time*
you're wasting and I've told you over and over that I
don't have much of it left!"

"Okay. Okay, but I think you'll have to come with
me."

The trip to the clinic was completed on the verge of

more ugly argument. Never had there been such tension between them. When they got to the clinic desk, the loud nurse was, thank God, not behind it. Still, by the time they were in the room, Bill was so on edge he knew he would have trouble.

"What do you want me to do?"

"Alice, please. Try to be . . . try to be a little gentle. This kind of talk just isn't conducive . . . "

"Shit, Bill, here you are, a guy who has been coming—and usually too soon—for years and years. Suddenly somebody's jammed in a cork?"

"Nice talk. Very romantic."

She swept up to him, undid his pants, dropped to her knees. Normally he would have been jumping at this but her way was so cold, so cruel.

"Okay, what now? You call the shots."

"Maybe if you were almost naked. And I think the lights should be off."

She tore at her suit, undid her bra, rolled down her black pantyhose. She slammed off the light.

And then, somehow, in all that swimming darkness, she seemed to Bill to be more tender. A stranger maybe, but a woman kinder than the woman he'd been living with in recent weeks. He reached for her, tried to give her some pleasure too. There was some response. Bill began to forget himself. To swim, to swim, in gradual search of a far shore. Then suddenly, that shore was in view. In fact it was rushing up to meet him at alarming speed.

"Alice, quick! The bottle!"

"Where is it?"

"On the counter."

"I can't find it. Oh damn! Now I've knocked it on the floor. Where's the light?"

"Too late."

Alice was so furious she put on her clothes and left without him. He knelt on the floor and pushed the sperm from the checkered linoleum into the plastic cup. He couldn't help thinking that there was going to be small man boot mud in his sample. In a sense he was right. When he phoned three days later, the loud nurse wanted to know what he had done to his sample.

"It sort of went on the floor."

"Well, it's no use to us contaminated that way." Her voice was crisp, full of scorn. "You'll have to come again."

Bill and Alice were no longer a talking couple. They moved in broad circles around each other every morning and both came up with frequent excuses not to be there in the evenings. Bill worked very hard at his job and got a small promotion.

He had trouble believing this had happened to him. After nine years that such a wall could suddenly erect itself between them; it was unthinkable and yet it was there.

When the thing hadn't blown over in a month, Bill began to plead with Alice. He would give the sperm sample, he only needed time. Time to get the right attitude going for him. Positive attitude had always worked for him in the past and it would work for him now. She seemed to relent slightly. They even made love once, but when he did not seem to be getting the positive attitude or planning to give a sperm sample, the temperature of their marriage again fell below zero.

It was about two and a half months after Bill's last failure at the clinic that he received a call from Alice at work saying that he must come home immediately. They had to talk. He could not judge her voice. It seemed to contain both elation and coldness.

Bill drove home recklessly. When he entered through the front door, Alice was sitting on the sofa,

94

bathed in afternoon light. The sheers diffused the light in such a way that Alice was edged in a soft glow like someone in a perfume commercial. She did not speak as he got out of his coat and shoes. When he did enter the living-room, something in the way she sat, the way her legs were up under her and away from him, made him sit separately on another chair.

"Well?" he said.

"I'm pregnant."

Bill was up out of his chair and halfway over to her, his face split in a grin, when the real import of that statement struck him. He stepped backward and sat.

"It's . . . "

"That's right. It's not yours."

"Who?"

"A fellow I've been seeing. You don't know him."

Bill took his head in both hands and held onto it firmly. Thoughts would not come and, finally, as he had always done in their years together, Bill asked Alice to explain what it meant.

"It means we're getting a divorce."

The central heating cut in three times before Bill could respond. "I guess that means I'm infertile," he said.

Alice was looking at him with a certain detachment, maybe scientific. "Maybe you should have it checked," she said.

Bill wasn't as destroyed as he thought he would be. He discovered singles bars and acquired a few casual girlfriends. He told them about his divorce in a way that made them sorry for him. He had been betrayed; he had been a victim of his wife's maternal desperation. But then, about a year after his divorce had gone through the courts, Bill found himself again at the infertility clinic, face-to-face with the loud nurse.

"My wife got pregnant by another man," he told her. "I have to know if my sperm work."

The loud nurse told him that they dealt only with couples. To do otherwise would be against clinic policy. But something made her relent even as she said this. She nodded in the direction of the room.

Bill didn't look at the magazines and he didn't think of the small man. He thought about Alice and he came quickly.

MELANIE MISANCHUK

Contraceptives

condom? what if it pops?
Pill? I'll gain so much weight!
diaphragm? yeah, who'll put it in there?
IUD? don't want no hardware
foam? I ain't no dessert
OK, no sex. Dinner, a movie
We won't let coitus
interrupt us.

SHARON MACFARLANE

Crucial Quiz

I left school thirty-four years ago, but I have a recur-
ring dream that I'm writing an exam for which I
haven't prepared. Last week my nightmare came
true. I failed a sensuality test.

With a much younger friend, I went to a Sleek
and Slinky lingerie party. The S. and S. representative
promised that she would show us exciting fashions—
teddies, chemises, camisoles and gowns—but first we
were going to have fun. She began to hand out paper
and pencils. Her idea of fun was to have us do a little
quiz. As a veteran of countless Tupperware parties I
was prepared for one of those fill in the blanks games.
You know the kind—each answer is the name of a
soap. (The ship floated out on the TIDE. When the
team scored the fans gave a CHEER).

Nothing so mundane for Ms. S. and S. This was a
SENSUALITY QUIZ. (Ten questions worth ten marks
each.)

1. *Are you wearing matching bra and panties?*
A. Beige bra and green cotton panties. They are both faded
    but I guess that doesn't count.   0%

2. *Has the man in your life ever bought you sexy lingerie?*
A. My husband doesn't buy me clothing. The sizes
    confuse him. When you buy a blender, one size fits
    all.   0%

3. *Would you buy sexy underwear for him?*
A. Of course not. He has a whole drawer full of boxer
    shorts. What he really needs is a new hedge-
    trimmer.   0%

4. *Did you ever take a day off work to be with him?*
A. Often. But we spent those days harvesting—he in the
    combine and me in the grain truck.   0%

97

5. *Have you ever given a massage to a member of the opposite sex?*
A. Yes, after one of those harvest days. But I don't think rubbing Sloan's Linament on an aching back is what S. and S. has in mind.   0%

6. *Have you ever taken a bubblebath by candlelight?*
A. Candlelight? How would I find the pumice stone I use on my feet?   0%

7. *Have you ever spent a romantic evening sipping cham pagne and nibbling caviar?*
A. No—but we once had chokecherry wine with tuna casserole.   0%

8. *Did you ever skinny dip with your man?*
A. Since we both swim like rocks, we don't dip at all.   0%

9. *Do you sleep in the nude?*
A. Are you kidding? We turn our thermostat down to 15 at night. I sleep in a flannelette nightgown with a high neck and long sleeves.   0%

10. *Would you agree to a night of beer, pretzels and acting out his fantasy?*
A. At last—a yes! Of course his fantasy is a wild game of cribbage, but no one needs to know that.
                                                             10%

We gave our scores. Giggling was rampant as one after another, the women reported 70s, 80s and 90s. My neighbour's perfect one hundred percent was greeted with applause and wolf whistles. She received the MOST SENSUOUS WOMAN certificate and a bottle of perfume. My ten percent got me the booby prize—a box of chocolates.

When I got home I shared the candy with my husband as we watched "The Journal." We've been married for thirty years and he still hasn't discovered that I'm not a sensual woman. With any luck he never will.

MYRNA GARANIS

Undergarment Trilogy

On post-Christmas coffee breaks, we women discuss who got what. Louise's husband gave her an expensive negligee, filmy, pink. We all ooh and aah. But she's indignant. She returned it *toute de suite*. They couldn't afford anything like that, she said. "Aaaah," we chorus.

* * *

This guy goes to the lingerie counter, asks for a black bra. Clerk sez, "What size?" He sez: "You know, two fried eggs." She brings the fried egg one.

* * *

My Aunt Mae keeps lengthy rolls of elastic on hand as repair material for her underpant waistbands. This is known as frugality. A survey of my aunts (I have seven) reveals two more repairers, three recyclers and one d.k. (don't know). My mother favours safety pins. This is known as false frugality.

MARLIS WESSELER

Indecent Exposure

You'll never guess what happened at work yesterday. Weird things don't usually happen in our office. I mean there's some pretty strange people that come in to apply for UIC and stuff like that, but nobody's ever really *done* anything before. Anyways, there was this guy in yesterday who was hanging around exposing himself. I always wondered what I'd do if anybody ever did that in front of me, you know?

Well Shirley said that a guy did the same thing to her at a bus stop once. He walked up to her, threw open his coat, you know, just like in the movies, and he said, "What do you think *this* is eh?" in kind of a whiny nervous voice, and Shirley told me she looked at him and said—get this—"It looks like a penis to me, only smaller," and then she walked away, real cool and collected.

Well, I don't know, do you think that she really said that to him? I mean maybe she couldn've said it, but she wouldn't have acted so calm and cool like she said, right? Really, I think sometimes you can't believe, I mean not that she actually tells lies, like she's my friend and everything, but I really think sometimes you can't believe a thing she says.

Like, one time she told me she was going out with this real hunk, right? So one night I dropped over to her place when I knew he was coming over and jeez what a wimp. I mean, I don't always go out with prime specimens myself but even Harold wasn't as bad as this guy. For one thing he came from Moose Jaw. Yeah, talk about nerd capital of North America, well. So anyways, there I was trying to talk to this gormless wonder for half an hour while Shirley got ready to go out. I could tell she was embarrassed, but what can you do? I'd be embarrassed too if I was so desperate I'd go out with some loser from Moose Jaw and my friends saw him.

Harold? Oh, he was dust two months ago. I only went out with him about five times, just long enough to get to know what a nit he was. He was always forgetting his wallet, you know the type? And let's face it, I only went to bed with him on our fifth date, I thought he was holding off because he was shy, and I thought, *Is this unusual or what*, and then I thought it was kind of cute. So one night I decided tonight's the night, just like in the movies and so I put on perfume and shaved my armpits and everything, and after the show at the Capitol he brought me home and I invited him in for a drink.

Get this. I lit candles and turned on the stereo, you know, mood music and all that. And when I finally got him into bed he was, you know— He couldn't do anything. He was a nit anyways even not counting that. All he ever talked about was high school and what a good old time he had back in Smuts or wherever his home town was. Yeah he could be a big cheese back in high school, as long as he made sure to go out with girls who wouldn't expect anything.

So there I am, in bed with a loser and wondering what the hell I'm supposed to do with him. I mean he wouldn't say anything even when I asked him questions about it like, "Does this happen often?" He just laid there like some kind of vegetable, looking at the ceiling. I could've used a vegetable right then like a carrot or a cucumber, eh, but there he was, more like a squash. He finally got out of bed, didn't say a word except, "Where's my socks," and left. I haven't seen him since.

Anyways, a few days after that I found out I had an

infection and I wondered if frustration can cause it, you know? Then I thought jeez maybe he has herpes or something and that's why he couldn't do anything. That put me in a real panic I tell you, so I finally went to the clinic about it, but it turned out to be nothing.

But jeez. You know when you have an internal and there you are, feet getting cramps in those metal stirrups or whatever you call them and the doctor keeps saying, "Relax dear, just spread your knees and relax." I could gag. And then I always hold my breath when he slips that metal thing in, you know? I'm sure my doctor keeps his in the fridge. Well there I was, looking at the ceiling counting the little dots on the tiles, just waiting for it to be over, thinking only a couple more seconds, when in comes a couple of *in*terns. And my doctor says to them like he's inviting them to view his stamp collection or something, "Here, have a look at this. It's a classic example of a yeast infection." A classic example, jeez. And there I was, I mean, I just about died.

I felt like a tourist attraction you know? Like the Grand Canyon or something, eh. I was just ready to say something like "Do you mind?" when in comes this nurse who goes, "The plumber's here and he wants to know which office has the plugged sink." Well I was just about crying, I was really pissed off, so I go real loud so I bet they could hear me in the waiting room, "Oh well, ask him to come in why don't you, maybe he'd appreciate a good look too." They all looked up and gawked at me, like they were surprised I had a head.

But what is it with men anyways? I mean, jeez, talk about egos. Old Harold was totally crushed and hates me because he couldn't, and then there's the guys who always have to prove that they can, and think they're real Casanovas. I mean really. There's this guy

102

at work that I do some typing for, he must be fifty-five if he's a day. Well I got to joking around with him you know, thinking of him as a nice old geezer. And then like two days ago it was secretary's day and he took me out for lunch and then I had the rest of the day off so he drove me home and guess what? Surprise, surprise, he started coming *on* to me, right in front of my apartment building.

I just got pissed off and said if I wanted to get close to fossils I'd go to the Natural History Museum. I mean here's this guy who's been married for thirty years, who got me to help him buy an anniversary present for his wife and stuff like that, treating me like a kind of niece or something and suddenly I find out he's after my body. Those were his exact words in fact, "I'm after your body," if you can believe anybody would actually say that.

I was stunned for a minute, and then I thought he must be joking, so I just laughed. But then he said, "I've been wanting to throw my arms around you for a long time," and you know for a second I had this picture of a kind of circus act, where I was standing in front of a target, and all these guys would get up on stage, take off their arms and throw them around me, not at me you know? They'd kind of swirl through the air like boomerangs and go in curves right around me.

Anyways, then I said about the fossils and that and got out of the car. Now he hates me too and not only that I still have to work for him. I mean I was really stupid to say that, I could have trouble with my job. And then to top everything off, the next day this flasher I started telling you about came into the office. I tell you it never rains but it pours.

So anyways, this flasher. He just— Well, I was putting away some files and noticed some guy just standing there trying to catch my eye and I thought he needed help or something so I just ignored him kind of, you know the way it is when it's busy and you don't want to be bothered. You kind of pretend you don't see them, really. So anyways he stood there for about five minutes before I even noticed! And so finally I looked at him, you know, as if I'd just seen him, and the funny thing was he looked really normal, I mean he didn't look like a perv or anything.

He had kind of short brown hair and was a bit on the skinny side but not short, really. And he wore a nice sports jacket and pants, he wasn't one of those slobs in old jeans or anything and what was the strangest thing—I don't know why I should think this is so weird but I do—he had these stylish glasses on, like the kind Snoopy wears when he's the Red Baron or whatever, only smaller. I really like those glasses. He had a moustache too, and there he was, it was just out. Just hanging there, like those sausages at Safeway, and this guy had kind of a grin on his face. Jeez I'll never forget it.

I screamed, right? I'd never screamed before in my life, you know. I mean not really, just when I've been at the lake with some guy and he tries to throw me in or stuff like that, just fooling around. Well I really screamed and everybody came hot-footing it to my area and I go something like, I mean I can't remember the exact words, but it was something like, "Call the police this guy's a pervert."

So that's it. He just stood there in the middle of the room with all these people around, and this big smile on his face, as if he'd won the lottery or something.

A City Woman's Guide
to a Country Man's Farm

The Harvest

I remarked to a farmer I am intimately acquainted with that I was thinking of writing something for publication on the harvest. He drew himself up to his full height and looked down at me with unconcealed menace. *"There is nothing funny about the harvest!"* he tried not to screech.

So. Here is the section about The Harvest: There is nothing funny about the harvest.

Any farmer will tell you that. Any farmer's *banker* will tell you that in spades.

Checking the Rear Tires

Checking the Rear Tires usually occurs late at night while driving home from a party. One undergoes the experience of having the pick-up truck brought to a screeching halt, and watching the farmer scramble wildly out the door, saying he has to check the rear tires. One then hears what *could* be described as softly falling rain. If the farmer is endowed with a sense of mischief, he will tell you upon returning that he had a transmission leak.

At any rate, it is a comforting thought to know that farmers will stop at any hour of the night or day, regardless of the weather, to maintain their vehicles, especially the back end of the truck. Farmers are quite likely the most conscientious group of men one is apt to run across.

Oh yes. Rural women do not check the rear tires. They instead Examine the Upholstery by clutching the edge of the seat with white-knuckled fingers to see if it will hold up for the duration of the ride home. They are not known to say much, except for the tight-lipped phrase, "For God's sake, hurry up. I can't hold this forever."

The Hired Man

The Hired Man is a person hired to do work that farmers say they could do much better themselves. Why farmers hire anybody is a mystery to me, and seems to be a mystery to most farmers, for I have often heard the anguished cry, "What in the *hell* ever made me hire that man?" However, I have developed some possible theories:

A farmer who has time to kill will hire someone so that he can re-do everything the hired man has done, thereby nicely rounding out the farmer's day.

It simply makes a farmer *feel* good when he can say that any day he can out-work, out-think, out-do, and possibly out-lie his Hired Man. A farmer's best friend is his underdog, even though he does have to pay him.

A Hired Man is a handy thing to hang the blame on when a neighbour spots misses in the middle of a newly seeded field. Misses on the *outside* rounds are usually relegated to grasshoppers or "too many tire tracks," but having a Hired Man is essential for misses farther in.

Most farmers, at one time or another, have been their own father's Hired Man, and they have found out that hiring someone impartial to scream at is much nicer than yelling at members of the immediate family. This arrangement comes in really handy when the farmer would like a place to sit down at family reunions and holidays.

The Farmer's Wife

Any farmer's wife will tell you she is a patient, long-

107

suffering, kind woman. Any *farmer* will tell you she is a Master Engineer of Guilt, hands down, no holds barred. A farmer's wife may not be able to fix a faucet, he will say, but she sure can fix a farmer.

Example: Oh *yes* dear! I think your new truck is wonderful! Now I can sit in it and recover from the fumes the living-room drapes are causing by rotting to shreds on their rods.

Example: Oh how I *envy* your new auger. It works ever so much better than my mixmaster, now that the lefthand beater fell apart in the spring of '85.

Example: You're improving and remodelling your shop? Very *smart* of you, dear. Bankers are much more prone to allocate several thousand for building improvements, rather than a few hundred for a fur coat. And while I'm thinking of it, could you maybe deposit ten dollars in my chequing account? I need some iron-on patches for that old black thing I wear in the winter.

A farmer's problems are not all over with when the tractor is finally working right, and the combine is fixed. A married farmer is more sure of this than anyone else. (His *mother* could have told him *that*, but she had all those hors d'oeuvres thawed for the wedding reception.)

Checking the Sky

One of the first things a farmer does upon arising in the morning is to step outside the back door. He will tell you that he is "Checking the Sky." This is the farmer's quaint way of saying that he is going to deal with flatulence in a somewhat musical manner, while looking skyward with great concern and concentration.

If a farm wife is endowed with courage and an inquisitive mind, she may poke her head out the window and brightly ask, "Well, what do you think? Is there something blowing in from the east, or is there a slight leak in the propane tank?"

A farmer would be shocked, nay, scandalized, were he to find a woman Checking the Sky herself, and so he makes sure he passes along any meteorological material he has, as soon as he accumulates it. The farm wife shows her gratitude for his consideration by flapping her apron and praising things, yelling "Good grief! Good Lord! Holy cow!"

Litter
One aspect that is pleasantly evident in the country is the lack of debris along the side of the road. This is because farmers are very tidy people, and it upsets them to see anything left where it shouldn't be. There is no littering problem in the country. If one does see something lying by the side of the road, one only has to recall that time-worn phrase, "Some farmer will pick it up."

Careless people who have lost things out of the back of their trucks are aware of the characteristic neatness of rural men. When the truck driver returns the next day to retrieve what was spilled, he finds to his surprise that every bit of litter has been hauled away by some farmer—usually in the middle of the night, because farmers embarrass easily if caught doing a good deed. And a really good deed might take a few hours and one or two trips.

Successive generations of farmers seem to be bothered by the same kinds of refuse. It absolutely *eats* at some orderly agriculturalists to see a pile of 4-by-4s, coils of fence wire or bags of cement carelessly strewn in the ditch.

"Look at that," a farmer will say. "Somebody will probably pick that up, and it might as well be me." He then throws the objectionable material in the back of his half-ton and drives off with a happy smile, mur-

109

muring to himself, "Yessir, a guy could really clean up around here if he keeps his eyes open."

MARILYN CAY

George said about the speaker

"he was great, just great
he spoke for an hour and a half
and never said the same thing twice
never repeated himself once
the message he gave was wonderful
an hour and a half
never saying the same thing twice
never repeating himself once
for an hour and a half, I
just couldn't get over it,
how anyone could entertain a crowd
for an hour and a half
and never say the same thing twice
never repeat himself once, I
really admired that about him ... "

Where in the Hell Are We?

Nokomis
A dishevelled hairstyle, worn mainly by teenagers, rock musicians, and poets.

Pym
That spot on your back that itches and which you never can quite reach to satisfactorily scratch.

Brora
A conversation that never seems to end, has no real point to it, and which usually occurs between two people who really don't want to talk to each other anyway.

Inchkeith
The first indentation in your new suitcase that wasn't there when you left on your plane trip but that appears there now and will stay forever.

Waniska
The sound a windshield wiper makes as it scrapes across wet glass.

Wimmer
The eerie sound that the prairie wind makes as it blows past closed windows late at night.

Gibbs
A circular Christmas present, one you received last year and never used, but which you now pass on to someone else who you think can use it, but who, it turns out, had first given it, two years previously, to the person who gave it to you.

Adanac
A headache caused by watching too much hockey on television; what makes the headache unusual is that it usually belongs to the one who wasn't watching but had to listen in the next room.

Tregarva
The smell of a wet toothbrush after travelling with it for a week.

Sclanders
The food particles between your teeth that fly off and stick to your bathroom mirror while you are flossing.

Crutwell
A kitchen sink filled with one week's worth of dirty dishes.

Tantallon
The missing black sock in the laundry that you discover inside a shirtsleeve when you put your arm into it three days later.

Gorlitz
The floor of a movie theatre after the lights go up and all the patrons have left.

LORIANNA GUNDERSDATTER

Living in Small Towns:
A Guide For Decentralized Civil Servants

So you're moving to the small town
decided   to keep your
government job   after all
then I've got some advice for you
you stranger in   a strange land.

Country folk despise extravagance
so when you move don't use a moving van,
                    but pile your
furniture into a horse trailer
and drive into town with the dust.

And when they come to greet you
say that you hate your job
and are working only
long enough   to buy a farm
and learn to curl
and wear a baseball cap with
curved peak   and farm dealership
logo on the front   and inform them that
you're planning   to raise canaries and
will buy all the   canary seed
they grow under   the government
farm   diversification   programs.

Don't be upset by their daily talk of
sex in the coffee shop   cause when they
say   *did you get much last night*
they're meaning rain   and   *red and hard*
refers to spring wheat on the prairies
as does   rape   mean   canola
And if they say their rubber burst at Climax you

know that their tractor tire had a blow-out
on the way home from Swift Current.

Get your rye's straight   as Spring rye   is
planted   in the field   in the spring
and winter rye is that what you take
to the curling rink   in your pocket
to drink after each end
and "wry" is the kind of face you make when
they mention the government or taxes or heat or
drought or grasshoppers.

Plant a garden, but throw stones on it when
you are still working and they are
all at the lake or auction sales and
tell them that it hailed: they will give you more
vegetables than you can use.

Don't golf openly during seeding or harvest
but sneak your clubs into your car at night and
say you're going to look at crops
for four or five hours and
don't wear Nike Airs and don't jog on
a grid road   and it may be wise

to tape down three fingers so folks think
you cut them off in a power take-off
It also will make it easier
for you to calculate seven per cent GST on
everything you buy.

Above everything   don't be upset   if
someone you meet calls you an asshole.
In small Saskatchewan towns   *asshole*   is a
term of endearment.

CAROL ANDERSON

Getting Even

This is really my sister's story. She told it to me and she knew the woman who knew the woman that it happened to. Or maybe I should say she knew the woman who knew the woman that made it happen to herself. Anyway, my sister hasn't gotten around to writing it yet so I will. It's too good to keep.

Ben and Lucy hadn't been married all that long. Mostly farm people marry in the fall after the harvest is in but they had married in the spring. Don't ask me why. When you marry a farmer you have to remember that you can't speak to him in February or March when he's doing his income tax, or April when he's watching the spring run-off and calculating the moisture loss, or May and June when he's putting in the crop or any time between June and late August when he's worrying about it, or August to October when he's getting the crop off and still worrying about it or November when he's figuring out the debits and credits, mostly debits, and saying he never should have taken up farming. That leaves you exactly two months the way I figure it. If you're lucky.

Well, anyways, to get back on track: Lucy married Ben in June after seeding and she was a farm girl herself so she knew what she was getting. They were just the two of them and working round the clock with no time to talk or to even see each other really and, when they did, they couldn't keep their hands off each other. That's the way it still was with them.

Lucy was at the kitchen counter making pastry when she saw Ben come loping up through the yard, looking handsome and big and clean-cut in the green denim uniform she laid out for him fresh every morning. And worried. The screen door slammed and he came up behind her, cupped each breast in one of his big hands and held her that way until she turned her face up for his kiss.

"What's wrong?"

"Need a part. Can you run into town for me?"

"Sure. Write it down."

"Okay. While you're getting it I'll pull the combine up in the yard and have a look at her."

Lucy shoved her pastry back in the fridge, rinsed and dried her hands, grabbed her purse and the piece of paper he handed her and was out the door into the old Pontiac and kicking down the gas in three minutes flat. She was hitting sixty-five when she turned the corner into the highway, and eighty-five— ninety after that.

Time to grab a bag of fertilizer for her hedge, getting spindly now, and on to the next stop for chicken pick because the broilers needed killing next week, then the combine part at the next stop, having to wait awhile there because they were busy, and finally into the drugstore for a birthday card for her sister in Calgary. The fourth stop, the drugstore, is run by her friend, Natalie, and Natalie says, "Lucy, do you know you're wearing a large black hand on each boob? Hope this is the first place you've been in. On that white shirt it shows up real good. Harvest time or not, can't anybody say your old man's neglecting you."

Lucy said, "Son-of-a-bitch. I'll get you for that." And she's out the door and into the Pontiac like a singed cat and the card forgotten on the counter.

The combine is pulled up in the yard and a pair of green denim legs sticking out from under it. She turns off the engine, gets out of the car and walks loud and crunching on the gravel up to the house

116

and slams the screen door like she's gone inside. Then she takes off her shoes and walks soft, down-wind, down shadow, creeping up on that pair of legs. Then, quick as she can, she reaches under the combine, unzips him, and grabs.

Now three things happen all at once. Lucy realizes that the dick she's got in her hand isn't the one she knows and she lets it go like it burned her. Ben comes strolling out from behind the combine having heard the car drive in. And John Babiuk, who belongs to the legs and the dick and who had just come walking by and offered to see if he could figure out what all was wrong with the combine, well John sits up fast and cracks his head on the bar and falls back again unconscious, out like a light.

It was only a minor concussion but they kept him in the hospital over night for observation after Lucy and Ben got hold of one leg each and pulled him out from under the combine, him limp as a—well, you know—and loaded him into the back of the Pontiac and drove him into town.

Of course Lucy had to finally give in and tell Ben what had happened and he just about killed himself laughing. And not only Ben. Worst thing is that John Babiuk is the biggest mouth in the country and he's still telling that story in the beer parlour and they're still laughing and it's been two months ago now. Ben's hauling his own repairs. Lucy? Well she says, "Serve the silly bugger right. Why couldn't he stay home and mind his own business?" But she hasn't been in town since.

Dad and the Maz

It all started out innocently enough. I picked up the mail on the way in. I handed it over and got to set the table, make some ham and cheese sandwiches, and serve up the tomato soup while they went through their mail. Mom received her Drought Aid Assistance form in the mail. Dad went through his mail. No form. Mom read hers through and found an 800 number to phone if you had questions.

Dad hurried his soup and sandwich so he could get on the phone and get his form. The deadline was already closing in. Dad went into the living-room to phone while Mom pulled out her files so she could fill in her form. Dad ended up cursing the phone since he'd either get a busy signal or the phone would ring about twenty-six times and then cut off.

The next day, Dad was on the phone again. He still hadn't gotten through which was abundantly clear each time he slammed the phone down.

"Bureaucrats!"

Dad stormed out of the bedroom, went through the mail quickly and when he discovered no Drought Aid Assistance form he stamped back to the bedroom phone.

"Why isn't he using the phone in the living-room?" I asked.

"Doesn't work anymore. He wore out the redial button yesterday afternoon."

"Ah," I said and set the table.

"Soup's on," Mom called and Dad grumbled out of the bedroom.

We all watched "Midday" quietly. When it was over, I started cleaning off the table. Dad went to the broom closet and pulled out a small brown paper

118

bag. He threw it on the table, went into the living-room, pulled the plug out of the telephone jack and brought the phone into the kitchen. He went to his study and grumbled to himself a few minutes. He came back out with the white copy of his traditional three-part memo form, folded it up and threw it in the brown paper bag. He then took the phone cord, wrapped it around the handset and threw it in the bag. He got some masking tape out of the cupboard, folded the bag around the phone, and taped it shut. I kept clearing the table. Mom sat at the table, sipping her tea and smoking her cigarette. Dad stomped over to the pencil drawer, rummaged around and came back with a black felt marker. He started writing on the parcel.

"Who are you sending it to?"

"Mazankowski."

"You're going to get into trouble doing that."

He stuck on a return address label.

"What for? I'm sending him a letter and a phone. I'm a taxpayer. I can do that."

"It probably won't get out of town when they see where it's addressed."

"I've got a return label on it. It's to a member of parliament. I don't even have to put a stamp on it. I'm within my rights." He held it up. Honourable Don Mazankowski, Minister of Agriculture, House of Commons, Ottawa, Ont. K1A 0N2.

"Probably blow it up instead," I remarked.

"Not if it has a return address."

"Okay," I said.

"What's the letter say?" asked Mom.

"Just a second," he said and went to the bedroom. He brought back a file.

"Dear Mr. Minister, Enclosed is a telephone. I wore out the re-dial button trying to get through on your Drought Aid Assistance 800 number. I would like a Drought Aid Assistance form and a new phone. This one no longer works. I would also like you to either get more phone lines so I don't get a busy signal or some people who will actually answer the phone. I spent all yesterday afternoon phoning and either got a busy signal or it rang and rang and no one answered.

"Thank you for your assistance in this matter. If you cannot replace this phone, please send it back since we are poor farmers and my grandson likes to play with the phone. He can have this one since it doesn't work anymore. Yours truly—That's what it says."

He went to the hall, put on his jacket, and yelled that he was going to mail it right now. Mom looked at me and said, "He's going to get into trouble over this."

"But it will keep him busy."

"True. Want some more tea?"

On Sunday, my brothers, their wives, one nephew, and I all showed up for supper. As we plowed our way through chicken, potatoes and gravy, corn, salad, Coll's antipasto, and apple crisp, Dad told us what was wrong with the world and Mom informed us of her week's events. She saved what she thought was best for last.

"You remember your dad sending that package to Ottawa?"

"Yes," I said and told everyone else what Dad had done with the phone.

"Well, on Thursday, I was sitting and watching 'General Hospital' while your dad was having his nap. The buzzer went and I answered the intercom. They said they were the RCMP.

"I buzzed them in and went to the door. They showed me their identification and all I could think of was that some of you had been killed. So I let them

120

in.

"We went into the living-room. I asked them if they wanted some coffee or tea but they declined. I told them to sit down but they said they preferred to stand.

"One kept glancing down the hallway as though someone were going to pop out. I'm glad your dad stayed sleeping. Both of them were over six feet and in civilian clothes. I just dreaded what they were going to say. The older one stood in the centre of the living-room. 'Did someone here send a package to Ottawa in the last few days?'

"Let me tell you, I breathed a sigh of relief. 'Why yes, I said, my husband did.'

" 'Could you tell me ma'am what was in the package?'

" 'Well, you got it. You should know that there was a letter and a phone in it.'

"Then one turned to the other and said 'Ottawa will be happy to hear about that.' 'Could you tell us why there was a phone in the package?'

" 'Better than that,' I said, 'I can show you the letter.'

"So I went and got the letter. They read it over and thanked me.

" 'Ottawa will be relieved,' the younger one said this time. I asked for their business cards and then I showed them out."

"When I woke up," Dad said, "I was damn mad let me tell you. Coming in and questioning your mom without me being there. I sure want to know what they did with my phone."

"Probably the same thing they did with the coconut and the candles, blew it up," I said. "It was in the paper last week."

"Paranoids," Dad said. "If they were running the country better, they wouldn't have to blow up packages that people sent them in the mail."

"Oh, there was one other thing," Mom said, "After I saw them out, I went back to the living-room. They were just visible from the window. One of them was doubled over with laughter."

Dad set down his tea. "When I got up and heard what happened with your mom, I sent Mazankowski another letter asking for a form and asking where my phone was. Can't trust them to pass on the message to send a form."

"Good luck, Dad," Bernie said.

"Just hope that the post office delivers it," said my other brother.

A week passed, the form still hadn't come and the deadline was even closer. Dad was still phoning since he didn't trust the post office but he was alternating telephones. He hadn't heard back from the Maz yet either. After still another week had passed, Dad finally got two forms in the mail. One was from the local M.P. and one was from the department.

Dad also received a letter from the Minister's office. They said that they had no record of receiving a phone in the mail. So Dad wasn't going to get a phone. Dad then needed some information about how to fill out the form.

He phoned the 800 number again and actually got through. He said that he had two forms and wanted to know if he was only supposed to fill in one or both for the different quarters he had. The fellow on the line asked if he had submitted two. Dad said that he wanted to know if he had to fill in two. The guy said that if he had filled in two they could nail him for fraud but if he hadn't submitted them both, it was too bad. Dad got his name and wanted to talk to his supervisor, but the supervisor wasn't around.

So Dad wrote another letter. This one outlined the poor customer service, the delay in providing the forms, and a problem with the wording.

The way the form was worded, not only could the Ministry of Agriculture inspect his books but any agency or their appointees in the government could. He was not about to let the coast guard or Indian and Northern Affairs go through his books. They had lawyers on the government payroll who should be able to write a form so that everyone in the government didn't have access to check his books.

He also wanted a replacement phone. If the minister's office hadn't received his, perhaps they should talk to the officers from the National Crime Intelligence Unit who'd stopped by to check if he'd sent a package. Presumably they'd blown it up before they'd bothered to read the letter. If the minister and his colleagues were a bit better at governing, they wouldn't have to be so paranoid.

As well, it wasn't his fault that they'd blown it up. He'd put on the return label so they wouldn't. They could send him another phone that was just as defective. At least that way his grandson would have a toy.

The minister replied that they'd received the package but it had been disposed of. Dad wasn't going to get a replacement phone. He'd got his form. He should fill it in and be done with it. Well, it was a little more diplomatic than that but not much. They were probably upset about the paranoid comment.

In the meantime, Mom had crossed out the part on her form where the Government of Canada or its agents could come and inspect her farm books. She wrote in Agriculture Canada. She just didn't want everybody and his dog coming by to look at her books.

She got her form back saying that they wouldn't accept an amended form. She had to send in an unaltered form. She filled it in, added "under protest" and sent it. They didn't like the "under protest" and returned it. Now Mom wrote a letter. I began to wonder if the mandarins thought my parents were feisty or just stubborn.

Dad and Mom eventually filled in the forms the way they were supposed to. At one point, Mom was talking on the 800 line to someone who said that they had received a number of protests about the wording on the form. She said that she actually thought they were re-drafting the form. Mom asked for another copy. She got the same one that she amended the first time.

By the time all the forms were filled in, the deadline was past. Mom and Dad wondered if they ever would receive any money. The bureaucracy, in their eyes, was becoming unmanageable. There was no service. The minister didn't respond very quickly or sympathetically. The only bright point was that the local M.P. actually sent the form. Dad was very happy with him although he didn't think that Dad would get a replacement telephone.

Then Dad started getting lots of mail from the PC party, presumably since he'd written the minister so many times.It only confirmed his worst suspicions. He replied to requests for donations with requests for money to help out a poor farmer. Perhaps when they got around to paying him the drought assistance, he could possibly see his way clear to making a donation. The requests gradually became less frequent.

Eventually, my parents received some money. Of course, other farmers who had harvested better crops than they did made out even better. No word ever came back that the snarky guy on the phone who was waiting for Dad to commit fraud was ever disciplined. Dad never received a replacement phone. Mom and Dad didn't get any more visits from the National Crime Intelligence Unit. I figure that they probably got put on a list of subversives.

At one point, Dad actually did donate some money to the PCs. Of course, some time later, they phoned him asking how much his cheque was for because they'd lost it. Dad put a stop payment on it, and then the party hacks found it again.

Dad received another request for donations. He sat down and wrote a very thoughtful letter. It mentioned that he had thought very seriously about donating to the party.

However, he'd had a few problems with some of their members and the staff didn't seem to be on the ball either because they'd lost his cheque. He had thought of donating a certain amount. It just happened to be the same amount as the cost for replacing the phone that the minister hadn't returned. For that reason, he was going to decline again this time. The money just wasn't there.

Dad died in the spring, just before seeding. He was cremated and buried beside his father. Mom, my brothers and I discussed what type of headstone he should have. They talked me out of my suggestion which I thought was the best idea.

I was going to get in touch with an actor friend of mine in Toronto. I would get him to dress up as a telephone repairman and take one of Mazankowski's phones. I would then get it bronzed and we'd use it as Dad's headstone. It would be unique and fitting I thought. My brothers agreed but the minister wouldn't go for something that different in his cemetery.

So, in the enduring tradition of my family, I sat down at my word processor. I turned it on and when the word processing package popped up on the screen, I wrote:

"Your Grace, Re: Headstone Policy in Elm Springs Cemetery, Would it be possible to change the policy in regards to my father's headstone? I think that headstones should reflect the feelings of the deceased and their family. No doubt, you have already heard about the discussions held with the local priest.

"Could you please inform me as the possibility of change. I await your early reply in this matter. Sincerely."

I am now awaiting his reply. My actor friend is still on standby.

LORNE KULAK

Knowing the Game

I throw the very first pitch of the game, a nibble on the outside corner, right where I want it. Umpire says, "Ball one." I throw the next pitch in the same spot. Umpire says, "Ball two." So the catcher gives me the signal and we go into our plan.

The next pitch is the high hard one. The catcher pulls down his mitt and the ball hits the ump right in the Adam's apple. Lays him flat on his back. Ball three.

Once he gets up and ready I throw another nibble on the outside corner. Umpire says, "Strike one." Next pitch is about an eighth of an inch outside. Umpire says, "Strike two." So the next pitch I throw a whole quarter of an inch outside. Umpire says, "You're out."

You've got to know how to play the game.

LORNE KULAK

Old Jack

Back in 1953 we had a good year, just the right amount of moisture at all the right times. We had an unbelievable crop. Now, all our bins were full so we had to use these three old ones. One was a chop house, so it was small. The next one was an old shack, not the one I was born in, but the one we lived in for the first year. The third one was made out of rough poplar, and you know what that's like.

I guess Dad filled those bins more than he should have. He knew that, but he didn't count on the cattle rubbing up against them. We had to keep nailing and nailing them back together. Finally, Dad got a roll of barbed wire and we wound and wound it around all three bins. We didn't want to cut the spool off so we just left it and hooked it up to a Ford coil and a battery.

Now, these bins were out of view of the house. We didn't know old Jack, the hired man, had been going out there to relieve himself. But we found out. He went back there, let out a scream, then the seventy-five-year-old man ran seventy-five yards peeing on his leg the whole way.

LORNE KULAK

The Mask

One time I was catching and something distracted me. I don't know what it was but when I looked back toward the mound the pitch was a fastball three-quarters of the way down the pipe. The batter swung and missed on strike three and the ball hit me square in the mask and stuck between the two bars. Soft metal. Popped both lenses out of my glasses.

I hadn't caught it and the only thing I could do was trap it. The batter knew what was going on so he took off for first base. Meanwhile I tried to get the ball out of the mask to throw him out, but it was stuck.

It was time for a quick decision so I hurled the mask overhand, spun it like a discus, in an arc like a rainbow, right over the runner's shoulder to the guy on first who caught it like a football.

The umpire shouted, "You're out!"

AUDREY JOHANNESSON

Mother and the Bull

Colonel was a big white Shorthorn bull that my mother acquired by working as a housekeeper for a bachelor in a district in northern Saskatchewan. He was not your average snorting, bellowing, dirt-pawing menace, but rather a sneaky type of animal. He would wait around corners of buildings, or waylay you out in the open when you had nothing in your hands to defend yourself and no place to hide. He wouldn't run at you with his head lowered, but would stalk you and rumble deep in his throat.

I remember the day we brought the bull home to our own small farm. It was the month of July and school was out.

Seeding time was over, and my mother and little brother were coming home from the bachelor's place to stay. I was coming home too, after being boarded out close to the school. We were a whole family again, riding home in a wooden wagon with Colonel the bull tied behind. Mom and Dad sat on the spring-board seat, weaving fantastic dreams of the wonderful cattle herd they would have some day.

After we arrived home, Dad turned the bull loose in the pasture with our little bunch of three or four cows. During that spring, while the rest of the family was away, Dad had planted fifty acres of oats and it was coming along nicely. He had also planted a garden. Money was in short supply during the mid-thirties, but if a family had food and warmth they could wait until better times came along.

The next morning my brother and I were up early ready to re-explore our old haunts and get our bearings. Guess who was in the oat field surrounded by his new lady friends? You guessed it—Colonel the bull.

That was the summer that we turned the calves back on the cows and packed up every pail, kettle, and tub into the wagon to go north berry picking. We even took along the wash boiler and empty cream can. North of Bronson Lake there was an old unused trapper's cabin and pole barn where we set up our camp. We slept out in the open on the beach in one big family bed. Mom and Dad slept on the two outside edges with us two kids in the middle. What a comfort my parents were when I woke during the night to hear wolves crying across the lake.

After a few days of berry picking, when our food was running low and all our containers were full of berries, we headed for home. Everything was quiet and peaceful when we drove into the yard. In my dad's garden stood Colonel, with two hanks of pea vine hanging out of either side of his mouth. There wasn't a lettuce or a cabbage plant to be seen, and what hadn't been eaten had been trampled into the ground. That was the first time I actually saw and heard my mother weep. I guess in my innocence I'd thought only children cried.

From that day on, Colonel was in my mother's bad books. He put her in the hayloft one day when Dad was away, and it wasn't till Mother called and called to my brother and I to put the dog on the bull that she dared to come down.

When Dad first moved us onto that quarter section we'd found a nice little spring flowing in a ravine behind the house and garden. My Dad dug out a reservoir on the down side of the spring, put a cribbing in it, then covered it with slabs. Since the cow pasture fence was within twenty feet of the well, a trough could be filled with water through a couple of sections of eavestroughing, the cow pasture being down hill from the well.

I don't know what got into Colonel that one

particular day, because the cattle trough was still half full of water, but he must have broken through the pasture fence and approached the spring well.

The next morning, when my mother went for water for the house, she found Colonel sitting in the spring well. He had broken through the slab covering and fallen bottom first into the well. His head, shoulders, and front feet were on ground level, but the rest of the animal was jammed in the cribbing. We had to get the neighbour's big team of Percherons to get the bull out of the well.

Early that fall my father thought he had a firewood contract in the nearest town, so he decided to make an ox out of Colonel and use him to skid dead trees out of the bush, but that still didn't stop his sneaky habits.

One day my mother was walking home with us after she had been to a Ladies Aid meeting, and we had to pass through the cow pasture. We could hear the brush crackling behind us, and there came Colonel, grumbling down in his throat. We ran. My brother and I rolled under the pasture fence, but mother got hung up trying to get through the barbed wire and tore her only good dress.

What she said to that bull isn't fit to repeat. After all, to ruin your only good dress in those days bordered on a calamity. Later that same afternoon, when Mother went out to get the milk cows, she found them out in Dad's oat field again. She had had just about all she could bear. Taking the .22 rifle down from the wall, she went out and shot the beast right in the pants.

He let a bellow out of him and headed for the bush. Mother brought the cows home and milked them. The bull never showed up for two days.

Dad's firewood contract didn't materialize, so after much discussion it was decided that Colonel would have to be butchered for meat. We traded some of the meat off for cabbages to make sauerkraut and kept the rest frozen during the winter.

Colonel's meat was the toughest meat we had ever encountered. My mother got into the habit of grinding it with her meat grinder to make hamburger patties or meatloaf. One day she was grinding some meat for supper, when all of a sudden the grinder went crunch, crunch, spong, right in midturn. After closer examination, my dad extracted a .22 slug out of the remaining teeth in the cutting disc. Even in death, Colonel had had the last word.

ROBERT CURRIE

In the Beer-Parlour

Yeah out here everybody's got a nickname
Take this one jasper   soon's the crop's in
just about lives in the beer-parlour
hardly sees the light of day
Everybody calls him Paleface
His wife stays mad from harvest to spring seedin
Course they call her Stoneface
Worst drinker of all though's Dieselbags
Any night of the week he's there at closin time
hangs on till the last draft is dry
an they threaten him with the snowbank
When he finally does leave
there's a six-pack under his arm
an by the time he makes it home
he's always down to the last one
He'll drink anythin   whisky   beer   rotgut
even tea they say   though I never saw it myself
This one night I guess he runs dry early
don't have that last beer to get him home
It's colder'n a witch's tit outside
when ol Zeebo down by the tracks
he hears this poundin on his door
It bein late an cold an all
he just opens up a crack
but that's enough to see Dieselbags
shiverin away like somethin the cat threw up
He kinda slides past the door
an starts checkin the place over
      Got a drink? he says but already
he's spotted somethin on the shelf
one of them tall old-style beer bottles
He don't give Zeebo a chance to offer
before he grabs it   throws back his head

134

an starts to drain her down
That man's got a throat like a sewer
Well sir   it's all gone
an ol Zeebo's still tryin to warn him
it's diesel fuel for startin the fire
I'll tell you   Dieselbags don't move for a second
but he looks like a cross between an earthquake
an a bull with a bee up its ass
Then he just stands straight up
an pukes all over the wall
Woulda killed some men I guess but not him
He's through the door without a word
an next night right back in his corner chair
gripin away same as usual at closin time
Folks out here used to call him Teabags
but not any more

DOUG NELSON

The Winter of '49

The first two weeks of November my hound Caleb and me tramped out every morning looking for game. But we didn't see anything bigger, not even a track, than a rabbit or a squirrel. Every day the air was colder than the day before, and every day the country got quieter, and every day Caleb and me came home earlier.

Finally, near the middle of the month Old Man Winter quit fooling around and really threw us into the deep freeze. This one morning Caleb and me only made it a couple hundred steps from the door before that hoary-bearded old eunuch reached right through my red woolies and latched onto my ankles. As those icicle fingers crawled up my pants I turned around and legged it back for the shack.

It's lucky Caleb hustled his tail and scratched on the door. By the time Ma opened up we were so stiff she had to jerk us both across the threshold.

The next morning Caleb and me and the wife and all three boys woke up under one blanket. After she stoked the fire Ma figured she'd best get me and Caleb out of bed. She was talking about sending us out hunting again, but heck, I was still numb from the day before and it sure hadn't chinooked over night. Caleb and me fought to stay under the covers, but the kids kicked us out. As we thumped down on either side of the bed, the dog and me made a run for the stove, but Caleb was closer and he skittered under it first.

There wasn't much use hiding. Though we whined considerably, right after breakfast the old lady pushed my dog and me out the door.

It was quiet as a saint's conscience out there, and

the air was so cold that it felt like we were inhaling little slivers of sharp ice. I looked down at Caleb and he looked up at me. I shook my head and we started down the trail.

I was walking about as fast as a kid to his bath and hadn't made more than thirty steps when I turned to look for Caleb. And wasn't he a sight! That dog had stiffened up into about the nicest point position I ever did see. His nose was pointed ahead, with one paw tucked up under his chin, and his tail was sticking out the back pointing straight towards the cabin door. I just stood there staring and froze up stiff as a tree trunk myself.

I guess the wife, she noticed that we weren't back after a few minutes and sent a kid out with a rope so they could pull us in. Ma said I was solid and white, like one of those Greek marble statues. She said that I kind of clunked up against the door stop and they had to lift me up and carry me over to the stove. They were none too careful though—not having much experience yet in handling frozen folks—and when they bumped my head against the threshold they chipped this here piece off the top of my left ear.

Poor old Caleb, he wasn't so lucky. The kids brought him in after me so they were careful at the door, but when they stuffed him under the stove, one of them gave an extra shove. Snapped his tail right off! Didn't leave the poor hound with so much as a stump to wag with.

Now I can't speak for Caleb but after going through that thawing-out process, I almost wished they had left me froze. It was just lucky that the stove was small and they could only thaw a bit of me at a time. Since they started with my feet, my frozen numbed head wasn't getting the tingling, thawing-out messages from my toes: I didn't feel anything until up around my armpits. But when I did! Well, it sure makes me sympathize with those folks that they're freezing and preserving nowadays. If they ever get thawed they're all going to feel that tickling, tingling in their heads like I did that day.

The wife, she said that it was lucky I had a brain no bigger than a peanut shell, otherwise I might not have been able to stand her—the thawing pain that is.

After that last trip, even Ma figured we should wait until it warmed up before Caleb and me went hunting again. I doubt she could have got Caleb to go anyway. Even after he was thawed out he never moved for the longest time, just lay hunkered under the stove with his broke-off tail tucked between his front paws.

Me, I started spending a lot of time sitting in front of the stove, turning around and around in my chair like a rabbit on a spit. As a matter of fact we all five of us got to doing that: just sitting and turning like a bunch of loony folk. By spring those chair legs were wore down to stubs and the soles of our boots were thin as butter paper.

Turning round and round got to be pretty wearisome so once in a while I'd spit a shot of chewing tobacco up on top of the stove. Then we'd watch those drops sizzle and hop around like a bunch of little brown kids with hot feet. The wife she didn't appreciate my dirtying her stove top, but it got so as I could tell when the fire needed to be stoked by how high the tobacco juice jumped.

If the tobacco juice appeared to be losing steam one of the kids or the wife would dress up nice and warm and head over to get some more fuel from the wood box. Even though the box was inside the door, the wood got so cold that a kid could crack a couple blocks together and they'd split into chunks just the right size for the stove. You couldn't hit those blocks

138

too hard though, or the wood broke into a thousand splinters, and we sure didn't need kindling that winter of '49. The fire Ma started in the fall was an eternal flame that burned day and night until crocus time.

As snow melt water was pretty dear, Ma got the once a day dishwashing habit out of her head real quick. We just chipped our plates off after each meal until, after about a week, the plates got too disgusting—even for Caleb and me. About that time we usually needed more fuel from the woodshed anyway.

On wash-and-wood day everybody kept busy. The wife, she scrubbed the dishes in a pan on the stove and set them in the warming cabinet to dry. At the same time the kids were fetching blocks of fuel from the woodshed outside. One of the boys would run out and grab an armful of blocks and start back. When he froze up, the other two pulled him in with a rope tied around his waist, hopefully with his stiffened up arms still glommed onto the wood. Then they waited till that first one thawed a bit and another one took a turn and ran out to get another armload. The thawing-out part slowed things down so it took those boys most of an afternoon to fill the woodbox.

When the wife had finished washing the dishes it was time to dump the dishwater. Now you might not figure that dumping the dishwater was worth mentioning, but it took some doing that winter of '49.

We'd have to get the pan of water bubble-boiling before the wife grabbed it with her hot mitts. Then I'd take a run for the door and throw it open just before Ma went barrelling out at full gallop—we only made a bit of a timing mistake once all winter and I sure was glad Ma's arms stiffened up as quick as they did. Anyway, like I was saying, the wife, she'd go through the door like a stampeding buffalo and about the time I'd look around the corner she'd be heaving the water out of the dishpan in slowww motion.

As soon as the pan was emptied I'd start pulling on the rope to haul her back into the shack. First, though, I'd have to give a jerk to detach her and the lip of the pan from the big arch of frozen dishwater. One especially cold day I had to get the kids to help me tug her loose as she'd been kind of slow and had only half-emptied the pan before everything stiffened up. It took a lot of jerking to get her loose. For awhile there we thought maybe one of her skinny arms would give before the ice, but finally the ice broke.

After that extra long trip Ma got a taste of what I felt when I had my whole body unfroze. Because of her peanut brain remark I was tempted to thaw her out head first, but then I remembered which end her mouth was on, so we took her nice and easy and slow, feet to head. That's probably the quietest two hours I ever spent with Ma. When she thawed out, the wife decided the dishes could stay dirty a week longer and the boys could start earlier and haul more wood in so we only needed a wash-and wood day every second week.

I've got to admit I missed seeing those big arches of icy dishwater once a week. With the winter's sun shining behind them, those boiling bubbles would just sparkle; and when the sun sank low the arches got coloured up like a winter's rainbow. It made washing day something to look forward to. The wife—she never did have time for assthetics—she still didn't like washing day. She said she never saw anything anyway because her eyeballs got all frizzed up with the steam and the frost.

Ma's eyes weren't the only things that got steamed and frosted on washing day. There were two windows on either end of the old shack but by the first

140

of December there was an inch of frosting stuck to each one of them. We only got a look outside on wood and wash days. Heck, the whole darned world could have blown up out there and we wouldn't have known until the wood box was empty!

During that winter of '49 New Year's passed by before we even noticed that we'd missed Christmas, but the kids didn't fret much seeing as we didn't have a turkey, and seeing as nobody would have wanted to go out and cut a tree anyway. I promised those boys that next year we'd have two trees, and two turkeys. The thought of turkeys made the boys' eyes spark. Since Caleb and me couldn't get out to bag a rabbit or squirrel, everybody got to dreaming of eating something besides deer meat.

By the end of January, though, venison was starting to look pretty good, because even it was getting scarce. By the middle of February we were gnawing twice-boiled soup bones.

Caleb still had his detached tail tucked between his paws, but he got to eying it, and sniffing it, and one day in February he was just about to chomp down on his own wagger when Ma cussed and jerked it away from him. That next pot of soup tasted pretty darned good. Caleb, he liked the leavings well enough himself, picking away with his teeth at a finger thin line of tail bones.

The next day the kids were mumbling about roasts and steaks as they were turning around in front of the stove. I couldn't hear too well because of the scraping of the chair legs, but there was always at least one pair of those blue eyes sighting like a lighthouse lamp on my dog. Caleb was too busy chewing on the remains of his tail bone to notice, but I could tell that those boys of mine were figuring out where the T-bone was situated on a dog.

I craved a good feed myself, but the thought of

141

roast Caleb with onions on the side didn't whet my
appetite none. I explained to those boys that Caleb
was a valuable hound. He could chase cows, he could
hunt, he was a good-for-anything kind of dog. Him
and me, we were a perfect pair that couldn't be broke
up. I told those boys that I'd just as soon slice a chunk
off my own haunch as put a knife to my canine
partner. The kids seemed amenable to the change
and proceeded to study my rear end.

I could see that our meat situation was getting
pretty desperate—desperate enough to risk another
trip outside. One of the boys had been hallucinating
earlier that week. He had said that he saw rabbits out
in the yard when he was gathering wood. He said that
there were white ones all over outside. I'd laughed
with the rest at the time, but now I played the story up.
I said that we couldn't see out the frosted windows,
and said that maybe there were rabbits all over outside, and that we wouldn't know for sure unless we
looked.

The wife commented that maybe my peanut
brain wasn't over the freezing yet, and two of the kids
laughed. But the character that had been hallucinating he said he'd hold the rope if I wanted to go out
and shoot one of those white rabbits he'd seen. So, I
dusted off my squirrel gun, pulled on every coat and
sweater I had, and headed towards the door. Caleb,
he backed farther under the stove and I went out
alone.

It was squinty-eyed bright afternoon, but the sun
didn't have a matchstick's worth of heat to it. The
country looked like it was made of crystal glass and if
a fellow hollered too loud every glittery thing would
shatter and tinkle down onto the snow. I stood staring so long I almost forgot to look for imaginary
rabbits. But just before my eyes frosted over, I saw
them. They were hard to pick out white on white, but

142

looking close I could see pairs of button-black eyes and pink-edged ears. There were rabbits huddled together in the snow all around the outside of the shack. Like a darned fool I let my mouth drop open and froze up stiff as a popsicle before I could get a shot off.

Since my eyes were bugged out and my mouth was wide open when they pulled me in, Ma and the boys figured I must have seen something. While I was thawing out Ma wiped the gun with kerosene so it'd fire in the cold. Then she shoved me out the door again.

I kept my mouth shut this time and edged up to one of those big eared varmints. He didn't look like he'd be moving too fast but I wanted to be close enough so's I could just fall on him after I fired. That white rabbit was sitting full centered in my sights when I pulled the trigger.

"Kee-rack!" There was a puff of smoke, but instead of firing the whole darned gun blew apart. The lead bullet stayed in one piece; it dropped and rolled down between the rabbit's paws. He was sniffing it when I toppled over and wrapped my arms around him. A live rabbit doesn't carry like a block of wood, though. The beggar squeezed out of my stiff arms before Ma could pull me inside.

The wife and kids weren't too pleased with pulling me in empty handed again; but, because I had a bit of rabbit fur caught in my mitts, they were willing to give me another shot. As soon as I was close to thawed they started shoving me towards the door. I braced one foot against each side of the jamb and said I didn't have a gun. Ma handed me the 30.30, but I braced myself again and told her that my heart was starting to act up with all this freezing and unfreezing. I said that this would probably be my last trip, and didn't a man get one last wish before he went to meet his maker—all I wanted was to sit in front of the stove for a minute or two with a fresh chew of tobacco.

The wife, she ain't all bad. She quit pushing, cut off a plug of Old Mule and let me sit down to enjoy a turn or two in front of the stove. But I only got in one spit before Ma jerked me off of the chair and hustled me out the door again.

Now I knew there wasn't any use trying to shoot. Even if the gun did fire, a 30 calibre bullet would blow a hopper to smithereens. The only thing I could think of doing was to use the gun as a club. I had to act fast before I stiffened up so I lined up on a spot between the first two pink-edged ears I saw. That old rifle whistled through the cold air and landed smack dab between those ears.

Unfortunately, they weren't a matched pair. My Winchester shattered from stock to muzzle between two rabbits sitting side by side.

That was the last straw. First my dog lost his tail, and now both my guns were gone. In utter disgust I spat out my whole chew of tobacco. That pear-shaped plug arched through the air towards one of them rabbits and plunked down right between his ears. The old hopper he hunkered up like he was about to jump, and then keeled over—fresh killed and fresh froze all in one shot. I can't say I wasn't a little sorry to get the poor beggar that way, but it surely was either him, or me, or Caleb on the supper table that night. Anyway, I toppled onto that rabbit and tucked him into me like those football players do nowadays.

It didn't take me long to thaw out but when I did there was nothing but bones left, and the boys and Caleb were gnawing on them. The wife, she was smiling. She said that was the best rabbit she'd ever ate.

Well, I'd found a sure-fire way of getting those rabbits and I don't suppose I wasted more than two or three plugs through the rest of the winter. It was darned lucky that I'd stocked up on Old Mule in the fall. When the first chinook finally blew in, I was down to my last pouch.

I still keep plenty of chewing tobacco around the place, and I always stock up special heavy in the fall. A fellow never knows when there might come another one like the winter of '49.

PAUL WILSON

Outside/In

We talked north
west passage, those winter nights:
Hudson in his pitiful boat
cast off with his faithful cabin boy.

Our heroes were dead men, we imagined them
bent, hands frozen on their groins.
The path to the outhouse was our "passage,"
the journey kept us talking against urgency.

We learned to piss inside out,
faced the frost caked window
leaned into the draft
thighs pressed to the sill.

There were three air holes
in the bottom of the storm window
penis warm in cold fingers I'd aim
for the middle hole in case the hand should stray.

This was desertion and we practised it nightly.
The urine built up, a frozen scab
on the white stucco farm house. After the thaw
we were surprised to see our mark, the colour

below the bedroom window.
Nothing was said though I thought the stain
held the shape of Hudson's Bay.

ANDY SUKNASKI

Argument Over Snow

if my late mother and mary should be fortunate
      enough
to meet again somewhere beyond the abyss
i truly hope they never find anything to argue about
how could anyone in wood mountain ever forget them
those two neighbours once arguing over one last
      possibility
of snow in the spring?

beyond the marginalized kurdish woman in last
night's news
telling the world
"i am 96
have suffered so much
i am old and sick
but i'm home"
i imagine my polish mother again in her last years
of failing health and praying for early death
my mother always lonely
and hungering for a single letter from someone in
      the family
the day she trudges to village post office
where lee hands her a few flyers and says
"the radio sez it's going to snow tonight
mrs shanahsky"
she then responding beyond a certain joy
"dats be good moisture . . .
for ven ve plant garden"
they sharing some local news
before my mother slowly walks up small hill back
      home
to meet her romanian friend mary by gate
mother happy being able to relate fresh news

147

"good morrning mary! dha rradio say
it goying to snow tonight . . . "
mary wincing
"oh i hope it don' snow!
my arstritis is killin me!
mrs shanahsky . . . ull cum over for coffee
after my mail"
and i can see mary again
as she arrives at the post office wicket
where lee's day isn't going that good
as he maybe broods about something
while mary proclaims "MRS SHANAHSKY SEZ IT'S GOIN
     TO SNOW TONIGHT!"
lee dusting an waving cigarette in the air
to briefly laugh
"ha! mary it's spring now!
don' worry about mrs shanahsky or snow . . . "
and he stuffs a fistful of flyers in her hand
to fire up her cookstove and keep mary happy
in her gently flowering miseries of arthritis
and toes budding with corns . . .
finally i try to visualize mary that morning
mary a rippling bundle of controversy
as she arrives at my mother's place for coffee
to knock on porch door and then hobble right in
     saying
"mrs shanahsky! i jus talked with lee soparlo
an he says it's not goin to snow tonight
so we don' have to worry no more bout rasdishes
     planted early!"
my mother bruised and quietly murmuring
"mary? vhy you goink talk vit lee behin mine back?"
mary defending
"but lee soparlo said it's not goin to snow tonight!"
mother coldly correcting her
"i never say lee say . . . i say dha rradio say
it vil snow . . . "

148

"ah bullshit!" mary stomping out into porch again
"i don' want yer coffee!"

and so it all congeals into stony silence
my mother and longtime friend mary
no longer sharing a tea or coffee
nor watching "sanford an son" on tv together
    anymore
the good rains come and go
while mother watches the garden flourish
pumpkins and squash becoming a green explosion
    of vines
till by late summer
a squash vine creeps through caraganas and into
    mary's garden
a blossom opens up and withers among the tall tomato
    plants
a squash grows and ripens until one fall evening
mary finally finds it while harvesting tomatoes
she carefully cuts it from the vine
and proudly carries the huge squash in both arms
    to the fence
where my mother is gathering broad beans nearby
mother doesn't look her way till mary half whispers
"mrs shanahsky . . . look what i found!
this is your squash . . . it trespass through caraganas!"
as mary lifts it across the fence
my mother takes it in her hands to inspect it carefully
before commenting
"vat's be dhis? no be pumpkin! no's be squash!
look like some kine halfbreed squash . . . mary?"
my mother hands the squash back across fence and
    says
"mary . . . you be keep dhis halfbreed squash!"
and they both laugh till they weep a bit
mary's vision blurred
she tripping to fall into a heap of dry corn stalks

cushioning her and squash's fall
she and my mother laughing to weep some more
mother then suddenly concerned
"youz be okay? mary?"
        "yes! we're both okay" mary laughing
        "come on over for coffee! mrs shanahsky!"

GARY HYLAND

Local News
April 14, 1956

Meanwhile in the hills
southwest of Moose Jaw
crocus insurgents
have infiltrated
outlying regions

Early reports mention
purple squadrons
apparently armed
with stamens and pistils
of their own design
bombarding defenders
with frequent bursts
of fragrant air

So far skirmishes
have been inconclusive
but civic officials
expressed confidence
their defences are secure
*If the worst comes
we have tanks and jets
standing by* the mayor said

The guerrillas are reported
to be demanding equal time
with fiscal considerations
in public and private fields

The effect on school attendance
licence applications
and income tax returns
is not immediately known

Getting the Hang of Privatization

Everytime I turn on the radio there's something about privatization—Air Canada, the post office, and the government says there's more to come. So I went to a meeting a couple of days ago and finally found out how it really works. It's a great idea. I came right home and put it to work.

The first thing I did was to sell the front yard. The fellow who bought it keeps the grass down, sprays the dandelions, and for a small charge he lets us sit on the lawn anytime we want to.

I'm not so sure about his idea of cutting down the trees to build a fence around it, but I can see he's got to make a profit. He can't just have people wandering around enjoying the grass for nothing. He's got this great plan for attaching blades to the front of wheelchairs so handicapped people can mow the lawn. He figures they'll be glad to get the work.

I used to like that bit of wild bush down at the back corner with all the birds in it, but he's got a great idea for that, too. He's going to fence it over and raise pigeons. My kids are out right now leafleting cars with a three-colour brochure of recipes for pigeon pie.

I sold the kitchen to my youngest daughter who thinks she can cut costs and raise efficiency sixty per cent. She's got out tenders for cleaning the fridge and the oven, and is selling off the dishes. She thinks with disposable ones she can save paying us to wash them—says she knows a guy down the block who's going to recycle them in his mother's juicer.

My son's put up a sign down on the highway for bed and breakfast. That should feed in nicely to the kitchen operation, and I got a terrific rate from the guy who owns the yard to let us set up pup tents for the family once the bedroom business is booming.

You can't make much sitting around so we've sold all our living-room furniture—took a bit of a loss on it but it'll all come back eventually. We even cleared out Grandma's rocker. Actually we've cleared out Grandma at the same time but she loves it down at the combination senior citizen and day care centre, and it hardly costs us anything to pay her a visit.

I just had to stop a minute to give two of the younger boys some change so they could go out in the yard. They don't understand the benefits of privatization and I see they're setting up a picket line. They're talking about starting a union. Isn't that cute? I'm going to offer them a very attractive share package on the dog, if they'll agree to walk him when he's not rented out.

We've replaced the budgies with cornish hens which makes the cage a bit crowded, but if it all goes well, I hope to open a "cornish nugget" stand out of one of the basement windows.

My husband is talking of selling the guppies and stocking the fish tank with trout, and I'm sitting down right now to work up a share offering in the baby for a group of solid investors down the block.

ED UPWARD

dog's revenge

dog delighted in throwing things
up in the air
and catching them before they landed
    old shoes
        discarded newspapers
      a fat lady's panties
in blue pastel like the sky
    half a bra
that looked like the nose plate
of a soft missile
    a plastic barbie doll
that spoke to dog
and nearly scared him shitless
       a cat too
he would like to throw
if he could ever catch one
who was a poor climber
or had dull claws

he spent hours of good dog fun
just throwing things and catching them
    when he got bored though
he took to garden romping
and flower bed stomping
    old bones he would bury
like hidden treasure
in the petunias and snapdragons
    his hind legs flogging the dirt
dislodging dirt leaves and petals
he looked like a hairy backhoe

the banker hated dog
with as much passion as he loved money
    he would swear at dog
    "you mangy sonofabitch
    i'll cut out your gizzard
    and feed it to the pigs"
    "i'll send you to the lab
    you four legged turd depositing
    son of a mongrel bastard"
he threw rocks at dog
a deluge of rocks and insults

dog came back at night
and pissed on his hybrid roses

NEAL DAVIS ANDERSON

We Wait Around the Gallows

We were sitting in the kitchen on chairs at the table, talking about herons, when all of a sudden, we heard the sound of smashing glass. The shattering was a big sound, as though wherever the object broken had dropped from was quite a lot higher than the place where it had landed.

Kiki was not too worried. "What was that?" she said, as though it weren't obvious it was glass breaking.

"It sounds like some glass broke," I answered her, after thinking about it for a moment or two.

We glanced at the cat, who was perched over on the windowsill, looking up and to the left, then down, very casually at the goings on of the courtyard. I had thought for a moment he'd knocked over a glass from the counter and made it fall all of the way down to the courtyard. But he was sitting very still. So we started talking about tetanus, how it is also called "lockjaw" sometimes, as though nothing had happened, just picked up where we had left off, as though nothing had shattered.

But soon there was a louder sound, the sound of something more durable than glass, hitting a hard surface. It was clear to both Kiki and me that a pattern of some kind was emerging. Now we went over to the windowsill beside the cat and peered out. The cat didn't seem to mind us being there.

We were just in time to see the suitcase bounce. It bounced loudly on the pavement, two or three times. All of the stuff in the suitcase came out at once when the snaps broke with a loud click. There were toothbrushes—maybe only one toothbrush—a box of cotton swabs, some Vaseline, a crumpled box of

157

tampons. It seemed to us that all the suitcase's contents were bathroom things. They rolled and bounced uncomfortably about, and were still. It was soon clear that things were being thrown out of one of the top floor windows, up and to the left of my window, and down into the courtyard.

"It looks like someone's throwing things out of their window into the courtyard," said Kiki.

I was impressed with the deduction. "Yes, out of one of the windows," I said.

The courtyard had been pretty tidy before the broken glass and suitcase and things. If there were dead leaves there before, they had been swept up by someone. Simone came to her window, a floor below mine. She was wearing a black hairband in her black hair that day. This made her look Italian or maybe French.

"There's Simone," said Kiki.

"Yes, there's Simone," I agreed.

Both Kiki and I must have thought the same thing at the same time then, because we both said, "Maybe she heard the glass break and the suitcase fall, like we did." And then we answered each other, "You're right. Maybe." Simone was leaning on her windowsill, looking up and to the left, then down, always out, just like we were, and like the cat was.

"There's some really good stuff down there," said Simone, pointing at the suitcase and all of the other things, which were clearly in great pain from their fall. "Yes, there's some really good stuff down there," she said again. Simone uses my bathtub sometimes.

We were silent then for a moment, thinking about things maybe. Kiki said something about letters, how it was good to get them in the mail. I said yes, that it was great to get letters. Simone said she liked getting letters too, except when they were letters from certain people, or bills, which she didn't like at all and didn't even take out of the box when they came. Then we noticed something sailing downwards.

"Here comes something else." said Kiki as it fell.

"There's something else," I agreed, watching it. It was a plant in a pot and it landed upright, compressed deeper into its pot, saying maybe, "Oof"—something we could never have heard, given the thudding sound that accompanied its hitting the ground. Not a leaf was out of place though, and the bright yellow blossoms were intact. "It looks as if the plant made it okay," I said.

"That's a really good plant," said Simone.

"Yes, it's a potted plant," noted Kiki.

Then some other people, among them, Old Teddy, came to their windows, leaned on their sills. It was a pleasant evening and people seemed glad to get out. After all of the rain lately, it was good to see the sun and mildness. And besides the crashing once in a while, it was a quiet evening as well. I mentioned this to Kiki.

"Yes, it's supposed to stay pleasant through the weekend, too," she said. We looked up and to the left, then down, up and to the left, and down again as we spoke.

"That's good to hear after all of this rain we've had," remarked Simone.

Old Teddy asked from his windowsill, "Did you say it was supposed to be pleasant over the weekend?"

"That's right," said Kiki.

"Yes, I heard that too." said Simone.

"Oh, that's awful good to hear, after all this rain," said Old Teddy, very thoughtfully.

"I wonder if there will be any more good stuff," ruminated Kiki.

"Couldn't say," said Simone, honestly.

"You never know," I said. "You never know."

"Do you have a toaster?" asked Kiki of no one in particular, I thought.

"No," I answered.

"No, no toaster," said Simone, sadly.

Kiki's optimism showed then. "Maybe there will be a toaster next," she said.

"Well, that would be something," I said. We both looked up left, down, up left and down again.

"I don't have a toaster," said Simone again, recapping. Then, "So, if a toaster is next, I've got dibbs."

"Well, all right," I said, "though I don't suppose I'd mind having a toaster either." We watched the window.

"I know," said Simone after a moment. "You can have the toaster and I can use it when I come up to have baths at your place." We agreed then, that this would be the plan of choice when the toaster arrived.

"On the other hand, there may be two toasters," said Kiki, because Kiki is quite an optimist.

There was another projectile. Our interest was perked. It landed with the sound of a piano falling into a courtyard from a great height. There were wooden splinters everywhere. What had fallen looked like the top of a piano, the part you put the music on, sort of a music stand. I may be remembering the sound it made with some licence. Whatever it was, it was not whole now.

"No toaster yet," said Simone.

"Hang tight," said Kiki. "If there was a plant with yellow blossoms and a suitcase, then there must be a toaster."

"True. Though you never know for sure," Simone added.

For the shortest moment, the cat looked down at Simone, before he looked up and to the left at the top floor window again.

A bright red scarf fluttered down from the window toward the courtyard. Then a heavy bundle of clothing, shirts, shoes, and the like, wadded tightly, caught up with it and made it fall faster. The scarf and the clothing seemed to feel far less pain than the suitcase, for instance, had. There was a soft, muted sound when it landed. Kiki said something about the homogenization of cream you put into your coffee, or it may have been me who said that.

"Putting *sugar* into coffee is repulsive," said Simone and feigned gagging. We looked up to the left, then down. "But then," she reconsidered, "putting sugar into coffee isn't so bad when you think about it."

"I guess you'd like a cup of coffee," Kiki said to me.

"I wouldn't mind," I answered her.

"Yes, I wouldn't mind a cup either," she said. We continued looking—it was clear that we both wanted coffee more or less. Though the courtyard had recently been empty, now all of the things were starting to fill it up. There was a mound like the mounds in garbage dumps, what with the big things and all of the little ones, even the splinters from the music stand. The window on the top floor, to the left of us, out of which things were falling, or being thrown, slammed shut. The whole wall must have felt that.

We looked up. It seemed to be over. We looked down.

Simone and Kiki and Old Teddy and I and some other people, started to crawl out of our respective windows to get to the heap of good stuff in the courtyard. Kiki, or it might have been Simone, said something about a film actor who'd worn a different tie-clip in every scene he'd ever played. Forty films!

help

Talk to your plant, the experts say,
So I told it all about me, it took all day
And the day after that and the next day too,
I talked and talked till my face turned blue
And the plant turned yellow and withered and brown
With spots and bumps and bugs all around.

I talked a little louder in case it missed a word,
I told that plant every joke I'd heard,
I told it all of my bowling scores
For all of the games last year and more,
I recited it poems and I sang it songs,
I read it the dictionary. Gee it was long.

Till it moaned in a pitiful kind of way
And it feebly started to crawl away,
Pulling its roots right out of the pot
And its little plant toes curled up on the spot.
Can you think why? I'm sure I can't.
And I still had lots to tell that plant.

Blood and Guts

The hockey fan likes blood and guts, especially the enemy's guts and blood. But you can't always tell who the enemy is. One time I got highsticked in the chops and fell to the ice in a heap. Our trainer came running out and when he saw I wasn't bleeding, he gave me a little shot in the nose trying to draw some blood so the other guy would get five minutes.

Once I crashed into the boards with another guy and we started slugging at each other. A woman behind the screen said, Beat the snot outa that creep and I could tell she liked my style. I guess we would have killed each other, but the referee got in the way—stuck his finger in my eye and his thumb up my nose, which wasn't too bad considering it was supposed to be a fight, except that he was the brother-in-law of the guy that I was trying to kill and was trying to kill me.

Bomb Threats

In the event of a bomb threat at this rink the following procedures shall be followed:

1. The Receipt of a Bomb Threat by Telephone

    1.1 The recipient of the call should remain calm, courteous and listen carefully. Do not interrupt the caller, except to prolong conversation. Do not transfer the call. Keep the caller talking. Ask questions: Where is the bomb located? What kind of bomb? Are you a hockey fan? How do you know so much about the bomb? What do you think of Wayne and Janet's baby? Is the bomb in the Rat Room? Do you know the score of tonight's game?

    1.2 Make a mental note of any identifiable background noises such as voices, office machines, Zambonis, street traffic, Johnny Cash walking the line, party atmosphere, a woman yelling at kids in the pool hall, the sound of digging in the potato patch.

    1.3 Note distinguishing voice characteristics: loud, soft, high pitch, raspy, intoxicated, professorial, editorial, dictatorial, tory torial, bloodthirsty, drink thirsty.

    1.4 Is speech calm, slow, stuttery, nasal, slurrrrrd esseterrra?

    1.5 Is language excellent or good, fair or foul, buckbuckbuck, better than what the coach says?

    1.6 Does the caller have an accent? Grave or acute? Doth the caller lithp?

    1.7 Are the caller's manners calm, coherent, emotional, angry, rational, etc. Estimate the age of the caller.

    1.8 Attempt to find out the location of the bomb and identity of person or persons or team to whom the bomb is directed. Is the bomb in the Rat Room?

    1.9   Attempt to determine if the person has any knowledge of the building.

    1.10   Ask the caller when the bomb is to explode.

2.   Immediately After the Call

    2.1   Write your mental notes in the space below.

BIRK SPROXTON

The Hockey Fan As Professor

Gene has just moved from Las Vegas. He wants to read the signs. What are those gestures about? He says he really wants to know.

This is SPEARING, I say, tickling his ribs with the point of my stick, and this, I say with a quick spin, is an ELBOW as I jolt him off balance, and this is a BUTTEND, feeling out his solar plexus and this, turning on my other foot, is SLASHING (whack him across the knee) and this, as he bends over to catch his shinbone, is a CROSSCHECK, a clean ninety degrees across the back of his neck. And this, I carry him to the armchair, is HOLDING. Have a beer, I say, which he takes and lifts to his lips but I grab it, INTERFERENCE I say between swallows. And when you want to learn HIGHSTICKING, BOARDING and CHARGING we'll get skates on.

WILLIAM ROBERTSON

After the Revolution

The first way I knew it was rock and roll was it went
faster than all the other stuff
                              creamy driftings of
Ramblin' Rose, Moon River, Everybody Loves Somebody Sometime, lush pink clouds of Ray Conniff
and Billy Vaughn blown apart by Great Balls of Fire,
Twist and Shout, the click of my father's finger on
the selector button, his muttering down the miles of
change I knew was coming, sitting like a happy spy
in his solid house, my feet beneath his well-blessed
table, my white canine teeth snapping at his hand,
singing I Can't Get No Satisfaction, and his final
bewildered response: You call *that* singing?

In the shoe store I can't get no service before I get
10,000 watts of head-banging sound. And at the ice
cream parlour, the drugstore, the cane furniture
boutique. In the car every station I punch punches
back and I wonder what my parents are listening to
now.

On the Classics of Rock show I can see young Elvis
sneer but they don't say anymore what he sneered
at: Mitch Miller, Fred Waring and his Pennsylvani-
ans, how many of the Lennon Sisters his hip shake
shook out of the room, Kate Smith puffing offstage
to wrap herself in the ironsides of Old Glory.

I take my daughter to the teen store for blue jeans
and the woman who waits on us is my daughter's
age, nodding to the bounce of the walls, the same
beat her mother bounced her to. I want to open up
with Misty, A Taste of Honey, Chances Are, but I
don't stand a chance against the well-armed com-
placency of eight 12-inch woofers barking to the
cash register beat, our salesclerk chawing away at
her gum, safe in a changeless world

I just wanted to tell you, Dad,

my side won.

SHELDON OBERMAN

Angel with a Full House

I was feeling bad enough about Joey dropping dead without Tina dumping all over me.

"You ought to be ashamed of yourself, Swartki. Your pal for thirty years lying dead and naked on a slab of marble and you're just dealing out another hand." Tina could be one mean mountain once she got going.

I slammed down that deck in front of her and said, "There's nothing I can do about it, Tina! I can't make him come back. Do you think you can?"

"You're all animals," and her fat arm cut across the clubroom at the dozen or so guys playing poker or watching the ball game. "You're just burnt-out gamblers and two bit boosters. Yah, that's you, Bolo—a backyard toilet mechanic. You'd rip off your own mother to feed your shakes. And Caps; just a pimping cabbie. You can find every back alley whore in town but not the way home to your own wife! And Ritchie there thinks he's James Cagney in some worn-out gangster movie! What a sad old joke. You all make me puke!"

They were stonewalling her but the cracks were starting to show. Bolo is nobody's wimp. He's got a chest like a 402 Ford engine and here he was just brooding with those gritty fists rubbing into the card table. Caps screwed on his Expos cap and sucked his teeth. Richie, who does look like Cagney except that he's bald and maybe even shorter, stayed very cool with not a thread out of place. But his eyes were swearing low into his cards like they were fresh parking tickets.

"You'll moan bloody Doomsday on a fix gone bad but a pal dies in front of strangers and what do you?

168

You grunt like he's skipped town on a bum cheque. You gotta be swine!"

Finally Milt, who runs the club, spoke up from the snack counter, "Settle down, Tina. The man was fifty-six. He had a heart condition, for Christ's sake. He knew his stats. What made him wrestle some kid two falls out of three? He was looking for the god-damn heart attack!"

"Don't you look for it, Milt? With your cigars and booze? Everyone looks for it. At least Joe found it with class. He went down with class!"

Milt just slapped the rag into the sink and shoved around the dishes, 'cause how can you argue with a dame like Tina? I was staring at the door figuring on getting out. Tina's one of these red-haired Viking types and she was just warming up. Now generally, she can keep herself pretty cool. She can hold a poker table for two, three days while guys drop all over, the cards blurring out in their hands. But here she was on a short fuse. Shorter than I would have figured because in the middle of a curse she starts to gag and I think, "Good, go choke in hell." But she wasn't choking. She was crying. Tina, who could crack you in half with her sour stare, was sobbing for Joey.

Then it started to figure. She was in love with the guy. She'd always been in love with the guy. She'd sure seen enough of him over the years; him sweeping in with one fast broad or another. Tina would watch him pass like a parade she couldn't join. Joey was a handsome guy in a swarthy kind of way. He kept himself real clean and neat and he knew how to give a woman a good time, at least for awhile. But no woman ever kept his attention and soon she'd be stewing in some corner while he was shaking more hands than a crooked councilman and often enough there was a wad of bills in that shake because Joey was forever wheeling and dealing. Then there'd be some blow up and Joey would disappear. Eventually he'd come back—sometimes looking mean and rugged, sometimes tanned and cheerful, a few times he seemed real sorry, but he always looked relieved. Joey never intended to mislead a woman. It was just that once she'd want him to be more than Big Joe, the high roller, he was facing stakes he could not meet. Which I guess was everybody's loss.

Over the years, he'd probably spent more time with Tina than any other woman. But that was only at poker. Tina was the best in town. And they always played a real good game. They wouldn't talk much and Joey never took a good look at her except maybe to raise a bet. But I guess she'd looked plenty and felt plenty because here she was bawling like a lost child.

This set the boys into some confusion. They could take shouting better than tears. Bolo stuck out his greasy rag of a handkerchief as if to shut her up and Caps scrambled for the whisky behind the counter. It was like Tina's crying required first aid. Richie held her hand and started working on her. He is a real estate salesman and more used to dealing with the public. He gave her the big cheer, saying how Joey wasn't in the morgue at all, he was in this terrific funeral home.

"He's a Jew, Tina. They're like the Chinese. They take care of their own. I bet he's all dolled up in a sharp suit and tie. And he's lying on satin sheets. Joe was always a sucker for satin. I'll tell you, that guy's going out in style!" Richie could make a leaky bathtub sound like a jacuzzi even with you staring right at it.

The other guys took their cue and went on about Joe's great funeral; how they'd all show up and toast him and roast him, and make it one great party in his honour. Milt said he'd send flowers from the club and Caps would deliver them personally—maybe something in the shape of a horseshoe for good luck. This had considerable leverage and Tina wiped her runny mascara and heaved a great slow sigh.

"I guess it was just a matter of playing the odds," she said.

"That's right, Tina," answered Richie, "It could've been any one of us. It was just Joey drawing the low card."

"He always took it on the chin for other guys," said Tina, "He carried Milt for years to keep the club going and what did he ever ask for on account? Some free drinks after hours."

"And if he wanted something boosted," said Bolo, "He'd pay you right up front, before he even showed you what to steal. How many other guys would trust a booster that far?"

Caps was rubbing his nose with sentimentality, "And plenty of times he'd grab your traffic ticket and get it torn up for you. This man was a prince!"

I was feeling pretty soft, too. Me and Joe kicked around plenty. He used to call me his personal attorney because we'd always argue about what to bet. He'd tell everyone, "Swartki gives so much bad advice that he's got to be a lawyer!" Then he'd plough me on the shoulder or put me in a headlock and mess my hair. Not that Joey couldn't be a jerk, but he was always ready to apologize if unintentionally he ever got a guy burnt. And he pulled me out of more jams than he got me into. I thought about one time during a game when we went out on the roof for a smoke. The sun was coming and the papers on the street were all wet and catching the light. We were watching a Greyhound bussing out of the depot and Joey said, "Swartki, just me and you. Let's hop the next bus heading anywhere. We'll keep going till we're outa luck." Now this was no bluff on his part and I know he would never have said it to anybody else. That's the

171

kind of pals we were.

Then I heard Tina speaking really soft. "I just got to have one thing. I got to see him before he's dropped in that hole."

The funeral parlour's security system was pathetic. We moved through it like swiss cheese. But then Bolo, who used to specialize in B and E's, reminded me that funeral parlours don't bank on break-ins as there is a limited resale value on a corpse.

Joe was in his box looking a bit waxy and washed out but generally in good shape. He'd lost some weight and his face was smooth and rested. In fact, it seemed that being dead was doing Joe a lot of good. The surprising thing was that he looked like he was dressed for one of those Christmas pageants that I used to watch at the Skoloda Ukrainian Hall. He was wearing this long white robe and a black beanie. Caps, who had lots of dead Jewish friends, said that this was the standard gear for them to get buried in. We were all very impressed.

Tina wanted to give him some rouge but I said that would be embarrassing and out of place for Joe and she finally agreed. But I could see that she was uncomfortable about the whole thing. We all shuffled around the box trying to think of something special to say to Joe but he was just lying there very noncommittal.

Finally Caps said, "Let's make a night of it. I've got a deck of cards and Milt's got whisky in the car. We'll keep Joe company."

So we dealt out a few hands of Chicago just to keep things light. But, Tina's eyes kept slipping off the cards and back to the coffin in the corner. Finally she said, "Look. Fair is fair. If we're going to keep him company, then we have to deal him in."

Well, Ritchie wanted to debate the point but Bolo

172

shut him off. So we set up on the coffin right there and then. We slid the lid partly open and hoisted Joe like he's sitting up in bed and Tina dealt the cards. Now I'm not trying to say that Joey actually played 'cause dead is dead. It was Tina who stood beside him every bet and it was Tina who held the hand. Now maybe there was something psychological going on that night and maybe it's just that Tina played so well. But this was one time that Joey, dead or not, just could not lose. The two of them made quite a pair sitting close behind the cards and neither face was giving up a thing. So we kept shelling out and drinking and propagating every B.S. story that Joey ever told, which could have taken us through more than just one night. I got pretty soggy and most everyone else was passed right out but I can still remember the hand that broke me flat. I had a flush and bet the works. Joey saw me through and hit me with a full house of royal smiles. So calling it a night, I woke the boys and we said so long to Joe as best we could and Tina stayed behind to close the lid.

Before we left, we all agreed to come back for the funeral but she said, "That's not for me. I've had my time with Joe and I won't share him now with any crowd. You can go yourselves. I could hit the sack for two, three days." And when she left she seemed already dreaming.

Well, me and Caps were the only two to make it. I wore my Israeli beanie which Joe gave me for a souvenir. He got it on a junket tour he took to Israel which he said was one big disappointment after another. There was no nightlife there except for tank patrols and foreign movies. And no one even told him which trees were his. It seemed he once laid out a bundle so they could plant some trees and he figured someone could have tracked down one or two. But I sure liked this beanie which he said was a religious object. It had SWARTKI knitted right into the front and on the back there was ISRAEL showing up very clear. I used to sometimes wear it to the racetrack underneath my hat for luck and I have to say that it often did me very well.

When we got inside I could see that the word had been spread because the show was already half sold out. There were lots of street people on one side. And on the other was a more fashionable crowd which I figured was connected to Joe's last wife and a couple of her earlier prototypes—all of his wives were Jewish because Joe was a great believer in tradition.

We got stuck beside a real ghoul, all pulpy white and crusted with make-up. I thought she'd look pretty accurate sitting in for Joe. She had a head like a chicken hawk and was deadly sharp on the cross examination. She tried to pump me for what I had on Joey but I just acted stupid until she shut the heat. Then she started telling me more than I needed to know about herself.

It seemed she was a real fan of funerals. She studied the obituaries like it was a dope sheet and always checked her choice of the day. She'd even visit the predeceased in hospitals—for a bedside chat. She called these her charity calls; gabbing with the ones up to bat, as it were. Now I don't see how someone looking like her would lift anyone's morale, especially since she mainly talked burials and autopsies. She had high hopes for this particular show and favoured it over the funeral of a certain gynaecologist whom she said had caused many of her acquaintances personal anguish. She picked Joey because she considered him a legitimate gangster. That was something Joey would have been pleased to hear.

As she was gabbing, I spotted Mad Jerry sniffing at the front doors and to my surprise the old ghoul identifies him as an orthodox rabbi. This was definitely news to me since I've known Mad Jerry since he was booted out of the Hutterite colony. He claims to hear these radio stations from outer space. Well, as you may know, Hutterites are a very religious tribe of farmers. They all wear black suits and beards and are not supposed to be listening to anything unspiritual like radios much less having them broadcast in Martian from inside their heads. So they gave him a bus ticket to Winnipeg and Jerry began his personal crusade against Satan's UFOs. This meant preaching in the beer halls until someone would buy him off with a drink. I was about to tell the old lady that she'd tangled her family trees but she kept rattling on about how this rabbi was some unknown second stringer transferred from the big league in New York. This was to be his first home game funeral.

Meanwhile, Mad Jerry went straight for the coffin which was parked in front of the pulpit. He stood at the head of it mumbling out of his big black book. The book was actually an old short wave manual he'd found at the Sally Ann. He was probably reciting transmission codes but it was working just fine for the audience. They were nodding and whispering about how pretty and pious it was. Even Caps was getting misty.

Then Jerry pressed his forehead on the coffin and took a deep breath. This got a rise out of the old ghoul who hunkered a sob into a wad of Kleenex. Personally I wasn't moved at all. But then I've seen him do the same thing on the hood of an '81 Trans Am. It was Mad Jerry's way of tuning into his UFO radio band. I guess he wanted some word on Joe. After all, Jerry always pegged Joe as a special case, being what he called both A Wayward Hebrew and A Leader of the Outcasts, which was the Main Street crowd. He'd always stop Joe on the street and offer him The Secret of Salvation which had something to do with lunar modules and secret code words he got from the CKY top ten song charts. Joe would laugh and peel a fiver from his roll saying, "Jerry, you sneak me into heaven and I'll bring you back ten per cent of the take."

I could see that some of the front rows were getting a number on Jerry. Maybe they were down-wind of him or noticed how his clothes weren't up to the spit of your average orthodox rabbi. Anyway, there was a general change of tone and two of the bulkier mourners were making a cautious approach.

Jerry was going a bit slack and running his hand along the top of the coffin. I guess he didn't know the rules because before anyone could do a thing he slipped that lid right off. Now, I've seen the look on a crowd change but I've never seen a shift like that. It was a kind of facial landslide. But Mad Jerry was in another world. He was high-beaming at the inside of the coffin like he'd just broke the bank at Vegas.

"Joseph," he shouted, "is an angel in the house of the Lord! Wrapped in the robes of glory! He was wagered with the spirit and been blessed by the three kings of Israel; by Saul, David, and Solomon, and by the two queens of the land; Queen Esther and Sheba!" Then he reached into that coffin with both hands and lifted a pile of big bucks high over his head, "And he has returned with those blessings!"

That last line pulled a high whining scream out of the old ghoul which definitely broke his train of thought. Then a half dozen guys jumped him and Jerry was carried twisting down the aisle shouting for his ten per cent of heaven. He had to be the most active body every transported through those doors.

Most everyone was rubber necking at the front doors but I checked the coffin. Joey was still in there, safe and sound in his holy land outfit and beside him was the rest of the take from last night's game. I guess

Tina just didn't want Joey leaving without a bankroll. The poker hand that took the last pot was in there, too; a full house of three kings and two queens. But the last thing I saw, before they closed the lid for good, was that Tina had pinned the queen of hearts and the king of diamonds together on Joey's chest.

CATHY JEWISON

God Lives in Saskatchewan

God lives in Saskatchewan.

In a four-house town
with a gas station
and a grain elevator.

Saskatchewan is God's Own Land.

He cleared away all the mountains
and the trees
so He could see forever.

He sits on his porch
and keeps an eye on the cosmos
and listens to the music
of the spheres.

And He watches the Ontario drivers
zip through to Banff
as fast as they can
without even looking around.

Then He carefully jots down
the license numbers
in a book
for future reference.

EUGENE STICKLAND

Lobsters of the Air

Say it ain't so . . . . People change, not schedules. I'm still here, an hour from Winnipeg and the people in this airport are starting to get me down. They're too enthusiastic, somehow. They actually seem excited about flying. Go figure. Me, I'm flying to Winnipeg which doesn't make for a whole lot of enthusiasm or excitement. Maybe if I was on my way to Vancouver or Halifax I'd have more of an edge. But for the most part Winnipeg just doesn't cut it.

The rednecks in the fluorescent hats keep drifting up the escalator: pink, yellow, orange, green. Where do they go, I wonder. Do they find some mystical place where they hunker on down, get in touch with their feelings, maybe even write a few poems?

They're never on my little plane to Winnipeg, a short plane for a short flight. Short stewardesses with short tempers. One threw—yes, *threw*—my little plastic breakfast box at me the other morning. I was tempted to spike my fruit cocktail into the feet of the suit sitting next to me. But I didn't. It may have ended up in a brawl, even a hijacking. Some demented farmer with crutches screaming: "Take this plane to Moose Jaw!"

I travel a lot these days. Someone else is paying but it still gets me down. The suits get me down more than anything. After awhile, you come to realize that it's the same twenty or thirty guys going everywhere, going nowhere, clutching on to their oversized sample cases. The suits look at me warily. They see me on the flights, in the airport bars, here in the restaurant with my little notebook, watching them, scribbling. And I can tell they all wonder to themselves: "Who is this guy? What's he selling? Where's his suit?!"

They don't like sitting beside me and I don't like sitting beside them. I've developed a little trick to make sure I get to sit by myself. Just after take off—about that time when you used to be able to light up a smoke and try to forget how close you are to death up there—I slowly pull the air sickness bag from the little pouch on the seat ahead of me. Then I lean in, just a fraction of an inch, to the person next to me. That's the kicker: leaning in, just a fraction of an inch. Opening and closing your fingers and staring into the palm of your hand has dramatic results as well, but it doesn't usually come to this . . .

Just finger the bag nervously, but of course subtly, and lean in a fraction of an inch. If the person doesn't bail out, try swallowing a bit of air and breathing just a little faster. If things become really desperate, you can always lean in and say: "Gee (urp!)—excuse me—Funny, eh, they make these bags so little! Heh heh." Do this and you'll never have to share your arm rest again with some donut salesman wearing a forty dollar suit.

Some of my non-flying friends and I were talking about lobsters one night. Someone remarked that lobsters are much like seagulls. Scavengers. If you were sitting on the ocean floor, a lobster might come up and steal the french fry right from out of your hand! If lobsters are the seagulls of the ocean, then it must be that seagulls are the lobsters of the air.

We are all lobsters of the air, scavengers, greedily flying after the worst crumbs.

"73!" The guy in the Lacost shirt has scored himself some scrambled eggs. "74!" Nothing against eating, but some mornings it just ain't an option. "75! 76! 76?!" Where did 76 go all of sudden, we all wonder suspiciously. 76's disappearance causes a bit of unrest here in Regina airport. What, did he pay for his eggs and then just wander off to look at the stuffed animals? Where could he be? Or she? What if 76 is a she? What then? Suddenly the air thickens with suspicion and distrust. Suddenly, nothing is as it seems.

"76!?" There's only about ten of us here in the airport restaurant. It's only about 8 o'clock in the morning. How could they be up to 76 already? I wonder just when, exactly, they began counting. We're talking about yesterday's numbers here. Yech! I also wonder why everyone is suddenly eating in here. Something's going on here, no doubt about it.

The worst thing about 76's disappearance is that it makes the rest of us worry that 76 knows something that we don't. Maybe the flight's been called. Maybe we've slipped into some kind of time warp. Maybe as we're sitting here playing with our stir sticks, 76 is sitting alone in the plane out at the end of the runway ready to take off. It happens.

It's also possible that 76 is somehow privy to certain information not usually leaked to the public for security reasons. Maybe 76 has a contact with security. Maybe a bomb threat was phoned in and 76 decided to bail out till things cool down. Meanwhile, the rest of us wait to fly to our doom. I mean, who orders and pays for breakfast at these prices and then just disappears? The more I think about it, the more I don't like it.

A "special" constable of the RCMP cruises by, casting a cold eye on this little hotbed of squalor. He's been carefully trained to ferret out suspicious activity, and the suspicious candidates behind the suspicious activity. I wonder what he sees here? Well, desperate measures for desperate times, they say. I want to grab him, take him down to his little concrete room with his steel desk and his girlie calender and level with him: "Something's going on here man, and it's up to you to save my hide! Find 76!"

Well, someone claiming to be 76 just went up and claimed a grilled cheese. I'm planning on keeping an eye on him when he goes through security. You can't be too careful these days.

I used to love coming out here to this airport. There used to be some magic out here. The addition of jetways was the beginning of the end. Nothing like walking across the tarmac at forty below: "Welcome to Regina." Right. But it used to be, you could sit in the restaurant, or better, the bar, and look out at the planes landing and taking off out there in the middle of the prairie. So flat out there, you had to wonder that they even bothered building a runway.

Apparently, that had to end that for security reasons. Too many crazed farmers coming into the cocktail lounge with their hunting rifles, ordering rye and Cokes, taking pot shots at the fuselage of the Saskatoon express. So they bricked up the windows and put in a skylight. What choice did they have?

A guy I went to high school with worked out here for a while. He found out young that people on the run are the true scum of the earth. He couldn't handle it. He started drinking. In grade eleven! Lemon gin and loganberry wine. Projectile vomiting after KFC. A couple of car accidents that would have killed him if he hadn't been so relaxed he just slid down to the floor and passed out until the ambulance came by. He was the classic high school lush. Just before passing out, he used to say to no one in particular "Man, I'm goin' go out there an' pook all over 'hat fuggin' airport, man!" A noble sentiment. And that was before the renovation!

This same guy ended up selling vacuum cleaners

184

for a living. The only thing he knew about sales he must have learned from Blondie and Dagwood cartoons. I saw him walking one day with a cane. He told me he'd actually put his foot in the door on some reluctant customer, an elderly woman, and she just kept slamming the door on his ankle until he cried "Uncle" and limped off to the emergency ward at the Grey Nuns for X-rays.

Another time, he encountered some deranged biker who told him to "Faggoff!" and slammed the door in his face. So my friend ran around the house and knocked on the back door. The biker opened the back door and punched my friend in the face, just punched him in the face without saying a word, leaving my friend reeling around the back yard, clutching his water-vac in one hand, his broken, bleeding nose in the other.

I wonder where that guy is now? He probably gives this place a wide berth.

For some reason the clocks in this airport are not highly visible. For some reason I cannot wear a watch. I'd love to, but they just stop on my wrist, just as they stopped on the wrist of my grand-father. Chemical or magnetic, they can't tell, but something's got to be wrong when a hundred dollar watch just grinds to a halt after you've worn it for only half a day.

You might think I miss a lot of planes because of this, especially here in Regina airport where they have no clocks. Actually, it just means I usually arrive for all my planes at least an hour early, which usually works except for days like this when they can't get the plane started and make us sit around worrying and drinking coffee at great personal expense.

Wait a minute! Listen! That low muffled sound must be them calling the flight to Winnipeg. They deliberately keep the volume low enough so the only way you can actually hear the announcement is if you're standing within six feet of the gate. Certainly they wouldn't want you to be able to hear in the bar or restaurant that your plane is about to take off.

I guess it's time for me to put my notebook in my little carry-on bag and move the show to the next town over. Remember what I said about sitting alone: lean in, lean in!

BRUCE FINLAYSON

Cruising

A young man from Fort Resolution
thought the military was the solution,
till he got a bad bruise
from a low flying cruise.
Now his head needs reconstitution.

JUDITH KRAUSE

Standing By

On Northwest 568 from Memphis to Minneapolis, the keynote speaker for tonight's banquet in Cedar Rapids, a well-known psychologist from Texas, offers to buy me a drink if we both make it on board, and we do, out of breath, heaving our bags into the overhead bins and buckling ourselves in with a mixture of relief and pity for those who didn't make it, the aircraft moving off at last. After takeoff, he leans into the middle armrest, asks me if I'm married, then wonders out loud if it was another woman, the most common cause, he says, for his clients. The lady in the window seat looks as if she too would like to comment, shifts her weight and looks at her watch. Now, who's better, he asks, leering into his second bourbon and Coke, your ex or your boyfriend? When he gets up to go to the bathroom, the lady taps me on the arm, tells me she's a Baptist and nobody oughta have to listen to talk like that.

GLEN SORESTAD

Sunday Afternoon At De Keulse Pot

We pulled up our bar stools in the tiny place
and ordered glasses of Amstel, served in tumblers
reminiscent of 50s Coca-Cola glasses.
At the bar were a group of five in Sunday dress,
two men and three women, articulate and animate,
a family group it seemed. We nodded all around.

Before our beers were drunk two more glasses
appeared unbeckoned before us and the host
offered an explanation: *birthday* we understood.
I assumed the birthday to be one of the family,
raised my glass to them all and called, "Sköl!"
They raised their glasses. We all glowed.

On the wall behind the bar was an unexpected aid—
a Molson's Canadian sign. I pointed to it
and indicated to them that we were Canadians.
The father beamed and roared, "Hey, KAH-na-da!
CHEERS!" We all drained our glasses. More glows.
More beer appeared. The two men exchanged
a rapid-fire excited volley of Dutch, the father
growing louder and more animated. The daughter
closest to us whispered in English, "My father
is talking of the war . . . and of Canadian soldiers."
"Hey KAH-na-da! Cheers!" he shouted out again and
the Amstel gushed down our throats once more.

The spirit of this celebration had by now
gained a firm hold on us all. A small man now
appeared bearing a tray of cheese and meats.
"KAH-na-da, EAT!" the father roared,
his voice a hearty testimony of hospitality.
We ate. The barman replenished the beer.
I had by now decided that a Sunday afternoon
in Amsterdam was decidedly superior in every way
to any I had known before in Saskatoon.

The daughter assumed the role of language bridge
and soon the information flow matched the beer,
each new revelation greeted with another toast.
We soon raised our glasses to each in turn by name.
Even the barman beamed with the growing camraderie,
though he was hard pressed to keep the glasses full.
And so it was we swallowed an Amstel afternoon.

When at last we slid from our stools and parted
in a great hubbub of handshakes and hugs,
it turned out that the birthday we had celebrated
was not the father's, nor any of his family.
Our barman's little girl had just turned two.

MARILYN CAY

canoe trips

far away
on a lake I imagine cool and blue
you dip your paddle
and aim your canoe across the perfect water
to where the river sneaks away
and rushes to the rapids

men do this—
drive hundreds of miles in hot trucks
so they can carry canoes and supplies through bush
and sleep in two man tents
and dip their bare bums in ice water
when morning comes
man stuff

the rapids are inside my mind
they fall and tumble periodically
I see you bobbing at the water's whim
I know you are testing yourself
I have confidence you will win the day
my canoe is a couch and it is comfortable
I think of you during the commercials

JIM MCLEAN

the well-equipped carman

steel-toed boots & hard hats
sparkers & goggles & mitts
overalls parkas & flashlights
gaskets & heavy tool kits

pulling hooks & oil cans
tacks & bad-order cards
little black two-way radios
so you won't get lost in the yards

blue flags & steel wheel gauges
3-buckle felt overshoes
itchy woolen underwear
an increase in union dues

temp sticks & ball-peen hammers
it's enough to drive you berserk
& under all of these burdens
you're expected to do some work!

so just hand me that big old shovel
stick a switch broom straight up my ass
I'll plow my way to quittin' time
& pray for the winter to pass

JIM MCLEAN

I'm sure the C.P.R. invented Spring

I'm sure the C.P.R. invented Spring
it's just like them to do that sort of thing
when you think that you will crack
swear you're never coming back
to lie down on the ground
in the snow to curse and pound
at those frozen Wabco brakes
till your whole damn body aches
and you start to shout and yell
that you'd rather live in hell—
someone wires Montreal

then the flowers start to bud
the snow melts into mud
and the sun fills up the sky
so dazzling blue you want to cry
and you pity those poor jerks
stuck inside as office clerks
and you tip your hat and sing
to old Van Horne who dreamed up Spring

oh, I'm sure the C.P.R. invented Spring
it's the way they have to keep you on the string
with the robins and the crows
you forget your frozen toes
when the sun begins to shine
why, the trains get back on time
and you settle right back in
forget your oath to pull the pin
decide to have another go
ah, when those summer breezes blow
who minds a little snow?

but pretty soon the leaves begin to fall
and you realize you haven't tried at all
to get a job where you won't freeze
(with a receptionist to squeeze)
teaching English   selling cars
waiting tables in the bars
cooking french fries   anything!
when you feel old winter's sting
you *know* the C.P.R. invented Spring

each year I tell myself that it's the last
when I'm shaking in a January blast
and I can almost see the day
when I'll just quit and walk away
to start my new career
down at Molson's   testing beer
but then I turn and hunch my back
tramp another mile of track
tell myself I'll never leave
that it's only make-believe

oh, it's such a sneaky rotten thing
I'm *sure* the C.P.R. invented Spring!

JIM MCLEAN

the interpreter

ve lay it d'steel
and dey bring us
d'bunch Portuguese
can't any speak it d'English
not von vord
don't know even
d'east from vest

bot dey know it
vat direction is d'Vinnipeg
and vat direction is d'Wancouwer
so every time ve vant move it d'rail
ve holler dem

yo! Vinnipeg!
yo! Wancouwer!

ERIK WATT

The Day We Burned the Iglu Down

We burned the iglu down at dawn.
I, half-asleep, with nothing on
inside my bag (your body heat
radiates if you strip complete,)
vaguely sensed that Josipee
was flashing up the stove for tea.
Then, to my vastly pleased surprise,
Warm sunlight bathed my sleep-gummed eyes.
Well, I'll be damned! I thought.
It's odd . . .
My frozen hands have barely thawed
and look at this!
It's springtime here!
I sat up, yawned . . . and gasped in fear!
That warm glow from no sunshine came;
our iglu was a sea of flame!

That scene from Dante, who'll forget?
The two Inuks, in silhouette,
Frozen against a roaring wall
of fire, flames leaping key-block tall;
The leaking campstove, wreathed in flame,
about to blow!

Reaction came.
A blur of motion and a crash
as Guy dove through the wall!
A flash
of singeing hair as Eric bent
to grab the Coleman!
Seared hands sent
it spinning through the gaping hole
hard-headed Guy had made!

(The toll
exploding naptha, close-confined,
could take, much later came to mind.)

In that wild moment, instinct said
we'd beat the fire, or we were dead,
for Guy alone was fully-clad.
The other choices which we had
were limited to burn or freeze . . .
and make your minds up quickly, please!

We flailed with parkas, kamiks, pants
to halt the leaping flames' advance.
They roared their pleasure as they fed
upon the gas-soaked furs we'd spread
to insulate us from the snow.
But inch by inch and blow by blow
we beat them back!

Two minutes?
Five?
Who knows?
Exhausted, but alive,
we sagged, half-blinded by the smoke
and steam, which made us gasp and choke,
and, one by one, grew swift aware
of heat replaced by Arctic air.
The fire was out!
One crisis past . . .
But,
Wow!
Let's get some clothes on, fast!

The jokes came later, after we
were thawing out with fresh-brewed tea,
the blackened campstove now absolved
of blame.
Pure error was involved.

The valve, left open, dripped all night;
the stove itself was working right.
But SOMEONE had to take the rap
and I became that lucky chap.

The boy who stood the burning deck
makes better legend stuff, but, heck!
I've learned to treasure my renown:
The guy who burned the iglu down!

BRIAN LEWIS

Wailing

A Pangnirtung whaler named Bayles
Liked singers, especially males.
He cut a whale in ten places,
and out jumped ten basses,
because people like singing in Wales.

LEE GOWAN

Going to Cuba

There was a sign at the front of the bus:
YOUR DRIVER IS:

> SAFE
>
> COURTEOUS
>
> RELIABLE

There was another sign at the front of the bus:

> PLEASE, DO NOT TALK TO THE DRIVER
>
> WHILE THE BUS IS IN MOTION

There was no sign that said:

> BE NICE TO THE DRIVER:
>
> YOUR LIFE IS IN HIS HANDS

A woman wearing a crumpled yellow hat climbed onto the bus. "Does this bus go to Penticton?" she asked the driver.

"See the sign on lane two? The one with EDMONTON at the bottom. What does it say in the middle?" the driver snarled.

"Penticton?"

"Very good," said the driver.

The woman skulked away.

"Safe. Courteous. Reliable. Dickhead," the man across the aisle said. He smiled through a lock of black hair that hung over his eyes. "The driver is a dickhead," he said.

"It's part of the job," Bob nodded. "The responsibility sends you over the edge to dickheaddom."

"You a driver?" the man demanded, sweeping the hair from his eyes.

"No, a perpetual passenger," Bob said.

"Get around a lot, hey?" the kid asked. He was getting younger: the black stubble on his jaw masked his youth.

"I rode to school on a bus every morning for

198

twelve years, and then rode home in the evenings. An hour both ways," Bob explained.

"Yeah, across town?"

"Cross country. I lived in the country."

"Yeah?" the kid said. "I ride a bike. Big bike. Harley. Laid her down last night in Surrey. Bad damage. Gotta leave her behind. Gotta work tonight. Mission. That's where I'm from."

"Mission?"

"Yeah."

The bus began to move.

The driver's voice came over the intercom: "This is a non-smoking bus. I repeat. This is a non-smoking bus. There is no smoking what-so-ever allowed on this bus. And that includes the washroom."

"Dickhead," the kid said.

"Once we had a driver who let us smoke on our schoolbus."

"I got a bike. Nobody tells me I can't smoke on my bike."

"It must be difficult all the same," Bob said.

"What?"

"Smoking on your bike. You must lose the cherry a lot."

"I don't smoke on my bike," the kid said.

"But you could if you wanted to," Bob said.

"I sure as fuck could."

"The driver on our schoolbus let us smoke and run up and down the aisles. We even crawled underneath the seats. We pretended our bus was a spaceship and we were crawling through the heat ducts to sneak up on aliens."

"He let you smoke?" the kid asked.

"Yeah," Bob said. "He smoked himself."

"Good guy, hey?"

"He drank too."

"He drank on the bus?" the kid asked.

"Naw. Before he got on. Every payday he was drunk."

"Did he let you drink on the bus?"

"Oh yeah. A big kid at the back sold us shooters of vodka."

"Party time!" said the kid. "I got some Comfort in here." He unzipped his bag and pulled out a bottle. "Don't let the dickhead see." He passed it across the aisle. Bob took it, slouched down in the seat, and took a slug. It tasted like cough syrup. A little girl peeked at him over her seat.

"It was kind of scary for the younger kids, I think. We had to threaten them so they wouldn't tell their parents."

"They were squealers?" the kid asked. "Only thing to do with squealers is introduce their tongue to a switchblade."

"It's part of being a little kid."

"Squealerdom," the kid said.

"You understand," Bob said.

They weren't even out of Vancouver yet. First Avenue was familiar, but from the bus it looked strange and remote. Perhaps it was the tinted glass, perhaps that they rode so high, or perhaps as you left a city it became the same as any other city you would pass through on your way to where you went: transitory images marking the passage of time, but not really even part of the past.

"History," the kid said.

"What?"

"My bike. She's history."

"Oh yeah? Well, at least you have your health."

The kid sneered.

"Dickhead," Bob said, motioning toward the driver to redirect the hostility.

"What's he gonna do if I smoke? Kick me off? I'd like to see him try. I'd kick his ass if he did."

"So smoke."

"You got any butts?" the kid asked.

"Nope," Bob said.

They were merging with the highway.

"We should have your guy driving," the kid said.

"Who?"

"Your schoolbus driver."

"Charlie? He can't drive. They took his licence away forever."

"Figures," the kid said. "They're all dickheads."

"Last day before Christmas," Bob said, "Charlie was pretty drunk when he picked us up. Some of the little kids were crying cause he was swearing at 'em. He was slurring so bad you couldn't understand him."

"Pissed," the kid said.

"So we get out on the highway, and its pretty icy, and Charlie's sliding the bus all over the road: right from one white line to the other."

"Crazy shit," the kid said.

"We were missing head-ons by a few inches and twice we went down in the ditch, but he drove her back on the road."

"In Sane," the kid said.

"And then we've got a cop on our tail with blue and red flashing, but instead of stopping Charlie decides to try and lose him."

"No shit? With a schoolbus?"

For a moment Bob watched the trees pass.

"Well," the kid called him back. "What the fuck happened."

"He laid her down," Bob said. "Went off the road and rolled her to the bottom of the coulee."

"Crazy shit!" the kid said. "Anybody hurt?"

"No," Bob said. "All dead."

"What about you?"

"I lived."

"No shit? Any brothers and sisters?"

"Nine or ten," Bob said.

"Big family," the kid said.

"Was," Bob said. "They were all over the insides of the bus, hanging from the seats like empty parkas."

"Fuck," the kid said.

"I kicked out the emergency window and climbed into the air. It was a sunny day. Cold. I walked to a neighbour's farm. Schultz's. There was nobody home, but the door was open. I went in and phoned the ambulance. When they got there I was watching 'The Partridge Family'."

"You remember stuff like that," the kid said. "I remember some graffiti on the building by where I laid my bike down that says DOWN WITH THE DEAD."

"Reuben had a bet with Danny that he could quit smoking longer than Danny could stay on his diet. I'd never seen Reuben smoke before. Did you know Susan Dey was eaten by a shark?"

"At least you didn't get hurt," the kid said.

"At least I have my health," Bob said.

The kid sneered.

"What about your driver?" the kid asked.

"Charlie? He took the steering-shaft through the heart."

"You said he lost his licence."

"Posthumously," Bob said.

"I didn't know they did that," the kid said.

"You name it, they do it."

"Dickheads."

"They can't help themselves," Bob said.

"They could sure as hell try a little harder," the kid said.

The Fraser slipped below them, brown and oily, worn out from its roller-coaster ride through the last ice age. The child in front of them stood on her seat and peered down at the river.

"Sit down," her mother said, and the little girl disappeared.

"It must have made the news," the kid said.

"It did."

"Dead people always make the news," the kid said.

"Some of them were important."

"Who? Some of the kids on your bus?"

"Some of them." Bob nodded.

"Like who?"

"General Patton. Roberto Clemente. Marilyn Monroe. John F. Kennedy."

"John F. Kennedy was on your bus?"

"He sat next to me. Used to fart a lot," Bob said.

"You're full of shit," the kid said.

"General Patton would confiscate your lunchbox if you forgot to call him sir."

"You're full of shit," the kid said. "Everything you say is full of shit."

"Not about the aliens," Bob said.

"Dickhead," the kid said.

After that the kid wouldn't speak. He got off at Mission without saying goodbye.

The sun sank behind the line of a mountain so big its slope stretched from the bottom right to the top left corner of the window. Disembodied voices rose and fell as though the night itself were speaking. An old man grunted, "Huh? You'll have to speak up a bit," by which he meant he was hearing the teenage girl's saccharine voice through the echo of five years driving without earmuffs in a negligibly insulated tractor cab.

"I'm from Golden," the girl spoke up.

Everyone on the bus analyzed the importance of this information and, finding none, returned to the misery of their stiff necks and sore bums. Everyone, that is, except the old man.

"Rosetown, Saskatchewan is my home, and I'll be glad to get back to it and away from this rainy country."

"You don't like rain?" the girl called across the aisle.

"Well, you know, it's a funny thing: you spend half your life waiting for rain, and it's sad coming to a place where they got so much they don't know what to do with it all."

"You don't have to shovel rain," the girl said.

"That may be," the old man said, "but you can't walk on it, you have to walk *in* it."

"APRIL SHOWERS BRING MAY FLOWERS," Bob shouted.

There was a moment's silence.

"Who was that?" the old man asked.

"Who knows," the girl said. "All sorts of freaks ride the bus."

"That's true," the old man said. "You can't be too careful these days."

"THE RAIN IN SPAIN FALLS MAINLY ON THE PLAIN," Bob shouted.

"What's he sayin'?" the old man asked.

"Who knows," the girl said. "There's people who live on the street in Vancouver who you see talking to themselves all the time. My Mom says they're talking to God."

"I don't know," the old man said. "Maybe the devil."

"I'M JUST WILD ABOUT NICKY," Bob shouted.

"I'll tell you one thing, there ain't no people like that in Rosetown."

"What do you do in Rosetown? Grow roses?" the girl asked.

"Ha! No no no," the old man wheezed. "Nothing but the wild roses and they grow natural. No, no. I farmed for years but I'm out of it now. My son has the place."

"Your son?"

"Yep, my son."

Bob began to sing:

So I just did me some talking to my son
Told him
I
Dinna like da way he held dat gun
Creepin' like a dog
And
I'm never gonna get the blame by refraining
Just wait and see
Me an' my Greyhound is free.

The driver's voice came crackling over the intercom at 105 decibels: "Please keep it down back there. Other passengers are trying to sleep."

"Courteous," Bob said.

There was a moment's silence.

"Was that for us?" the old man asked.

"No, that was for the singer," the girl said.

"They don't sing any more. They just scream and moan about things best left unsaid."

"My uncle farms too," the girl said.

"Does he now?"

"He has pigs. What did you have?"

"What's that?"

"My uncle has pigs. What did you have on your farm?"

"Oh, well, wheat. Yes. Strictly wheat."

"I guess wheat doesn't stink anyway. My uncle's pigs stink."

"No no," the old man laughed. "Smells pretty sweet in the hopper."

"DURUM IN THE MORNING, DURUM IN THE EVENING. DURUM AT SUPPERTIME," Bob shouted.

The little girl peeked at him and the shadow of

205

her mother's head appeared over the seat, struggling to make out the shape of madness through the dark. This was happening all over the bus, everyone waiting for Bob to sing again, his voice a monster surfacing like a memory of hell.

"What were you going to say?" the teenaged girl asked.

"I don't remember," the old man said.

Nonsense. They all remember hell: sulphur fumes burning the sinuses and the eyes in the back of the head. The torture was incidental. Mostly hell was boring, hardly happening. The kind of place you remember on bus rides.

"I spoze you go to school," the old man said.

"Yes. I finish next year."

"What'll you do then?"

"I'm going to Cuba," she answered instantly.

"You're goin' where?

"Cuba. Down south. It's an island."

"I know what it is," the old man scolded. "Castro."

"Ummm hmmm. He's the President."

"He's no President," the old man said. "Who elected him?"

"The people."

"The people? Maybe the goats maybe. It weren't no people that voted for that bearded devil."

The girl briefly considered the possibility of a devil ruling paradise, and then dismissed the idea.

"Oh, I was there last summer with Mom and Dad and it's the most beautiful place in the world."

"Your mom and dad got no business taking you to a place like that."

This silenced the girl again. Bob wondered if he should go up and help her out, but she didn't need any help: a moment later she was on him again.

"Have you been there? It's not that different from Canada, you know. It's a lot like Canada really."

"Not my part of Canada. We're free in my part of Canada."

"You should see the beaches. If you saw the beaches you'd change your mind. And if you met Ramon. He's way better than the boys in Canada. Way nicer."

"You've never met my son. Finest young man who ever lived, and do you think he can find a wife? You come to Rosetown and I'll introduce you to my son."

The girl laughed nervously.

"But I'm in love with Ramon."

"Ramon? What kind of name is that?"

"It's Cuban."

"He doesn't love you. If he loved you he wouldn't want you to go to Cuba."

"He's in Cuba," she said.

"Is he a communist?"

"No."

The old man grumbled. "Well, I suppose a person can't help where he's born, can he?"

"It's a beautiful country really. I don't know why anyone would want to live anywhere else."

The old man didn't speak for awhile, and Bob wondered if he should go up and help him. This wasn't necessary either.

"You don't. Well, I'll tell you why then. That country's a dictatorship. Would you want a dictator telling you what to do all the time?"

"No one told me and my parents what to do when we were there."

"They did," the old man said. "They did. You just didn't know they were doing it."

"Like how? We could do anything we can do here, plus we could swim in November."

"Did you ever try and take a picture of a bridge? If you did they'd arrest you."

"I didn't want to take a picture of a bridge."

"But that's the point, don't you see? The point of freedom is being able to do something when you want to."

"MIND IF I BURN?" Bob shouted.

"And I'll tell you something else. Those people just want to keep spreading—those dictators—that Castro and the likes of him. They want their people to keep spreading until they rule the entire world. Those countries don't produce anything but people. Look at how many of them are coming to live here. Pretty soon their people'll be in control of this country too. They want you's what they want, and they'll do whatever they have to, to get ya." He snorted. "Ya can't just give yerself to them."

"We had to wait a month for a visa just to visit," the girl said.

"That don't mean nothing. They let you in, didn't they? You know why they let you in?"

"Why?"

"Because they want your money so they can buy missiles to shoot across the water and bomb you with over here."

"KABOOOOM," Bob shouted.

"KEEP IT DOWN BACK THERE," the driver's voice crackled over the intercom. "Your high jinks are distracting me and as such are a threat to the other passengers."

"Safe," Bob said.

"I bet you never thought of that," the old man said. "I bet you never realized that you were payin' for the missile that's gonna drop on your house."

There was no response. Everyone on the bus considered the idea that they might be buying their own death. Each person shivered. The driver turned up the heat. Bob felt a rush of hot air across his cheek which he'd pressed against the tinted glass to feel the cold air outside. The bombs fell all around them now,

208

blossoms of fire, bought and paid for by the sweat of a free man's brow. They were dying slow horrible deaths. Bob hunched forward, held his ankles, sweating.

"I don't know," the girl said. "Cuba's just like Canada."

"Except the boys are nicer," a new voice said, and there was an eruption of laughter from various uncharted troublespots on the bus: five or six different cacklers finally acknowledging their position as audience. The driver allowed them this liberty. There was too much resistance. It was a critical moment: if he tried to suppress them he might lose control altogether. On the other hand, by allowing them this limited freedom they were themselves wiping out the insipid conversation, going on at a dangerous volume—almost crossing the line between conversation and oration—with the devastating weapon of humiliation.

Bob calculated fractions: two hundred miles gone, eight hundred to go. Swift Current was the *one* waiting at the end of a fraction of motion. A million stars were out. All numbers except zero are the same fraction of infinity. There was this constant battle to make the trip longer—even more boring than it already was; he watched the second hand count off one more minute of the fifteen hundred or so total it would take to get there. Time would stop when he saw the Peavy Mart.

"When are you going back there?" the old man's voice said.

Did he not realize what the laughter was about? Or did he not care? Maybe he wanted them to listen, needed to be heard, saw himself as the voice of their resistance—the calling together of the forces that would overthrow this bus and drive it to heaven, where they'd live with the rest of the happy dead. But the girl didn't answer. It was she they laughed at, not the old man, and so she ignored him now, wiser, unwilling to let them laugh at her dreams again, perhaps even a little less willing to dream, sensing for the first time all of the variables involved.

"You come to Rosetown," the old man muttered. "I'll introduce you to my son."

Given time she might marry someone like the old man's son, who would take her to Disneyland or Las Vegas every few years. She would forget palm trees and beaches and negroes happily cutting sugar cane and old cars patched together with tin. Given time. But who can? Even the rich can only *take* time, bundle it in a plastic bubble on a slab of cardboard with pretty pictures to represent what has been taken from us forever—what we need or want, and would kill for, that can never be given back.

A blinding light approached.

"Kamloops," the driver said. "We have a twenty minute rest stop here. Please be back on the bus in twenty minutes. There are other drivers waiting down the line."

"Reliable," Bob said.

A cinnamon bun with butterscotch frosting had the advantage in bulk. A substantial snack. The nanaimo bar was ahead in regards to taste: the chocolate and whatever that yellow stuff was in the centre. Behind him the frozen lineup murmured curses while he weighed degrees of sweetness for a correct answer.

"Take both," the clerk suggested, smiling, amused at his quandary and perhaps grateful for the rest he was giving her.

Given time.

A man slapped down a dollar for his coffee and brushed Bob's back as he passed.

"Okay, both," Bob agreed. She rang it up and he

210

paid. A smattering of applause rose from the lineup. Bob turned and bowed. Puffy eyes, bedroom hairdos: they looked like old comfortable lovers. Only the drivers hid behind their uniforms or in the shadow of the next replacement who waited down the line, like this one, marching up to Bob's table, who was not Dickhead himself but wore his sore red eyes.

"Now you listen to me, Mister. I've had enough complaints about you to justify leaving you here. The last driver told me this has been going on since Vancouver. So I'm going to give you one last warning: either stop disturbing the other passengers or you'll be walking. You hear me?"

"Walking," Bob said.

Neither the cinnamon bun nor the nanaimo bar were what he wanted: a date square. Sure the date squares were a little squashed, but they reminded him of the lunches his mother used to pack in the grey plastic lunchbox.

He ate what he had and then played with the salt shaker until the driver ordered them back on the bus.

A bar of purple appears above the crest of foothill in the sky and below the foothill in the lake. Purple becomes red and then orange, spreading across the horizon, filling the lake with light. Bob walks toward the bus, which is parked on the shoulder of the highway. He just wants to get back on and go home. He'll be no more trouble. He regrets the problems he's caused; if they let him back on he'll behave. He wants to go home.

The windows on the bus are smashed out and from each opening a rifle barrel protrudes.

"Don't shoot," he calls. "I want to go with you."

The driver's voice comes over the intercom.

"This is not a rest stop. There's other drivers waiting down the line. FIRE!"

The first volley misses, shells whistling by his ears and others hitting the earth, spraying up clouds of dust around him. He almost runs but resists the urge; instead, slowly walks away. A second volley is fired, this one more ragged, so that he detects the path of each bullet, calculating which side of him it will go wide before it arrives, as he continues to casually walk away. His back taunts them, tells them it will be they who die, not him, and their shots become more frantic, less accurate, missing him by whole yards as he gets farther from them, nearing the top of the hill already—how did he cross the lake?—so that the distance has grown too great for anything but a lucky shot, maybe aiming above his head to compensate for fall, but even this doesn't succeed. Bob is blessed. He steps over the crest of the hill and falls off the edge of the earth, leaving behind the dawning sky, the mountains pressing behind the bus, and the driver, who is still looking for blood.

"What's that you're reading?" A voice from across the aisle woke Bob. A very lonely man was speaking to him—only the lonely would dare and try to strike up a conversation with a sleeping bus passenger at 5:30 in the morning.

"I'm asleep," Bob said.

"You are not." The man chuckled as though sharing a joke.

"I am so."

"Well, I just assumed, because you've got a book open in your lap and you're the only person on the bus with a reading light on, I just assumed you were reading. I'm sorry."

"My eyes were closed," Bob said.

"No, actually your eyes were wide open. They did look a little glassy, I must admit, but they were open."

"I was asleep," Bob said.

"And just now you said 'Don't shoot', so I thought

212

it must be a very exciting book to get you talking out loud like that. I measure a book by how much you talk to it. The only book I talk to is the Bible. I get reading the Bible and it's 'Watch out, Joseph' or 'Get him, David' or 'Walk on that water, Jesus'."

"I was asleep," Bob said.

"You must have been dreaming. It must have been a terrible nightmare. Who was gonna shoot you?"

"Nobody."

"You can't remember? Maybe it had something to do with the book you're reading. Is there shooting in the book?"

"Yeah," Bob said.

"What's the book?"

Bob held up the book so the man could see the cover: *Cheyenne Autumn*. The man took it from him and read the advertising blurb on the back.

"*Savage heroes*," he murmured. "Why are you reading this?"

"Why not?" Bob said.

"No reason. I just like to know why people read the things they do."

Bob tried to stare him down, but he couldn't see his eyes.

"You really want to know?" Bob asked.

"Yeah."

"These Indians—the Cheyennes—were the descendants of the greatest warrior tribe in North America. The U.S. government took away their land and put them on a reserve in Oklahoma. Then they tried to starve them to death. Extermination was their policy: 'If we kill them we won't have to feed them or pay for their land.' You see their reasoning. But the Cheyenne broke away from the reserve and with less than a hundred men they managed to fight off more than ten thousand American troops."

The man nodded. "So how come you're interested in that sort of thing?"

There was a long silence. The driver coughed.

"It's a good story," Bob said.

"Oh, that's it. You're not picking sides then," the man said, as though he was relieved.

"What? How could I help it. I identify with the Cheyennes," Bob said.

"You do? Have you ever eaten raw meat? Have you ever spent a winter in a tent? Have you ever scalped a man and then raped his wife?"

"Not recently," Bob said, "but I'll tell you what I have done. The Cheyennes were trying to escape to their homeland, over fifteen hundred miles north of the reservation. I'm trying to escape to my homeland too. And do you know how many minutes I'll have been on this bus by the time I get there?"

"How many?"

"Over fifteen hundred minutes."

"Isn't that something?" the man said with about as much sincerity as a long distance operator. "Soooo . . . what is it you're running from?"

"I can't talk about it," Bob said.

"Did you do something very bad?" the man asked.

"You can't imagine how bad," Bob said.

No one else, except the driver, was awake. They coasted down from the mountains onto the prairie. The sun had broken the horizon.

"I might suggest that you'd find the answer to your troubles much sooner if you were to read the right pages. I understand that the Indians were a beautiful beautiful people, but they were also pagan. Let me remind you that they've long since found their solace in Christ. You'd be wise to follow their example and look for your answer in the Bible too."

He passed a tiny copy of the New Testament across the aisle. When Bob didn't take it the man

214

placed it on his leg. It was two inches by three inches and had a red cover: the same as the one the Gideons presented to everyone in Bob's grade four class.

"I've read it," Bob said. "Revelations is a gas."

"You liked Revelations?" the man encouraged him.

"Yeah, fine stuff. What kind of drugs you figure John was using?" The man didn't answer. "Must have been opium. What else would give him dreams like that: a dragon with a dozen heads ridden by a sexy lady in a red dress. And then there were all those dead people. Sign of a guilty conscience when you dream about crowds of dead people; sign of a craving for power."

"I refuse to even consider the idea that the greatest gospel writer used narcotics. We're talking about the man who wrote the lines, 'In the beginning there was the Word and the Word was God.' How dare you infer that the Word was drug induced?"

"Performance enhanced," Bob said. "How else can you put flesh on a word? It's easy enough to kill with a word. John knew that: he had heaps of corpses in his dreams. He controlled the twelve churches like a general from his island. 'If they want to feed you to the lions, let them. How else is anybody gonna feel sorry for us? We need more sacrifices.' And there's this greasy little guy with food in his beard who always follows John around asking him questions like, 'Why is it that your followers are martyring themselves while you live safely out here on this island, giving out orders?' John spits on a rock, glancing at the greasy little guy who's one of *those men who call themselves Jews* and says 'My blood is not worthy enough to be spilled for our Lord.' The man with the food in his beard smiles and says 'Lucky for you, eh John? Healthier to have bad blood these days.'"

"MAY THE LORD HAVE MERCY ON YOUR SOUL," the

man shouted as he marched toward the front of the bus.

"Thank you," Bob said.

The woman in front of him, wakened by the shouting, peered back over her seat. She had bleary morning eyes. Bob smiled. She frowned and ducked back out of sight.

Calgary prepared to surround them.

"That's it buddy." The driver grabbed his arm when he stepped off the bus. "I hope this was as far as you wanted to get, 'cause you aren't goin' any farther."

"Why?" Bob asked.

"The last driver told me you had one more chance."

"What did I do?" Bob asked.

"I got a complaint from one of the passengers. That man." He pointed to the Bible man, who was waiting for his suitcase.

"Him? He woke me up and started preaching to me. I'm the one who should be complaining."

"You should get the police," the Bible man said. "He told me he murdered somebody."

The bustle of action stopped. The crowd forgot about their luggage for a moment to stare at Bob. He smiled. A beefy man who'd been unloading luggage grabbed him and pulled his arms behind his back. The crowd escorted him into the terminal where they found a policeman. The Bible man told his story. The policeman asked for Bob's I.D., then escorted him to a phone and ran a check on him. The crowd milled about at a safe distance, waiting for word of blood.

"We have no reason to hold him," the cop told the Bible man.

"You can't let him go. Just mark my words: any minute now somebody's gonna come across a whole family he murdered."

"Did you murder someone?" the cop asked Bob.

"No," Bob said.

"Why did you tell this man you did?"

"I didn't," Bob said. "I said I did something very bad."

The cop looked at the Bible man, who blushed and nodded.

"What did you do?" the cop asked.

"I watched a man die and then got a sandwich during the commercial." Bob held up one finger. "I drank coffee out of a styrofoam cup." Bob held up two fingers. Someone in the crowd laughed. "I carved my initials in my favourite poplar." Bob held up three fingers. "I never said thank you to my mother." Bob held up four fingers. "I threw up on a stranger's shoes." Bob held up his thumb. "And I used the Lord's name in vain." Bob held up the middle finger on his other hand and aimed it at the Bible man who had already begun to slink away.

"You people are wasting my time," the cop said.

"Can I kick him off the bus," the driver asked.

"That's up to you," the cop said.

"Can I sue him for false arrest?" Bob asked.

"That's up to you," the cop said.

"Oh forget it," the driver said. "The next driver can worry about him. I'm going home."

"Me too," Bob said.

The cop shook his head and walked away. What was left of the crowd began to disburse.

Bob had scrambled eggs for breakfast. The coffee was crude.

Bob didn't speak until the last stop before Swift Current: Gull Lake.

"Is anyone sitting here?" a woman asked. Her finger brushed the blue Naugahyde next to him.

"Your eyes will tell you," Bob said.

She thought about this for a second.

"Oh," she said. "Very clever." She sat down, then offered her hand. "I'm Michelle."

"John Smith," Bob said. Her grip was limp.

"Pleased to meet you, John," she said.

She rubbed her back against her seat and gave a satisfied sigh as the bus pulled away from the curb.

"Just holidaying at the lake?" Bob asked.

"There is no lake," she laughed. "That's just a name. I have family there." She sighed again.

"You have a good visit?"

"They're nice people, but I don't think they understand me."

"You remind me of someone," Bob said.

"Really? Who?"

"A woman," Bob said.

"Well isn't that a coincidence. I am one."

"A lover," Bob said.

"Oh." She blushed.

"She died."

"She died?"

"Yes."

"I'm sorry," she said.

"It was my fault," Bob said.

"No it wasn't."

"How would you know?"

"Because. I know I've blamed myself for things I shouldn't have. It's human nature. And it doesn't do anyone any good."

"Unless it really is your fault and you're just not taking responsibility. Then you have to face up to it and take the blame," Bob said.

"I don't think so. Everybody I know seems to carry around a lot more guilt than they need to."

"Not me," Bob said. "I never feel guilty. That's why I'm so dangerous."

"You sure sounded like you were feeling guilty

218

just now."

"Nope." Bob shook his head.

"How did she die?"

"Murdered," Bob said.

"Oh my God, that's terrible," she said.

Bob nodded.

"Why . . . how could that be your fault?" the woman asked. "Unless . . . " She was leaning away from him. Her face was pale.

"When I was young I loved my soul," Bob said. "I cradled my soul like a sleeping child inside of me, you know what I mean? I loved my soul but I hated my body and because I hated my body I would get these huge eruptions of pus all over my back and my chest and my face. First they'd swell up so that every time I sat down it would hurt me because the chair rubbed against them, and every time I moved it would hurt me because my shirt rubbed against them and I couldn't sleep at night because the sheets rubbed against them. And then they'd explode and the pus would come out smelling like peanut butter and honey whenever I ate peanut butter and honey so I stopped eating peanut butter and honey. I stopped eating sugar and I stopped eating meat and I stopped eating any kind of fried food or milk products, but nothing helped. After they'd burst I'd bleed all over my shirts and I'd know people were looking at my shirts and wondering what was underneath. When I stayed at people's places I'd bleed all over their sheets and I'd know that they were wondering why I bled all over their sheets. And I never took my shirt off. Never. I even slept in a T-shirt. I knew that people'd be repulsed if I ever showed them my body. I knew that any woman who looked at my body would either laugh or throw up. But then I met this woman . . . "

He was silent.

"And she loved you?" the woman asked.

"Yes. She even loved my body."

"I see," the woman said.

"No you don't," Bob said. "You don't, because you never saw how repulsive I was. She did, and she loved me anyway, and that's when I started to get better. And when I was better I left her and went off with another woman. And then, years later, I went to visit her again and she was dying. She was dying for love and they'd cut off both of her breasts. I still loved her, but I only loved her soul, I didn't even want to look at her body. Just imagining it repulsed me. She told me that the doctors' cure was too painful, that she wanted to stop, that she believed only her soul could heal her. I agreed. Three months later she died."

Bob turned away to the window. A farmer on his tractor glanced up at the window and saw Bob crying before he had time to look away.

"You shouldn't blame yourself," Michelle said.

"It doesn't matter what I do," Bob said. "I won't feel guilty anyway."

"I don't believe you," she said.

"What you believe doesn't make any difference," Bob said.

"I don't believe that either," she said.

"You're a product of the times. No one has any faith anymore. Twentieth-century syndrome."

"I believe that you could be a great healer," she said. "I believe that you could heal me."

"What's wrong with you?" Bob asked.

"Breast cancer," she said.

Bob looked at her chest. There wasn't much there.

"I'm sorry," he said.

"Don't be sorry," she said. "Heal me."

"I can't," Bob said.

"Yes you can. If you touch me I'll be healed," she

220

said.

Bob shrugged and touched her arm.

"I think you should touch the afflicted area," she said.

"Is this a come-on."

"We're talking about my life."

Bob studied her, wondering where she'd got the idea that it was possible to talk about somebody's life.

"Take off your shirt," he said.

"Can't you heal me through the shirt?"

He shrugged.

He touched her.

"Thank you," she said. "You've given life. Now you don't need to feel guilty."

"Oh, I see," Bob said. "This was all a little game."

"No," she said. "I really did have cancer."

"You're lying."

"Scouts' honour," she said, and saluted.

"You're too young."

"So was your lover."

"I'm a virgin," Bob said.

"You were lying?"

"I guess."

She turned away, and he guessed that would be the last thing she'd ever say to him—that they'd be the last three words he'd ever hear when St. Peter stopped him at the Pearly Gates. He'd have to prepare a more convincing answer.

"I really did have cancer," she said, surprising him.

"It's not fair," Bob said.

"It's my own fault."

"No it's not."

"Yes it is," she said.

"You shouldn't blame yourself."

"I had silicone injections."

"Oh."

Now she couldn't look at him and he couldn't look at her and he thought perhaps they'd shamed themselves into silence.

"It doesn't matter," she said. "You cured me."

"Why did you have silicone injections?"

"Economics," she said.

"You're a model?"

"No, a receptionist, but I used to act."

"Will you go back to acting now?"

"I doubt it. There's no jobs," she said.

"You could try."

"You think I should?"

"Yeah."

"Okay. I'll go back to acting."

Bob glanced out the window. The dirt road he saw didn't stop at the top of the hill, the way it did for everyone else on the bus. It led over the hill past Klassens, and continued on from there until it ran out in a small grove of poplars that someone had once planted.

"What sort of acting did you do?" Bob asked.

"Mostly commercials."

"Commercials! Don't go back to commercials. You'll get cancer again. Commercials have been linked to cancer."

"Is that so?"

"Scouts' honour." Bob saluted her. "Get into some serious acting."

"I played Hamlet once," she said.

"Really. Experimental theatre?"

"No, very conservative. I played it as a man."

"That must have been difficult," Bob said.

"Not so much as you might think. I used to be a man."

"Uh huh," Bob said. He turned to the window. "And your family doesn't understand you."

"No," she said.

"I sympathize."

"With me or with my family?"

"Yeah."

"Jesus was a woman in one of the twelve gospels and gay in another one. Did you know that? The Gnostic Christians ingested semen as their communion. Did you know that?"

"Don't tell my parents," Bob said.

"There was a woman inside me."

"I sympathize. I let her out on weekends."

"You go drag?"

"No, naked."

She laughed.

"Is that true?" Bob asked. "You were a man?"

"I have a man inside me."

"I sympathize," Bob said.

There, across the service road, beside the railway track, in red and white plastic, was the Peavy Mart sign.

"Tell me," Bob said, "when you were growing up in Gull Lake, did you ride a bus to school?"

"Yes."

"Did your driver let you smoke?"

"No," she said, "but often, in the evenings, as we were driving home, and everyone else had already gotten off except me and my brother and my sister, and the sun was falling into the earth, making the snow golden, suddenly the bus would take flight, and we'd look down from the sky and see my father walking across the yard toward the barn to do chores, and he'd hear the sound of our engine and turn and look up, and we'd open the windows and wave down to him, and he'd smile and wave back."

"I thought so," Bob said.

They didn't speak until the bus stopped at the terminal.

"This is the end of the line," Bob said.

"Does that mean I get off?" she asked.

"No. I'm passing the torch to you."

They shook hands. Her grip was stronger.

"Goodbye," she said.

"Drive on," Bob said.

He walked down the aisle and stepped off the bus. The buildings gathered round like they'd waited years for a visitor.

MARILYN CAY

to the man who didn't wave
the woman who never says "hello"
the person who honked his horn behind me
while I waited for the train to go

. . ! .
      /

STEVEN SMITH

visits

there are many who keenly anticipate visits to earth by
aliens. there are even more who fear extraterrestrial
intelligences drawn by our oscillations.

not counting natural radiation
earth is still a very bright star
especially in the invisible spectrum

we are constantly broadcasting
radio & television messages
to outer space

aliens have seen
the Man from Glad
Charlie's Angels
The Price is Right
Ed Sullivan
Mork & Mindy
Morris the Cat
Red Fisher
I Love Lucy
Howard Cosell
Family Feud
& the Pillsbury Dough Boy

we have nothing to fear
they've turned us off
realigned their receivers
fired the retro rockets
& sped from our bright & lethal glow

The Rabbit

Your neighbours have a rabbit, a pet rabbit they keep in a cage. And they feed it greens from the kitchen, and they recycle the little bunny turds, you know, throw them in the garden, where they grow their own organic food. They have a complete little eco-system over there. You have a dog. It shits all over the yard. It eats meat. You eat meat. You have to step over the dog shit to get to the barbecue that pollutes the atmosphere with the smell of burning dead cows. Yet you are friends with your rabbit neighbours. Your kids go to swimming lessons together. You take turns driving them, you in your Ford, they in their Volvo. They give you zucchini from their garden, you make five loaves of zucchini bread and eat one. The rest you hide in the freezer.

One weekend they go away. They have asked you to keep an eye on their house. No problem. That evening you go to the video store to rent a movie, you come home, the gate is open, the dog is gone. You call, "Rusty, Rusty" the dog's name is Rusty and the dog appears, wagging its tail with a foolish grin on its face. Rusty has returned from the neighbour's yard. You go into their yard, and there, lying almost neatly on the compost pile, is a dead rabbit, a dirty dead pet bunny rabbit. You know Rusty is a killer. If this is what Rusty will do to a rabbit, what might Rusty do to small children? But Rusty is still standing there with a foolish grin on his face, still wagging his tail. It's clear that Rusty is denying everything. He seems to be saying, "Is there a problem here?" Yes Rusty, there is a problem. Mentally, you are lining up the sights between Rusty's loving stupid eyes and you shoot him. But you can't.

While you drive Rusty to the vet, who will do what you can't, your loving wife has taken the dead rabbit into the kitchen. She washes it in the sink, then takes her hair drier and blow dries the dead rabbit's fur. She fluffs it up. It looks almost as good as new. By this time you have returned from the vet. The children are silent. You take the dead rabbit and put it back in its cage. You prop it up. You give it a carrot. It looks like the dead rabbit is eating the carrot. You go home.

The next day your neighbours return. You give them time to be home for awhile. Time to unpack the Volvo and put things away. There is unease in your house. Your wife is trying to unthaw a loaf of zucchini bread.

You go into the back yard and start scooping up dog shit. Your neighbour is in his back yard digging a hole. You ask, in a friendly neighbourly way, how their trip was. He answers, it was fine, the trip was fine, but that something really strange had happened here, here in the back yard. You feign great interest. Your neighbour says that someone dug up their pet rabbit and put it back into its cage.

You swallow an apple, your voice breaks. "Your rabbit died?"

"Oh yes," says the neighbour. "It died last week."

BRUCE RICE

Celestial Orinthology

God sees the little sparrow fall.
So what does She make of it, does She
give a damn?
Does She call up Mr. Tweel
Ornithology Dept./sparrow division
and say
See here, Tweel.
There's a sparrow down
at 16 Romanow Road.
Could you send a car around
to look into it? Well,
when will one be available?

I ask you, what does She think
when these cranks call in
five minutes to closing?
Does She gaze at the moons of Her fingernails,
      muttering
life would be simpler if Administration would vet
      these
confounded claims?

And on Her way Home does She send out a flash:
      Tonight, Mike
Duffy gets something to think about. I bet She
knows all the good fishing spots.

Is God a one book author?
Does She have a standard contract:
"Publisher retains copyright for life
plus fifty years?"

There are things it would be useful to know about Her.
Does She have Her MBA? Who is God, anyway?
Maybe She's the kid who comes to my door selling
    chocolate bars
so Her choir can go to Vienna next year. Is She put
    off
by people who slam the door in Her face, and others
who pretend they're not home?

But I suppose the worst thing
is this damn sparrow business.

GEOFFREY URSELL

There Ain't Nobody Here But Us Chickens

The Boss comes running through the back door, laughing like a loon in heat. Then he starts singing "The Zombi Jamboree," his favourite song. He's singing "Back to back, belly to belly, We don't give a darn, 'cause we done dead already!" as he zips by his office and then the stairs going down into the store-room. But he doesn't slow down in time to stop before he hits the grease I'm wiping up, so he goes down on his fat little ass and slides feet first right through the swinging doors. But they're so busy out there taking orders and making shakes and sizzling chips and frying dogs and burgers and packing chicken that they don't even see him coming through and then coming back my way on his feet again. He's the runt of the litter anyways, so unless you're eyeballing someone's ass, you're looking too high up to see him. The Boss has to stand on a barrel to bust a chicken in the beak.

Anyways, he fights his way back through the swinging doors, and I've got the grease cleaned up. So he bounces up and down on his tippy-toes and yells at Mike. Mike's down at the other end of the 48-burner side, slamming lids closed on the cookers, so he don't hear the Boss at all. And the fat in the open pots is sizzling, and the gauges on the closed pots are pumping steam and jumping, and the vent fans are on full throttle, so even I can't hardly hear him, and I'm standing right next to him.

"Faster, boys, faster!" he's yelling. "We got a line of honks out there nearly two miles long!" And then he dances back into the office, clapping his hands like he's a little kid at a birthday party and his cake just arrived.

232

That's because it's a fucking Specials Day. And it's the Sunday of the long weekend. And it's Dominion Day. And the city can't seem to get enough of our special fried chicken—89 herbs and spices in a secret recipe, not deep-fried, but sealed in a delicious coating at 452 degrees for 9 minutes and 33 seconds in a pressure cooker.

And it's a fucking pressure cooker all right.

Two buckets for the price of one. Two barrels for the price of one. There's 18 pieces of chicken in a barrel, 24 in a bucket. The last Specials Day, we put through 3000 buckets and 1700 barrels. That's 94,800 pieces of chicken. You get 36 pieces in a pot. So that's 2370 pots of chicken.

I'm the one that hauls it out of the cooler where it's packed in wooden slat boxes with chips of ice. And then Mike and I dip it in eggs and milk (I got to crack the eggs and beat them up with the milk). Then we flop it around in the flour and spices (I got to mix that in big steel buckets, measuring out the spices from the drums in the basement—they're shipped in all the way from Tennessee up here to Saskatchewan). Then we set it on trays and carry the trays over to the open pots and flip the chicken in. And you got to do that fast and careful, cause that grease is at 452 degrees and when it spatters on your wrists and hands it leaves these little puffy bubbles of cooked skin. Looks like plucked chicken skin by the end of a Specials Day.

Mike's made it all the way down the 48 side now, and he sees me standing there, taking a breather, and he kicks me hard in the ass. When he's got my attention, he says, "Pull those fuckers!" and he points at the other range.

"Jeesus!" I yell. Cause 9 minutes and 32 seconds have gone by and that chicken has to come out right on time or it gets brown and hard. So I grab my padded gloves and run right down to the other end of the 36-burner side. Mike's right beside me. And we flip off those gauges, slam open the pots, hook out the baskets of chicken, and dump them on a tray Mike's grabbed on the way by the tray pile.

Out those pieces come—breasts, thighs, keelbones, drumsticks, wings—golden brown. Perfect.

By the time we've opened all those pots and reached the end of the burners nearest the swinging doors, there's Belly-belly standing there. She's in her tight white uniform with her long black hair pinned up in that little white cap. But my eyeballs are so hot that I can't even see how gorgeous she is. She's just a beautiful blur. She stacks a couple of trays piled with golden chicken one on top of the other and whams her ass into those doors and is gone.

And I don't have time to think about what she and the Boss are up to, cause those empty pots have to be drained and refilled with filtered grease from the grease tubs down at the far end. So I start helping Mike carry them and dump them and fill them up again. And I notice the thermometer over the tub just as it pops its top at 160 degrees, and that red stuff inside gushes out and falls into the grease. I scoop that grease into the pots anyways. What the fuck. We'd never have time to drain that sucker and get some new grease hot. It comes in big white blocks—reminds me of ice cubes, and melts about as fast.

Then it's back to dipping and breading and then the 48s are ready to pull, and we do that, and then I got to go into the walk-in to grab some more crates. I slam the door behind me and stop for just a minute. I keep a jug of root beer in there, and I open the top and tip that jug over my shoulder and guzzle it down. It's so icy cold, my throat almost seizes up, but I keep it pouring down. I can feel it making a cool pool in my

234

stomach. A sudden vision of a big lake, full of beautiful cold water pops into my head. My family's there right now, at Waskesiu, and I sure as hell wish I was there instead of here.

Instead, I'm trying to catch a breath and watching steam rising off my bare arms. I drink some more root beer, top it, and set it down in the corner. Then I go over to the stack of chicken crates.

When the day began, this place was jammed with them. Now it's only three in the afternoon, and there's a big clear space in the cooler where crates used to be. And all at once I wonder if we're gonna run out. We're already over 2500 barrels and 1500 buckets. There's two miles of cars out there, full of hungry honks, and the supper rush is just beginning to roll. Jeesus, I think, counting crates. The Boss didn't order enough.

Then the door is swinging open and Mike is there. "Are you finished jerkin off or what?" he yells. "Fuckin teenager! We got pots to pull!" And he's almost gone before I can shout at him, "Mike! Come and count these crates!" And he comes in and slams the door. "What the fuck for?" Steam is just shooting off him. I mean, real steam. "There ain't enough," I say. "We're gonna run out."

"Let me see." he says, pushing me aside, and stabbing his finger at the crates, counting out loud. "Eighty-nine!" he says. "Eighty-nine?! That won't last more'n two hours! You asshole! Why didn't you tell me sooner?!"

I don't have to answer that. He knows we've been running around cooking chicken like we were chickens with our heads cut off.

"Fuckin asshole Boss!" he yells. "Let me at that fucker!"

Mike is six foot three in socks. He has muscles on his arms the size of baked hams from slinging those

235

pots for 10 years. He's been with the old El Diablo since it started. Which means he's nearly 30 now.

He swings around and slams that cooler door open and nearly knocks the Boss ass-over-pecker down the stairs into the basement storerooms. The Boss just gets one hand on the handrail before he takes the tumble. Mike sticks out an arm and hoists the Boss back onto his feet. But he don't let him go.

"What the hell are you doin in there?!" the Boss screams. "There's chicken burning!!"

He's right. There's smoke coming out the top of about four pots, and I know others are gonna start unless we pull them right away. I start to head for the burners, but Mike puts out his other arm and grabs me by the collar. I'm still walking even though I'm being held off the floor.

And it musta looked pretty funny to Belly-belly, who comes through from the front just then, looking for more trays of chicken. Mike's holding me off the floor with one hand, and lifting the Boss up in the air with the other so he can look him right in the eye.

"We're countin fuckin crates! There's only 89!" Mike yells at the Boss.

The Boss starts to move his arms like he's doin the breast stroke, and kick his feet.

"Let me see!" he yells. And then, "Put me down! Put me down!"

So Mike puts him down, and me down, and they go into the cooler to count crates again while I go and save what I can of the chicken in the pots. I just turn the burners off under the ones that are smoking. They'll have to wait. And I open up the next eight. We put them on eight by eight, leaving two minutes between each set, so we can fit all the dipping, breading, and dumping in.

The next eight aren't bad. Pretty brown, but not hard as iron yet. So I pile them on trays and give them

236

to Belly-belly. My eyeballs have cooled off enough now that I can see her fine, which is nice, cause she's been sweating so much that her uniform is plastered to her curves.

"You look real good when you're hot," I say. But she just ignores me, like she always does. I have to be careful what I say to her, because she could get me fired if she wanted to. She puts her nose in the air and goes out again.

Then Mike and the Boss slam out of the cooler, and the Boss runs for his office and Mike comes my way, carrying two crates in each hand by the wire wrapped around them.

"He's gonna try and order more," he says.

"But it's a long weekend," I say.

"He knows the packer," he replies. "Asshole better try to get us more or he won't be shippin us another crate." He sets the crates on the double sink by the breading counter. "Do these," he says, "and I'll handle all the pots for a while."

So I go to it, pulling chicken out of the ice till my hands are aching with cold, then dipping and breading, and passing the trays to Mike while he passes the cooked stuff back to me, and Belly-belly takes it out front.

And before we know it, we're down to our last crates, and it's only 4:15.

The Boss runs out of his office, yelling. "I finally got through to his kid. Packer's at the lake, but his kid says there's a semi-trailer on the way from Regina. He thinks it's full of chicken. It left more'n a coupla hours ago, so it should be almost here. He's gonna meet it at the plant and send it here."

"Good!" Mike yells.

"I also called the cop shop," the Boss shouts. "They're gonna send a squad car so it can get through all the cars out there."

So Mike and me cook up the rest of the crates, send it out front to the steamer, clean up all the pots, and put new grease in them. Then we tackle the burned ones, pulling out the chicken, that looks like a bunch of coal chunks, and dumping that grease in a coupla buckets. I get to carry it out to the pit at the back, across the gravel parking lot. It's a beautiful warm day, and the lot's jammed with cars, new model 59 Chevys and Fords, some Oldsmobiles. They all got their windows rolled down, and moms and dads and kids are all chewing on chicken, licking their fingers, slurping down shakes and slushies, and chomping on burgers and dogs and fries. Just about makes me sick, all those mouths moving, throats swallowing, bellies filling up. Especially those fries. I know who's cooking them.

But I make it out to the back gate, where the Boss's car is parked. It's a brand-new 1959 baby blue Caddy, and it's hitched to a 200-horsepower, dual-outboard, cabin cruiser. Then through the gate to the dump, where I slosh that burned grease in. Down at the bottom a coupla rats are prancing through last night's garbage. Almost get em with the hot grease. Almost have Tennessee-fried rat.

Wouldn't have been any worse than some of the chicken I've had to cook. Had some crates once been on the truck a week too long, and they still wanted us to take it. Stuff was crawling with maggots. Not even the Boss would let it hit the pots. And it has to smell pretty high before he gives a damn.

When I get back, the Boss tells me to get out front and lend a hand. That I don't mind at all. The air-conditioning actually keeps the place only hot, not like the hell-hole I usually spend my time in. So out I go, through the old swinging doors.

At the front counter, by the sliding windows where all the trays of food go out, Lorraine is perched on a stool. She's tall and lean, but pretty. "Welcome to El Diablo," she's saying in this low, purry voice. "May I take your order puh-lease?" And she flips the switch so some honk can ask for "Two buckets and three chili burgers and four, no, five fries—" And while he's still saying this, and since there's no one at the order window waiting for their order, I call out, "And one roll in the hay, puh-lease, Lou-lou, honey!"

Without even turning around, and still writing on her order pad, Lorraine says, "Well, if it ain't Little Dipper. If you don't call me by my real name, dip-stick, I'll make you hard and snap it off." And without missing a beat, she flips the switch again and, sweet as a Green Apple shake, repeats the guy's order and says, "Thank you for your order, sir. Will that be all?" And he says, "Four shakes—two chocolate and two vanilla." And she thanks him again and flips the switch to OFF and belts the order out.

And Jazzbo whaps another three patties on the grill, calling out, "Hey, it's the Big Dipper! Hey, well all right!"

I watch Belly-belly for a while, stuffing buckets with nearly the last of the chicken, then adding the "homemade" buns we get from McGavin's every week, and a container of "Down South" gravy. We make the gravy out of what the Boss calls "cracklings." That's the flour and egg sludge left on the pans after the dipped chicken's been thrown in the pots. I scrape it off at the end of the day and we cook it overnight, and make it look nice and brown with food colouring.

Then I stroll over to where Jug-jug is fixing the shakes. She's 19 and in First Year University, and I'm only 17, so I know I don't stand a chance of a date unless I'm always nice and only call her by her real name, which is Nancy. So I say, real polite, "I don't mean to bother you, Nancy, but would you mind makin me a strawberry shake? It's just so darn hot back there cookin chicken." And she smiles and says sure, so I stand there a little while watching her make the shake, putting in a bit of extra strawberry, cause she knows I like it. And before she hands me the shake I drink her in. She's really cute, but she's already going with a guy in Third Year University who drives a heavy Chevy from '55.

When she gives the shake to me, I say thanks, and tell her the Boss sent me out here to help out, and can I give her a hand? She says no, she's got things under control. And we both know what the Boss meant was for me to help Jazzbo on the grill. So I head over there, trying not to look at Zits.

Zits does the fries. I never eat fries. Zits has zits, big, white, juicy ones, all over his face. They drip. He tries to stop them by taking a fry just out of the oil and zapping his zits with it. I dunno what he thinks he's doing, soaking it up or searing it shut. Then he flips the fry back in the grease. Like, puke city. No one who works here ever eats fries. Except Zits.

I make it to the grill and have a flipper in my hand just before the Boss sails through the swinging doors. He's yelling, "God, God, God, where's the fuckin semi?!" before he sees there's a honk at the order window, so he makes a detour behind Belly-belly, ducking out of sight until the honk pays up and leaves. Then he goes to the till, dings it open, and pulls out the stacks of bills. He peels off a few to put back in the till for making change, then fishes some rubber bands from his pockets, rolls up the bills and snaps the bands on them. You can almost see the dollar signs dancing in his eyes.

Jazzbo's flipping cheese slices on some of the patties, cooking onions under a metal lid, frying bacon strips, toasting open buns. He's got it down to a science, so I just look occupied and keep out of his way.

Then we hear the sound of a siren.

The Boss goes nuts. "It's here!! The chicken's here!! C'mon, Dipper!" He rips out the swinging doors and I'm right behind him. "Fix up four buckets!" he yells at Belly-belly as he's going past.

The cop car has led the semi into the yard through the EXIT gate. The Boss goes scurrying around the lot, telling everybody parked there to move outta the way. Engines are revving up, the siren wailing, kids are bouncing in the back seats with excitement and spilling their shakes all over the upholstery. Finally, the cops take over the operation and the lot gets cleared in no time.

"Back her in here!" the Boss is yelling to the driver of the semi. His rig has "Chicken Licken Ranch" in big yellow letters on the sides. He wheels it around smoother than butter on hot bread right to where the Boss is guiding him. Which is a chute leading down into the basement storerooms.

When the rig's in place, the Boss runs over to Belly-belly, standing at the door with the four buckets, grabs two and tells her to come with him, and presents those buckets to the cops. "For you and all the other boys at the station," he says. "Compliments of the chef." The chef is leaning against the door, picking his nose and swigging root beer.

The cops spray gravel, siren still blaring, and race downtown.

The rig driver steps down from his cab. He's a thin, little guy, bald on top. Looks like his head's been pecked by a buncha chickens, it's all pocked.

"You wanted the chickens?" he asks the Boss, with a sorta puzzled look.

The Boss yells, "Open up those doors and send them in!"

The guy looks even more puzzled. "You want

241

them down in your basement?" he asks.

"Fuckin right!" the Boss says. "And now! Right now!!"

The guy objects, "But—"

And Mike steps up, towering over him. "Do what the Boss says, fuckface."

The guy backs off. "Sure thing. Whatever you say." And he heads for the doors on the chute.

Mike and the Boss turn and walk back through the door, with me trailing after them. The Boss says to Mike, "We'll rip those crates open and dump the ice on the floor down there. She'll melt down the drain.

Mike agrees, "Yeah, that'll get 'em unpacked faster."

The driver's opening the chute doors. They're up a coupla feet on the backwall, about loading dock-level, so's to make it easier for deliveries. He gets them open wide just as I'm going in behind the Boss and Mike. I guess he's gonna open his rig doors and back the rig right up snug, then go in to unload the sucker through the side entrance on his rig.

"Let's check those pots," Mike says to me. So we go over to the burners while the Boss heads through the swinging doors. I hear him yell, "Chicken's comin! Tell 'em chicken's comin, Lorraine!" He sounds like he's just won the Irish Sweepstakes. Then he comes sauntering back through and heads down for the basement, to see how the crates are piling up.

We've got all the burners going full blast, just primed for chicken, when we see the Boss come ripping up the basement stair three at a time. And when you got legs the length of toothpicks, that ain't easy. "Son of a bitch!!!" he's yelling. He races out the back, and I follow to take a look, stopping in the doorway.

Like I figgered, the rig's up real snug to the chute

and the little guy ain't nowhere to be seen. Must be inside the rig. The Boss goes racing around the rig, then comes back underneath at full tilt. He doesn't even have to duck.

"Where the fuck is he!?" he yells at me.

"Inside," I say, and point.

The Boss leaps up and down, hammering his fists on the side of the rig. "Open up, you son of a bitch!! Open up!!"

But it's obvious the guy can't hear him in there.

When I turn around and look back inside is when I hear the first "cluck-cluck-cluck." There's a chicken, a real live chicken, sitting on the post of the handrail at the top of the stairs down to the storerooms. And then there's another one. And another.

I run inside. Mike is still at the pots, I yell at him and he turns around. He nearly drops one a them pots.

"Chickens!" he yells. "It's fuckin chickens!!"

There's a tide of chickens, big suckers with long white feathers and floppy red combs and real chicken feet, rising up the stairs. The ones in the lead come strutting towards us, going "Bawk-bawk-bawk, bawk-bawk-bawk!"

The Boss comes scurrying back in. "I can't reach the fuckin door!" he yells. "You!" he stabs a finger at me. "You get the hell out there and tell him to stop!"

So I go out and climb up and open the side door on the semi, and walk in. It stinks of chicken in there, but there ain't a chicken to be seen. Just the rig driver standing in the narrow corridor between rows of cages that go from floor to ceiling. Empty cages.

"You send them all down?" I ask.

"Yep," he says, this little smile on his face. "Hope you had the pen ready for them. I called down before I started, to let you guys know they was comin. You couldn't wait to have 'em killed, plucked, and gutted, eh?"

"Guess not," I say.

"It's no fun," he says.

"It might be," I say, jumping down from the door.

As I come through the back, I yell at the Boss, "He'd finished before I got there. I was too late!"

The Boss can see that now. Up the stairs is rolling a flood of chickens. "Herd 'em back!" he yells. And he grabs a broom and starts swishing it at the chickens.

That's the wrong thing to do. Those chickens get excited, and start scrambling to get out of the way. A whole bunch of them run into where the pots are sizzling away. The chicken on the handrail post squawks and lays an egg. It rolls off the post and smashes on the floor.

The Boss goes nuts. He starts chasing chickens, waving that broom. The chickens make a run for it, moving in little waves this way and that. There's more of them coming up from the basement every moment. Our kitchen is filling up with chickens. They're laying eggs everywhere, eggs are dropping and rolling all over the floor. The Boss steps on a couple and goes down. He gets up again, slamming the broom at the chickens.

Mike starts to wade through the chickens, waving his arms, going downstairs, trying to drive them back. Chickens fly up in his face, and he has to cover his eyes and turn back. I can see he's getting mad. He grabs a chicken and wrings its neck. It doesn't even have time to squawk before it's dead chicken. He grabs another one.

The Boss joins in. Soon the floor is littered with the bodies of dead chickens. But more chickens, a great flood of chickens, keeps rising out of the basement.

"Help us kill them, you asshole!" the Boss yells at me. "Kill! Kill!!" He's starting to froth at the mouth.

Mike is a lot better at wringing their necks, but I can see he's gonna go off his nut anytime.

The air is filled with the noise of chickens. I can't hear anything else. Chickens clucking, chickens flapping, chickens squawking their last. The chickens are so scared, they're shitting themselves, and that don't help the footing.

I see the face of the rig driver at the back door window, waving the invoice he's finally made up. All of a sudden he ducks outta sight. I hear that rig fire up and pull out faster than you can fry an egg.

Through the glass in the swinging doors, I can see the faces of the whole crew, Belly-belly, Jazzbo, Jug-jug, Lorraine, and even Zits, staring in. Then they try to come in to help, and that's a mistake, cause the chickens see a way out and they make a mad dash for it. There's a hundred chickens through that open door before you can say "Easy over." And there's a thousand more trying to follow.

Then Mike does crack. He grabs a coupla dead chickens and heads for the burners, sliding and slipping on the broken eggs and chicken shit. He dips those chickens in milk and eggs, he rolls them in the flour with the 89 secret spices, he drops them into pots. The fat hits feathers and spews into the air. But Mike don't care. He slams on the lids and turns around for more. He doesn't have to look far. There's chickens jumping up into the milk and eggs, so he just wrings their necks, flours them, and puts them into a coupla more pots.

Some chickens jump on the burners. Their feathers get singed. The stench is awful. Mike dunks them in milk and eggs to cool them off, kills them, pots them. I yell at Mike, "Gauges, Mike! Gauges!!" But he can't hear me.

Then the Boss yells at me, "We gotta keep 'em outta the front!" like he's just figgered out what the honks are gonna think when they see a buncha live chickens staring back at them from the order window. He swats his way through the swinging doors and a lot more chickens follow him. So do I.

Things look calm in the front. Everybody's at their posts. Jazzbo's working the grill, Nancy's making shakes, and Zits is on the chips. Lorraine is perched on her stool, shouting into her mike, "That's two buckets, one burger with cheese and onions, two cokes, and one choc-o-late shake!" Or trying to shout, cause it sounds like a henhouse that a mink's just visiting, and the honks can't tell a word she's saying.

Only Belly-belly is sitting on a chair, sobbing. With a coupla chickens perched on her lap, giving her sympathy.

The Boss tries to grab a chicken, and the chicken leaps onto a counter, and then into the air. Well, it connects with the overhead fan, and all at once there's feathers and chicken parts flying everywhere.

A honk pulls up at the window, takes one look at what's going on, and lays rubber. Another honk pulls up, takes a look, and also lays rubber. I haveta agree, it ain't pretty. And it don't sound nice either.

The Boss is cursing, Belly-belly's wailing, Lorraine's screaming orders back at the honks, the chickens are going berserk.

Then the first pot blows.

There's just a moment after the first huge "WHOOOMP!!!" when it's totally silent. Even the chickens pay attention.

And then the shock wave blows the glass outta the swinging doors and everybody dives for cover. Except the Boss, who yells, "Holy shit!!" and heads back for the kitchen.

Mike shouldda put on those gauges, I think.

Then the next pot blows.

We all know how to take a hint. Lorraine is the

first one out the order window, sliding on her belly right into a T-Bird convertible that's just pulled up. She turns to the tanned young guy driving his trapper's wagon and says, "Let's see the world, honey," and he floors it and away they go. That's the last any of us ever see of them.

Then I help Nancy to go through, and she crawls out backwards, real ladylike, followed by a dozen chickens.

The Boss keeps prancing towards what's left of the swinging doors, then back again. "Mike! Mike! Get outta there!!" he's screaming.

Another pot goes.

Jazzbo is fixing up the rest of the burgers and dogs on the grill. He bags them, then hands them to me, and hops outta the order window. I hand him back the bags, then a coupla trays of drinks and shakes Nancy had ready.

Zits is next in line. He's so scared it looks like all his zits have popped at once. His face is a mess. I hand him a counter towel and he wipes his face off. He tries to hand it back to me, but I just point to the floor and he drops it. With all his zits cleaned off, he don't look that bad. Out he goes. Along with 50 more chickens.

KABOOM!!! KABOOM!!! go some more pots. Flames are starting to appear behind those doors.

At last the Boss decides Mike has to take care of himself. He goes over to Belly-belly, who hasn't moved and hasn't stopped wailing through all of this, helps her up, and they go out through the order window.

Followed by yours truly.

The lot has cleared out completely, except for the Boss's Caddy and boat.

And somebody musta called the firemen, cause we can hear sirens wailing in the distance. Flames and a big pillar of black smoke are rising up higher and higher from the building. The fire engines don't have a chance.

All of us trek over to the Caddy. We climb up into the boat to get a good look at the fire. Chickens are still pouring out the order window, strutting around in the gravel lot, pecking and squawking.

And who should we meet up there in the boat but Mike himself. He's a little singed, but not crazy any more.

"Sorry, Boss," he says. "I shouldda gone down with the kitchen, but I just couldn't take any more of those chickens."

The Boss pats his arm. "S'okay," he says.

Jazzbo passes out the burgers and dogs, Nancy hands around shakes and cokes. And we stand up there, along the rail, eating and drinking, watching the old El Diablo burn, every once in a while another pot going off with a big, muffled "WHUUMMP!!" When the fire engines arrive, they can see there ain't nothin to do except wait around and hose down the coals. So they leave one pumper and all the rest head back for the station.

As the fire burns out and the sun goes down, the Boss pulls out his rolls of bills and peels off a bunch. "Here's what ya wouldda earned for the rest of the summer," he says to us all.

He turns to Belly-belly. "How about you an me headin for the Coast?" he asks her, and she nods yes.

The last we see of them is when they drive away in the baby blue Caddy, pulling that cabin cruiser off to the ocean. The Boss don't even offer us a ride into town. And neither does the pumper when it takes off.

So we gotta stand around, breathing in the stink of exploded chicken, and listening to the live chickens that are left finding a roost on the fence that goes all the way around the gravel lot. They're all clucking away with these quiet little satisfied clucks, like

248

they've just found a home away from home. I figger the rats from the dump are gonna find themselves in chicken paradise tonight.

Finally, Nancy's boyfriend arrives at midnight, and the rest of us all catch a ride with him.

"Hey," says Jazzbo, as we hop in the car, "whadaya say we all head out for Waskesiu?"

"Whiskey Slough? Great idea," Nancy's boyfriend replies.

So off we all go, speeding through the night.

RICK HILLIS

Gulls

Gulls strut the shopping mall
tarmac because they're too heavy
for their wings.
            They step goosey and click
their beaks like 1950s fingers. Gulls
are out of style. Just ask Neil Diamond.
          Gulls are louder and more stupid
than ducks whose dainty woodwind lips sound
like saxophones (and ducks themselves are stupid—
              ducks live programmed lives;
              not gulls). No,
a gull's life is a random grey whirl
torn into the sky above sewage lagoons and garbage
   dumps.
            Some live miles from the sea and
    probably
don't even know it. Gulls are incongruous
wherever they are except on the crossed masts
of fishing boats where they perch like cats
in apt. windows and erect chalky cones of shit
everywhere.
          Gulls,
               gulls are stupid fatties
who walk on matchstick feet. They have brains
the size of pocketchange. They hop from trash
can to trash can screeching and slapping each other
with empty-gloved wings. They remind me of
politicians or stage actors
overdoing it.

                    They squabble
all the time and sprint around parked cars,
wings aloft like wind-inverted umbrellas or feathered
serving trays. They think they're so important.
I'd like to blunderbuss the species.
                    And you can't trust gulls
like you can a dog. A cat you can trust to do
as it pleases, but gulls aren't trustworthy.
They don't make good pets because they aren't
consistent. Of course what's consistency to
a gull? Who cares?
                    They remind me of
my neighbours who roam the block for mattresses
and wrecked car parts. They are scavengers
who breed like insects (gulls, that is),
                    and they have
generations of marble-eyed, slope-shouldered
offspring (my neighbours, I mean).
                    I'm afraid
they'll mate with each other and the headline will
    read:

        Seagull gives birth to strapping
        3-toed humanoid with dime-size brain

and it'll live next door to me. Where's
Dave Winfield when you need him?
                    Ah, gulls.
They're no magpie or chicken, I can tell
you that.

RICHARD STEVENSON

Fubar

Fubar
It looks like any other government acronym,
sounds like "Podzol" or any of a dozen
specialized designators for the acidity or
alkalinity of soil, amount of sand or humus,
and might well be the scientific name
for the soil conditions in this particular plot,
but, of course, it's not; it's what Woody chose
to fill in the blank this particular day
after filling out a thousand similar field reports
and finally coming across a type of soil he couldn't
identify. It's an all-purpose, all-weather,
generic acronym. It means it was hot out,
it had been a long day; the mosquitoes were
particularly bad; that there was a glacial lake
reportedly full of Dolly Varden in the vicinity;
that it was after lunch anyway, and Woody
was hungry. The guys had been in the bush too long
and needed to knock off. It meant the soil
had finally become what it is for most of us:
dirt, and nothing special you'd want to muddy
your knees in studying too long. The same stuff
caked into the treads of all our boots:
lumpen dirt. Full of clay certainly; hard to
get off, and full of the smell of rot, if not
septic. Sedimentary certainly, and as old
as an extinct species of flora or fauna
you care to name. Old as Methuselah, who
never had the good fortune to work for this outfit.
Fucked Up Beyond All Recognition, but
officially FUBAR, duly logged and accepted,
for Woody's the soils expert around here,
has been in these woods a long time; he ought to know.

JUDITH WRIGHT

The Land of the Lizards

In the Land of the Lizards
We eat our heads, and save our tails
We speak in tongues, we do not listen
Our hearts are deadly but we frequently mate
After watching TV we peel and groan
To the patter and the rhythm
Of the garbage men's feet
In tune with Death: a small black apple

In the Land of the Lizards
Where no means yes
And maybe and might are impotent
We pray to flowers and men-like things
We furnish our homes with dragon wings
We sing and croon, in love with Dying
And make our bed to the thump
And the shuffle of the garbage men's feet
Bright beetles of knowing: escaping

In the Land of the Lizards on a Saturday night
We all get together and begin to fight
We pick our teeth with the bones of notions
We love our children but we poison our oceans
We eat our heads to save our tails
In the Land of the Lizards
We hunger

DAVID CARPENTER

The Prince and the Pelicans

A few miles from the town of Imperial (that's north of Stalwart) about three thousand people are streaming across the grid road into the Last Mountain Lake bird sanctuary: old folks with lawn chairs, school kids with plastic flags, cubs and scouts flashing regimental colours, soldiers in berets, birders with binoculars, tourists with cameras—conservationists all. A flag-snapping wind makes the grass lean one way and the people (from Saskatchewan and therefore stubborn) lean the other.

In the centre of a prairie the size of a galaxy, the lake is as long as the Americas. Next to the lake is a sage and gopher field as flat as an ocean (the nearest mountain is six hundred miles west). In it stands the red and white circus tent on which the crowd is converging. Gulls, hawks, swans, plovers, and cranes drift and teeter overhead. The wind wraps the flags around the poles and sends the ladies' scarves into the far north.

Three oldsters have taken shelter in a straggle of caragana bushes, huddling like teenagers in a blanket, a man between two ladies. The man in the middle says, "I'm just here t'see the copters."

"Oh, you're not," says his wife. "You're here t'see him."

Him. That's how most people here refer to HRH Prince Philip, the Duke of Edinburgh, President of the World Wildlife Fund. He is coming to celebrate the one hundredth birthday of the Last Mountain Lake sanctuary, the oldest in North America, latterly famous as the nesting ground of white pelicans.

A little background. About ten years ago the white pelican had declined to sixteen thousand

254

breeding pairs in Canada. In 1978 it was added to the endangered list, and the World Wildlife Fund and Canada Life, whose logo shows a white pelican, mounted a campaign to protect it. This April, when the population appeared to have risen to fifty thousand pairs, it was taken off the list of threatened species. Never before in Canada has this happened.

"This is a once-in-a-lifetime," the lady on the far end of the blanket says. "I collect royalty memorabilia. I have three hundred salt and pepper shakers alone."

From the other side of the galaxy through a tattered sky come three helicopters, scattering gulls and geese. The helicopters rock down and alight. Prince Philip is out at once to a ripple of applause, a tanned handsome man, regal as a ship, wearing an olive jacket, brown slacks, a golden duck pin in his lapel. Flanked by cabinet ministers and honoured guests (two separate categories in Saskatchewan), he strides over to the crowd and chats his way to the platform.

"Look at these," he says to the federal minister of the environment, indicating a swarm of kids in yellow and black tractor caps bearing the logo, "I ♥ No-Name." The Shop-rite in Nokomis has donated them for the occasion. The prince asks the kids what their caps mean and gets seven or eight simultaneous explanations. He asks the federal minister who tries to explain. Is it an Indian name? No, your Highness, uh, y'see, uh . . . and off they go again, past the applauding throng.

The ceremony begins. The regional director of the Canadian Wildlife Service does introductions. The federal minister delivers an environ-mental speech. Robert Bateman, the wildlife artist, presents a painting featuring white pelicans to Prince Philip; in turn, the prince presents a reproduction to the president of Canada Life. The provincial minister for parks, recreation, and culture reminds the crowd that his home town is Edinburgh. The Duke of Edinburgh smiles. An eastern kingbird loops the circus tent.

All through the ceremony, birds of every description glide by: a marbled godwit, a double-crested cormorant, a ring-billed gull. One by one, one per species, they swoop low across the army of binocular and camera-bearers, then swerve back into the wind. A meadowlark, a lesser Canada, a green-winged teal, a Caspian tern. An attempt to honour these nature lovers with a fly-past?

The binoculars and cameras remain trained on the stage. The prince and the dignitaries have risen to sign an agreement establishing Last Mountain Lake as a national wildlife area. A flotilla of pelicans lifts off from a marsh at the edge of the lake and wheels into the air, drifting in perfect formation around the crowd, riding the air currents in a spiral, the black-edged wings of each bird spread wide for soaring.

No-one looks up.

One by one they bring their wings in and dive, eighteen pelicans, eighteen identical snow-white Chuck Yeagers in perfect control. They pull out at the last moment over the lake and wheel back into the wind.

Nothing. The birds have been snubbed.

The prince walks off the stage. He stops to chat with a dandelion field of No-Name caps; he speaks to some legionnaires, who answer back shyly; he waves goodbye. There is, of course, one more thing the birds can do, but they have their orders from Pelican Central. No international incidents today, boys. Bring 'em on home.

TONY PENIKETT

The Politics of Moose

Nobody, perhaps not even the moose, knows for sure exactly how many moose live in my constituency.

The Yukon Government has often been criticized for its ignorance on this question. The opposition regularly demands to know what the Yukon is doing to raise moose populations. Hunters need more moose, the argument goes. Predators take too many. The government should therefore kill more bears and wolves. Of course, no one ever calls for the moose to be consulted, nor the bears or wolves for that matter.

There has never been a complete census of the Yukon's moose population. There may indeed be more moose than people. But moose do not have the vote, so as far as most politicians are concerned they do not count. This silent majority rarely attends public meetings and never writes letters to the editor. They do not demand jobs or housing. Regardless, I'm one legislator who thinks that not only do moose deserve a hearing, but that specific moose questions deserve more consideration in our political forums.

Representing Moose
Representing the moose in my district is not easy. They are a transient lot and, like Her Majesty, they don't have a lot to say. However, we legislators must do what we can.

Part of the problem is the moose's image. Thanks to a character in Archie comics children of the dominant North American culture are taught to think of moose as big and dumb. Al Capp's creation "General Bull Moose" associated the innocent mammal with unbridled capitalism. Neither of these characterizations can be completely fair. After all, who really knows what moose think. If they were enfranchised, one surely could not count on the support of a moose bloc vote at the polls.

Canvassing moose at election time is time consuming, and sometimes risky. Once a fine representative of the moose population suffered a hunting accident shortly after meeting with me. I sincerely hope that the two events—our meeting and the accident—were not in any way connected. This tragedy clearly demonstrates the need for both strict confidentiality when meeting with moose in the fall, and the difficulty of maintaining consistent contact with one's constituents.

Moose and Tourism
No one ever thinks of moose as tourists. But after all, they are always on the move. True they generally prefer wilderness over the historic site or the shopping mall, delighting apparently in the unguided summer tour of the Yukon landscape, far away from hotels and recreational vehicles. This is a pity, since many foreign tourists come thousand of miles just for a glimpse of northern wildlife. Because moose avoid the highways like death during the tourist season, they might be accused of not doing their bit for the Yukon's second largest industry. But consider the matter from their perspective. No sooner do they come down from the hills in August, than people in pickup trucks start shooting at them.

Moose and Land Claims
For some time, aboriginal claims have been the principal political question in the Yukon. Moose are obviously necessary to a just settlement of land claims. In fact, moose may be the one essential ingredient to a successful agreement.

What the moose want is a level playing field. My guess is that they need to know the score. What they have now is a confusing situation in which they are forced to live (and die) according to two conflicting sets of rules. Ever since the Yukon was created by an act of the federal parliament, non-native hunters could chase only certain kinds of moose in certain places at certain times of the year, while aboriginal hunters suffered relatively few restrictions.

This has been very confusing for the moose and bad for both their mental and their physical health.

Land claim negotiators have worked out new arrangements which guarantee a future for Yukon moose. All sides have expressed deep appreciation for the patience and understanding which moose have shown while this difficult situation was being resolved.

Gender, Age and Moose of Colour

Natural law is hard on both young and old moose. But human hunting laws have been particularly prejudicial to the adult bull moose. As a result, single-parent families have long been the norm for Yukon moose. However, at least things are improved somewhat from the days when the government permitted the hunting of cow moose as well.

One can't help noticing that most moose are dark in complexion. Remarkably, there is no evidence of discrimination against the rare albino ungulate. This is an admirable moose quality and one which obviates the need for any legislative intervention.

Moose and Diet

In the Yukon, moose stew, moose soup and chocolate mousse are popular dishes. In the aboriginal community, moose guts and moose nose are rare treats.

Yukon Indians are justly proud of their practice of eating the whole moose. Not surprisingly, moose are vegetarians.

Moose and Sex
We hear that Yukon moose horns are sometimes shipped overseas where they are ground into powder for use as an aphrodisiac. Does this, I wonder, explain the origin of the term "horny"?

The Politics of Moose
The politics of moose is a subject of endless fascination. I may never know how many moose there are in my district. I may never get their vote. But I'm happy to have had a chance to meet some of them and represent them in the legislature. Moreover, I have absolutely no hesitation in saying that the Yukon is a better place for their being here.

JON WHYTE

The Bannister Boys

The Bannister Boys are coming to town,
coming to town and making some noise,
raising the roof and painting it red—
they're known as the Sinister Bannister Boys.

Phimister Bannister, starting an escapade,
sliding the length of a rococo banistrade,
gave one banister a thunderous poke;
whereupon Phimister noticed the banister
turned on a lathe from a piece of stout oak,
under the stress of his rambunction broke.
It's known as The Banister Phimister Bannister Broke.

Winchester Bannister, brother to Phimister,
noting the banister's splinters of oak,
knew it was Phimister's way with a joke.
Slowly he reached deep down in his poke
withdrawing the moolah to make matters right,
to pay for The Banister Phimister Bannister Broke.

Senator Samuel, Ottawa Minister,
observing his brother, Winchester Bannister,
withdrawing the cash from out of his poke,
drawled out a warning, solemnly spoke:
"Do you think, Winchester, it is all right,
though I think that you are a very fine bloke,
to pay for the banister our brother Phimister . . .
to pay for The Banister Phimister Bannister Broke?"

The Reverend Bannister, Lester C. Bannister,
a Bannister brother, one of the folk,
declaring, "Phimister's he who's broken the banister
and it's he who should replace it of just as fine oak.
None of his brothers should have to dig deeply
into a pocket and into a poke
to pay for The Banister Phimister Bannister Broke."

Winchester Bannister swirled in his cloak
as to his brother he thunderously spoke,
"Now Lester C. Bannister, see here, Mister Bannister
you'll have to agree
we Bannister Brothers cannot be a joke.
You as a minister cannot be less sinister.
We must all share in the cost
for The Banister Phimister Bannister Broke."

The Bannister Boys have come to town,
they've come to town and they've made their noise.
Each of the boys is a very good bloke.
They're known as the Sinister Bannister Boys.

JAKE MACDONALD

Norris

"Which one do you want?" the man asked.

Six small pigs, no larger than four-legged watermelons, were nosing around in the strawfloor of the stall. The mother was passed out on the floor, huge as a beached whale. The smell rising from the stall was sickening. I should get my head examined, Sam thought.

"It doesn't matter, any one of them."

"A big one or a small one?"

"A medium one, I guess."

The man opened the door of the stall and slipped inside. The piglets started to run around the stall and the sow bucked to her feet. Once inside he pushed open another door that led outside and the sow made one quick circle of the stall and then bolted out into daylight, followed by six grunting youngsters. The man reached down and grabbed a piglet as it whirred by and scooped it into his arms. The piglet immediately began to scream, in such a bloodcurdling manner that anyone listening would have thought it was being tortured with hot irons. The man carried it outside and laid it on the tailgate of Sam's pickup truck and Sam brought some twine and the man tethered its feet. The woman was watching from the door of the house. It looked like she was holding her hand over her mouth but Sam didn't look twice. They spread some straw in the bed of the truck and laid the pig down beside the spare tire. It was no longer screeching but was choking and sobbing and rolling its eyes in horror. Its back legs were covered with excrement.

Sam got in the truck. "Thanks," he said. "I better get it home."

He drove slowly on the way home. It was a gravel road and he checked repeatedly over his shoulder to make sure the pig was all right. After five miles or so he heard it retching and he stopped the truck. It had gotten sick and there was yellow bile on the straw and its eyes were still clenched tight. Sam got a cloth and went down into the ditch and soaked it in the frogwater, then wiped off the piglet's face. "Try not to be such a pig," he said quietly.

Several miles further up the road he slowed down for a construction crew that was working on a culvert. He pulled to a stop on the shoulder of the road and waved to a large fat man in a hard hat who was wallowing around in the mud of the ditch. "Hey Norris . . . Come here. There's a lady here in the back of the truck that wants to meet you."

The man gave Sam a skeptical look. He grunted and jiggled as he climbed up the embankment and looked into the back of the truck. "Holy Jeez," he said reverently. "It's a goddamn pig. Hey look you guys. Sam's got himself a goddamn pig."

The flagman came over. "Hey, nice . . . what is it, a girl or a boy?"

"You know I never checked," said Sam, dismounting from the truck.

The flagman looked. "It's a boy. It looks a lot like Norris . . . Kinda smells like him too."

"That's what I think I'll call him, Norris the Second."

The tubby man laughed, flattered.

Sam took the wet rag and wiped off the piglet's face. It opened one eye and heaved a great self-pitying sigh.

"What are you going to do with him?" Norris asked.

Sam was patting the pig gently on the flank. "Throw a party and eat him," he replied.

264

Sam owned an island about nine miles north of town. On the map it was designated S-981, and until Sam shelled out fifteen-five in October of last year it was owned by a widow in San Diego, California. The island was located in a wild and uninhabited section of the river. Sam was planning to build a house and live there year-round. He'd wanted waterfront property a bit closer to town but he'd given up on that. All the serviced lots were sky-high and the crown was sitting on everything. When the island came up he realized he'd be living the life of a hermit but hell, he could go on looking forever too.

There were no buildings on the island and Sam intended to build a log house the following winter. For now he lived in a half-shot old houseboat that he anchored in a U-shaped notch at the south end of the island. The houseboat was temporary lodging, and was getting near the end of its days. It had once belonged to a wealthy car salesman from Winnipeg who had used it as a floating bordello throughout the summer and then in the seventies it was purchased by the people at The Keewuttunnee Marina, who rented it out on weekends to morons who drove it into every reef on the river system, and then Sam bought it for eight hundred dollars, again on the spur of the moment, when the proprietor told him he could pay any time and to please get it away from his dock or he was going to dump a jerry can of gas on it and go looking for a match. The superstructure was made of scaly blue-painted plywood that was slowly delaminating and the glass louvres in half the windows were missing or broken. The floor heaved, the pontoons leaked, the outer deck was rotten and the only method for heating the place was closing the door. Sam however filled the living-room with plants, carpets, driftwood artifacts, sea shells, Bob Dylan posters, book shelves, animal skulls, stereo speakers and barnwood furniture and decided it would have to suffice until he got his house built. As soon as the ice went out in the spring he pushed it out to the island with his twenty horse and nudged it into that U-shaped slip. Then he scrambled up into the woods and tied it down to the big pines with half-inch steel cable. Then threw down the gang plank. Then down went the old snow tires into the water, to cushion what remained of his flotation. The houseboat floated on a pair of steel pontoons, thirty-two feet long. The pontoons were painted with black tar and horribly rusted. Each pontoon was divided into eight compartments, and so many of the compartments were punctured and waterlogged that all he had to do was stroll down one side of the houseboat, clinging to the narrow walkway, and the old tub would heel over and almost dump him into the snags and lily pads, where there were leeches and dock spiders the size of his hand. Home sweet home.

Sam wasn't weighed down with a great need for human company but he liked the odd visit and conversation as much as the next guy. After spending a few weeks hard at work clearing the site, burning brush, dropping trees, he decided he'd invite all the townies out for a little party. He was browsing through a northern cookbook that night and he spotted a recipe for roast whole pig. A momentary image came to him, of a stuffed porker turning on a spit above a bonfire, with music, drinks, a big summer moon, barefoot girls and so on and so on.

When he got home with Norris the piglet he cleared out a space in the tool room of the house-boat, laid down a bed of newspapers and put the piggy inside with a bowl of grain and a bucket of water. "Make yourself at home," he said. He closed the door of the tool room and went outside and got his tools together to build a pigpen. The island was sixteen acres, about the size of a large city block. From the water's edge it rose in a series of granite ledges to a long humpback of open meadows and heavy mixed forest. Sam went to a shady opening in the side of the forest and began building the pen. Using two-by-sixes, ardox nails and a quartet of standing spruce trees he built a square corral with the approximate dimensions of a very small room. With two sheets of plywood he fashioned a low roof. By midafternoon he was admiring his work. Not bad. He'd lived in worse places himself. He went down to the houseboat to get Norris, who seemed to be adjusting nicely, curled up and sleeping in a corner of the tool room. He hadn't even dirtied the floor. Sam carried him up to the pen and Norris snuffled around in the straw. Welcome to your new home, boy. You won't be needing a door.

The word soon got out that Sam was raising a pig on the island and people began coming out to visit. At first the boats would troll slowly up to the houseboat, the people standing and waving tentatively at Sam as courtesy demanded, but as these people brought other people and the other people brought friends of their own some of the courteous behaviour began wearing away. Sam would step out the front door of his houseboat and he would hear voices up in the woods—more visitors. The police boat came by one day and bubbled hesitantly a hundred yards off shore until Sam waved them in. Chaput and Murphy tied the big inboard up to the tail of the houseboat and came aboard. The two big guys coming up the narrow walkway heeled the houseboat over and Sam had to yell a warning and they almost got dumped into the water. They crossed the gangplank onto the shore and Sam led them up into the woods. Norris, the local hero, peered up at them from the churned earth upon which he lay. His ears hung over his eyes like a coy hairdo. Murphy was of course an authority on swine management and he told Sam how to custom-feed Norris for that extra poundage. They all stood there silently for several minutes, watching. The smell of the black earth and the small fly-bothered pig was not unpleasant. Sam cleared the air by mentioning that they were both of course invited to the barbecue. "Hey, all right," said Chaput. Murphy asked who was going to dispatch Norris when slaughtering day came.

"I will," said Sam.

Murphy offered his services. He said he'd done it many times before.

"Okay. If I change my mind I'll let you know."

"This is the spot," said Murphy. He drew his service revolver and flipped Norris's earflap out of the way and stuck the gun muzzle right into the ear. "Bang," he said. "Out go the lights."

Sam went into town for a bag of nails one day and when he came back he saw a dirty old freighter canoe with an ancient Johnson six-horse pulled up on the shore on the north side of the island, half concealed by the shadows and undergrowth. He knew who owned the boat and he didn't waste any time motoring around to the other side. Smelly Mike and Johnny No Cash were standing beside the pig pen when he got there. Smelly Mike was wearing a big hunting knife on his belt and they both looked a bit guilty. "Thinking of having a pork chop for lunch?" Sam asked, with a big smile. They both laughed, as if this was the funniest thing they had ever heard. Sam went about the business of watering Norris and changing his straw and when it became apparent that he wasn't in the mood for inviting them to the barbecue they made their excuses and headed for their canoe. Sam didn't trust either of them. Johnny No Cash was a ratfaced and ponytailed little item who'd wandered in off the highway one day with his guitar in a black plastic garbage bag. Like a lot of people in Keewuttunnee he came from somewhere else, somewhere else where he had a proper Christian name and a social insurance number, but here in Keewuttunnee he only had his guitar, which he strummed in a futile bid for spare change. Everyone called him Johnny No Cash. Smelly Mike was a big man with broken knuckles and a soft voice. He was a biker from Oshawa who'd been around for two years, claiming that he'd be gone just as soon as he got the bread together to get his motorcycle fixed. He had a weedy blonde beard and fat arms and wore paratrooper pants with pockets and zippers all over them. The little Indian kids in town had been responsible for naming him. Whenever Mike walked by they held their noses and whispered to each other. "That guy's kinda smelly, or somethin." Sam got into the habit, after their visit, of locking Norris into the tool room whenever he went to town for the afternoon.

Sam had had sloppier room mates than Norris. When Sam got home and unpacked the groceries Norris would explore the forbidden territory of the living-room, or scratch at the door and grunt if he had to go out. He would sit obediently while Sam ate his supper, and if Sam offered him a morsel he would first sniff at it with his pink nose and then take it into his mouth as delicately as a cat. There was always a great display of pleading and whining when Sam closed him into his pen for the night and Sam was beginning to wonder how much pork he was going to be eating on the night of the barbecue. He decided to include lots of cobbed corn and baked potatoes on the menu.

At first he'd planned to invite people on an individual basis, to keep the thing from turning into a natural disaster, but a roast pig party wasn't easy to keep quiet. It seemed that everyone he met either wanted an invitation or already assumed they were coming. Lemon the bartender was working on posters and Sam couldn't bring himself to disapprove. Lemon had taken some art courses at the university and he was Keewuttunnee's resident artiste. He was developing a limited series of prints that would forever commemorate the event. One of the posters depicted a bacchanalian feast, with Norris impaled dripping on the spit and dozens of half-clad revelers dancing around the fire. Another poster showed a handcuffed Norris being smooched by officer John Murphy, whose nose looked slightly more rounded and porcine than usual. Burt Harrison had likewise appointed himself music chairman, and he was planning to come out any day with his thousand-megaton stereo system and wire the island for sound. Sam dreaded the prospect of Burt rupturing their eardrums with his Iron Maiden and Ozzy Osbourne tapes but probably no one else was willing to transport their precious stereo equipment out to the island to be nailed to trees and walked on.

Meanwhile Norris was spending a lot of time running free every day. Sam thought it would be good for him. He could get away from the biting flies and supplement his diet with the roots and truffles that grew wild in the woods. Visitors always commented on his increased size and Sam himself noticed, especially when he was lifting the pig in and out of the pen. He wasn't getting much fatter but he was certainly taller, with an adolescent's long legs and all the standard identity problems. One day a group of dogs arrived with a boatload of visitors and Norris reacted as if these were his long lost brothers and sisters. The dogs tore back and forth on the island, barking at squirrels, investigating rabbit holes, splashing in the lake, and Norris did his best to keep up with them. He could run almost as fast as they could through the woods but the moss-covered rocks at the water's edge defeated him. The dogs would wade in up to their chests, slap the water with their pink tongues, and then shake off and dash back into the woods. Norris would still be skidding and scrambling at the water's edge, falling on the greasy rock and squealing pitifully. For days afterward, when Sam patted him on the flank he would wag his tail.

Sam was having a lot of trouble figuring out how to make a rotisserie. His first option was to dig a barbecue pit, Hawaiian style, and bury the body in hot coals overnight. Checking around the island though, he couldn't find any suitable place with deep enough soil to dig a pit. He talked to the alcoholic cook at the hotel and learned that an above-ground barbecue pit, with Norris turning regularly over the coals for twelve or fourteen hours, would probably do the job. This still left the job of designing a spit to turn him on. A dry wooden pole would probably burn from the heat of the fire. A green wooden pole would probably sag under Norris' weight, which was getting close to a hundred pounds. Any kind of pole would have to be equipped with clamps of some kind, so the carcass wouldn't slip as the pole turned.

Sam finally swallowed his pride and went to see Smelly Mike, and asked him if he would weld up a set of clamps and a spit. Smelly Mike, knowing that this meant he would be invited to the party, was more than pleased to assume this important role. He and Sam went to the dump—he really did smell bad that day—and cannibalized an old Datsun, knocking off the drive shaft and radius rods and wheel rims and tossing them in Sam's pickup. Back in Keewuttunnee, at Steve's Esso, Murphy and Henry Yelle and Steve the Grouch and Sam stood around watching as Smelly Mike put on his gear and arc welded all that

271

butchered steel into a reasonable approximation of a rotisserie stand, with the uprights standing in the wheel rims and the drive shaft as a cross bar. Smelly Mike triumphantly removed his hood and the others stood there muttering in admiration as the steel cooled. Murphy, in uniform, planted his ass on the cross-bar and gave it his full weight. Steve the Grouch said that if that didn't break the rig nothing would.

All that week volunteer workers showed up at the island, using his tools, stringing lights up in the trees, cutting down logs for bench seating around the fire, and even cutting a small room-sized area out of the forest that featured a Christmas-light entranceway and a tin foil sign that said DANCE HALL. Burt Harrison came out and started wiring up all the trees with sound equipment: hi-fi speakers, car door speakers, tweeters, woofers, Eatonia shelf speakers salvaged from the dump, even a set of PA horns from the community hall. He set up a little orange tent in the bush and built the stereo inside, the chrome multi-dialed amplifiers and boosters and spilled guts of cord. Sam patrolled the job site, trying to ensure that any damage done to the local ecology was not permanent. Norris went around making friends with all his executioners. It was almost dark when they finally left.

The next day Sam went up to the terrace in the middle of the island and worked on the site plan for his house. The preparations for the pig roast were almost complete. Norris grazed in the undergrowth while Sam drilled holes in the rock for his foundation footings. The site was forty feet above the water and he could imagine he was standing on his sundeck, gazing aross the miles. Back in the bush there he'd put his pumphouse and wood shed, and maybe a little barn for his animals. On the slope here, there'd be a winding staircase down to the water and the dock.

When he finished drilling the footings it was seven in the evening. He went for a swim and fed Norris, then made himself a salami sandwich and went and sat on the shoreline with his sandwich and a Coke. Norris joined him. The execution was scheduled for tomorrow morning at eight. Sam, with his blue jeaned legs stretched out on the moss-crusted granite, finished his meagre supper and scratched Norris between the ears. Norris snuffled and wriggled his nostrils. They watched dusk come to the lake. The water was slack and one shade lighter than the storm-bruised sky. A loon was whooping maniacally somewhere down the lake. If it rains, Sam thought to himself, we might have to cancel the party. And if we cancel the party, I doubt if we'll go to all the trouble of scheduling it for another weekend. That's the only chance for a reprieve I think you've got, boy. Until then I think we'll just keep you in your pen.

Next morning dawned bright and clear. Sam didn't waste any time lying in bed. He went up to the woods and found the wall of the pen smashed down and Norris gone. Accustomed to having his freedom, Norris had obviously taken exception to being penned up like an animal. Sam fashioned a lasso at the end of a thirty foot length of yellow polypropylene and looped it, Roy Rogers style, over one arm. He filled a pail with grain and tiptoed into the woods. "Norris? Norrr-is"

He spotted the pig almost immediately. Norris didn't even flick an ear as Sam slipped the noose over his head but as soon as the rope tightened on his neck, some ancient and infallible swine-alarm circuit blew in his brain and he suddenly stiffened, loosed a wild squeal and bolted, hitting the end of the slack rope at full speed and burning a fast angry furrow in Sam's palm. Sam swore and dropped the rope and the pig galloped into the woods, with thirty feet of yellow rope bouncing behind him. When the execution squad arrived half an hour later—Murphy and Lemon in one boat and Johnny No Cash and Smelly Mike in another—Sam was kneeling at the water's edge, bathing his wounded hands in the water.

Lemon grounded the bow of his Starcraft and Murphy leaped out. Murphy was wearing a sweatshirt with torn-off sleeves and sunglasses. The handle of a revolver protruded from the waistband of his jeans. "Did you grease him yet?"

"Not yet."

"Do you want me to do it?"

"We'll have to catch him first."

Sam led them up to the pen and showed them how Norris had broken the two-by-six planks as if they were made of balsa wood. "You can't leave spaces or they'll bust out every time," Murphy said. They organized into one-man scouting teams. Sam drew them a map of the island in the dirt.

"He likes to stay in the woods during the heat of the day," Sam explained. "He's got a long rope on him already. Once you spot him, call out for reinforcements."

"I got my reinforcements right here," said Murphy, patting the revolver.

"Yeah great, but don't start shooting holes in the spare ribs."

Sam directed Johnny No Cash and Smelly Mike to the swampy end of the island. Murphy was to come in on a pincer movement from the north end. "He knows me, so I'll take the middle," Sam concluded. Lemon was already off in the bush somewhere, scouting.

Sam gave everybody ten minutes to get into position. He began working his way stealthily into the woods. Soon he was in the gloom of the early morning forest and there wasn't a sign of life. The ankle-deep moss sank underfoot and the ferns hung down. This is my island, he thought to himself. I own it. I own all these trees. I own Norris the pig. A frond of underbrush waved back and forth and he spotted Norris' curly-tailed rump sneaking away. The rope was no longer around his neck. He frowned. He called out "It's an island, Norris."

They combed the island for two hours and only spotted Norris twice. The first time when Sam spotted him and the second time Murphy got a shot. Murphy was a marksman of almost frightening skill but on this occasion he muffed a running shot at twelve paces. "Pretty small target," remarked Sam. Murphy and Smelly Mike and Johnny No Cash and Lemon went into town to have breakfast, swearing that they would return with reinforcements in several hours.

"Don't worry Sam," Smelly Mike said, giving Sam a consoling pat on the shoulder, as if a tragedy had come to his family. "We'll hunt him down."

Apparently after breakfast (more like lunch) they got temporarily sidetracked into the bar and spent several hours slaving over a hot pool table. It was late in the afternoon when they returned, with a flotilla of drunken reinforcements. Sam had already started the fire up on the hill. Smelly Mike was wearing cutoffs and a Harley Davidson shirt and was carrying a peeled spruce pole with a hunting knife lashed to the end of it. The others were carrying a motley assortment of weapons. Burt Harrison, stylish as usual, looked like a besotted Mexican road agent. His hair was swept back in a wild mane and he wore his shirt like a cape and he was grinning and brandishing a gaff hook. "I wouldn't go to a lot of trouble," said Sam. "It's too late to cook him now anyway."

"Hey man," Burt Harrison crooned. "It's never too late."

"It takes twelve hours, minimum, to roast a pig and it's almost six o'clock now."

Smelly Mike checked the lashing on his spear. "Yeah, but this is a question of honour."

"Right on," somebody replied.

Smelly Mike nodded. "A question of honour . . . RIGHT BOYS?"

There was a cheer and a waving of knives.

"Suit yourself," Sam replied. "But I'm going to start cooking the corn and potatoes."

"Oh man, look at these beer on ice."

"We'll have one drink," Smelly Mike decreed.

"He usually comes back for his grain at midday," Sam shrugged, explaining the pig's absence to Nimitz. "I haven't seen him since first thing this morning."

Burt Harrison had stumbled his way into the stereo tent. There was a horribly amplified scratch and sizzle from the trees and then the first chord struck, loud as a crashed helicopter.

"One drink," Smelly Mike reiterated. Nobody was listening to him.

More boats were arriving. These ones, thank God, containing a moderating element of females. Sam tipped his head slightly to avoid the swung knife-tip of Smelly Mike's spear. He glanced at Nimitz. "So tell me, you read any good books lately?"

All night long there were torchlit forays into the bush to look for Norris. Dim Harrison fell on his machete and the last thing Sam knew was that they took him back to town, bleeding profusely from the web of the hand. Johnny No Cash fell in the bonfire, for the second time this summer. He didn't seem to be burnt too bad, though it wasn't easy for Leslie the Indian Affairs nurse to give a physical examination to a smoking, semiconscious drunk by flashlight. By two in the morning the beer supply was exhausted and a lot of people were heading to home. The nicer people came by and thanked Sam for the party and a lot of them admitted they were a bit leery of the pig roast idea anyway. The corn and the potatoes were a better idea. Vegetables don't have first names, and they don't clog your arteries either. Smelly Mike and a few others loitered around the fire until very late but Sam gave up and went to bed. Finally, in the chill part of the morning, when the first squirrels were ratcheting in the forest, Sam was lying asleep in the houseboat when he suddenly heard Smelly Mike stumbling up the gangplank of the houseboat. Everybody had left without him, Smelly Mike had fallen asleep and now he was mumbling and shivering his way towards his freighter canoe, which he'd left tethered to the back of Sam's houseboat. Sam felt the houseboat tilt gently as Smelly Mike made his way down the side. He heard the muttered exclamation of alarm as the houseboat kept tipping, and heard the helpless clawing of fingernails on plywood and the long instant of silence and then the sudden, booming killer-whale splash. Sam smiled, how nice. He lay in bed, faking sleep, while Mike clambered out of the water sputtering and screaming profanities.

When the drone of Smelly Mike's freighter canoe faded around the corner Sam got out of bed and tiptoed outside. Up on the hill he could see the littered beer cans and paper plates and the un-greased spit. That's my party, he thought. That's the last party I'll be having for a while. He opened the door of the tool room and let Norris outside. The pig scooted down the gangplank and urinated, with a great groan of relief, against a bush.

Sam shivered in the sharp morning air. "Go and clean up that mess," he said to the pig. "And don't say I never did anything for you."

CHRISTIAN STUHR

Why Is It That We Do Not See
Tyrannosaurus Rex Around Any More?

Tyrannosaurus Rex
    to be succinct,
was nasty—and had trouble
    getting sex—
and is extinct.

Till debt do us part.

LORNA CROZIER

On the Seventh Day

On the first day God said
Let there be light.
And there was light.
On the second day
God said, *Let there be light,*
and there was more light.

What are you doing? asked God's wife,
knowing he was the dreamy sort.
You created light yesterday.

I forgot, God said. *What can I do*
about it now?

Nothing, said his wife.
But pay attention!
And in a huff she left
to do the many chores
a wife must do in the vast
though dustless rooms of heaven.

On the third day God said
Let there be light. And
on the fourth and the fifth
(his wife off visiting his mother).

When she returned there was only
the sixth day left. The light
was so blinding, so dazzling
God had to stretch and stretch the sky to hold it
and the sky took up all the room—
it was bigger than anything
even God could imagine.
Quick, his wife said,
make something to stand on!

God cried, *Let there be earth*!
and a thin line of soil
nudged against the sky like a run-over serpent
bearing all the blue in the world on its back.

On the seventh day God rested
as he always did. Well, *rest*
wasn't exactly the right word,
his wife had to admit.

On the seventh day God
went into his study
and wrote in his journal
in huge curlicues and loops
and large crosses on the *t*'s,
changing all the facts, of course,
even creating Woman
from a Man's rib, imagine that!
But why be upset? she thought.
Who's going to believe it?

Anyway, she had her work to do.
Everything he'd forgotten
she had to create
with only a day left to do it.
Leaf by leaf,
paw by paw, two by two,
and now nothing
could be immortal
as in the original plan

Go out and multiply, yes,
she'd have to say it,
but there was too little room for
life without end,
forever and ever,
always, eternal, *ad infinitum*
on that thin spit of earth
under that huge prairie sky.

Joni Went to Market

Lean sky and the anorexic prairie.
Highway unwinding its movie without beginning and
end.
                    Larry. Larry!
Jesus I told her a thousand times. Don't interrupt me
when I'm writing.
                    Larry! Please.
Can't hear a thing. There's a bird in a tree. The low
surf of traffic. The anorexic prairie.
                    Larry.
It's a delicate balance knowing how long you can
hold out before it's more trouble holding out than
giving in.
                    Damital Larry!
If she gets mad enough we have to fight. Silence.
Long silence. Can't write a damned thing now. She's
in my mind. Why'd she quit calling? Did she reach
the sugar herself? Carry the vacuum cleaner upstairs
herself? Game's over. Might as well get a drink. This
July heat is murder. Taste of salty sweat. House is
bloody dark. Blink out all that sun. Maybe I'll have a
game of solitaire till my mind clears itself out. Where
the hell is she? Not in the kitchen. Living-room.
                    Delores.
Silence. Where the hell's she gone? Bedroom.
Everything's in place but her. Upstairs. No, no,
can't walk upstairs. Look like I'm looking.
                    Delores you up there?
Nothing. What's she up to? Playing games? Car's still
out front. Should I try the basement. Maybe she's
hurt. Better check.
                    Delores? You down there?
Silence. Black feeling in my stomach again, like I've

had too much coffee. Okay, okay, I'll look in the closet, check if her clothes are there. Well I'll be a . . .

What the hell are you doing in the bloody closet? There she is sitting quietly in the corner under all her blouses as if she were just spending another day in the closet. In the closet!

What are you doing in there for Chrissakes!

Hiding.

Hiding?

What the hell for?

For the hell of it.

I've told her a thousand times I make the word plays around here. I'm the poet.

You miss me? she asks.

What?

When you couldn't find me anywhere. Did you miss me?

Don't be stupid.

You went all over the house looking.

I was looking for a deck of cards.

And then you looked in my closet.

Yeh.

So why look in my closet?

If you can't say anything real mean don't say anything at all.

We've never kept the cards in here.

Go ahead honey rub it in.

Can't say it? she asks.

Last time I said something nice we had twins.

Look, why don't you come outa there.

Must be hot as Hades in there. Come on, I'll give you a hand.

The hand of compromise. Try the magic word.

Please. Delores.

I like it in here.

You must be baking. It's like an oven in this

place.

I'd like a drink.

You'd like a drink? In there?

Yes.

Okay, I can arrange that.

Sometimes you gotta humour them. It's what you get for marrying a woman. Though there aren't many options. Okay, the tequilla, the tonic, the lemon juice, the Nanton water, the large glass, the ice. No ice. Nobody's perfect.

Where's my drink?

I'm breaking the ice, I shout.

Well, so to speak.

Hurry up I'm thirsty.

Give em an inch. Where the hell's the jigger. Doesn't matter. Captain's measure. Carry in two glasses, give her one, sitting in the corner of the bloody closet. Keep the big one for myself. I'm under a lot of strain.

Weird.

Come on in.

Uh, no thanks, I'm hot enough as it is out here.

Don't be a stick in the mud.

Can't think of the last time I heard that expression. She kicks off her shoes. I drink. She drinks. I drink. She drinks. Hot days have one advantage. A thirst that would make a camel proud.

Well drink up honey.

That's part of an old joke between us so I can use the word without committing myself. Irony is a wonderful glue. It sticks but it doesn't bind.

You want another?

Sure.

In there?

Mmm hmmm.

I go get two more. Captain's measure. Turn on the radio and get told to buy a hamburger, a car and to

284

go to a movie about poltergeists whatever the hell they are. I kill that junk and spin a disk. That's my era. So. Hot day cool jazz. Miles Davis "Kinda Blue." The perfect record for a hangover. Maybe I'll work on one. Listen to that music. The cool blue waves arriving on shore at regular intervals.

Where's my drink?

Getting a bit insistent she is.

Tequila coming in.

She's unbuttoned the top two buttons on her blouse.

Hot enough for you?

Come on in the water's fine.

Delores what the hell are you doin in the the bloody closet? Am I gonna have to phone a doctor about you? Do I have to bring you your meals in there? You gonna come out to go to the bathroom?

What were you looking in my closet for?

Oh we're back to that again are we. And what did you want when you called me?

I called you?

Silence. Tricked. Bone stupid.

You mean you heard?

Drink drink. That's one drink for each of us.

How many times did I call?

I heard once.

Oh.

Back she goes into the corner, into her steam bath.

You like Miles? I ask, as a diversion.

You put that on for me?

Uh. Yeh.

I'd like Joni Mitchell.

Okay, when the record's over.

Now.

Shrug. This is a thing I never argue about. I've spent thousands of dollars on records and a machine to play them on. When I get a request I fill it. Then I can buy another record and not feel guilty. What'll I pick. "Black Crow" I like. Travelling the highways and flying like that crow in the blue sky. Good hangover record. Ice cool voice. Stretched back face. Woman on the road. My woman in the bloody closet.

Well, there's Joni.

Only where the hell's Delores. The cupboard is bare.

Delores! Where the hell are you this time?
In the oven? Jesus Christ woman!

I'll be damned if I'm gonna look for her again. Kids'll be home soon. That'll straighten her out. I'll top up this drink. Upstairs. Under the bed. Study. My closet. Car's there. In your ladies chamber. God it's hot. Where the hell is she? Ready or not here I come. Home free. Once in a while. Basement. No, she wouldn't be there. Too cool and comfortable down there. Sensible. Probably did climb in the oven and turn on the time bake. Nope.

Delores.

Silence.

Delores! Damit Delores!

I'll keep my eye on the bar. Catch her when she comes back for a refill. Too damn hot. Maybe there's a breeze outside. Back to the patio. In this heat we'll all turn anorexic. Well I'll be a . . .

What are you doin out here? Goddarn it woman.

Having a drink. It's nice out here. And you brought me a refill. Thanks.

I give her my drink. Plenty where that came from. Now she's wearing a peasant skirt. Halter. My ball cap perched on the back of her head.

Why don't you get yourself a refill?
Will you stay put?
Maybe.
You like Joni?
Thank you.

286

Back down I go to the magic bar and put together takillya and mixins. Whistle it together. She's a helluva hot day. Oh oh. Out the corner of my eye. I see her. I see her. Sneaking back to the bedroom but she can't fool me. Come out of the closet honey.

> Howdy.
> Oh.
> Don't go into the closet again, please.
> Cheers.
> Cheers, I reply. You look kinda, uh, kinda . . .

Its the gesture that counts.

> How many times did I call you? she asks.
> I don't know. I don't remember.
> Guess.
> Well, five.
> Why did you look in the closet?
> I was afraid you'd left.

In tequillam veritas.

> Why would I ever leave you?

Oh oh. Trick question. Landmines all around that one. Cut her off at the pass or we'll waste all this good liquor. Truth is okay but you can overdo it.

> Can't imagine. What did you want me for?
> Can't remember.
> I'm sorry I didn't reply. I was working.

An apology. Think of that. Well, sort of an apology. More'n usual. I hold out my glass and we clink. Then she lifts her peasant skirt. And she is a peasant. She. I. She. I. Making the summer summer. I dropped my pen. Anorexia be damned. The prairie is a sandwich, white bread clouds, brown bread fields. We're the filling. Joni went to market and we stayed home.

A Cotton Flannelette Man

Annie feels like a car up on a hoist.

Her feet are held by metal stirrups. A steel speculum exposes her most intimate parts to the view of the mechanic, as an appallingly efficient fan simulates winter conditions in Alaska. Thousands of watts of fluorescent light illuminate her flesh.

She tries to think strong assertive thoughts.

The mechanic is Dr. Lawrence Comfrey, or Larry as she prefers to think of him. Under his lab coat he wears a thick tweed suit he must have had custom hand-woven in the Hebrides.

Ah well, at least one of them is warm.

Larry probes around inside, a perplexed look on his face. "Uh-hmmnnn," he says, ambiguously. He removes the speculum, to her great relief.

"I think we'd better just check the back passage too," he announces.

This is how he talks to her. Front passage. Back passage. Tummy. Very scientific. She wonders if he talks this way to the other doctors.

Larry adds more lubricating jelly to the middle finger of his plastic glove and makes the face he always makes when he has to negotiate the murky reaches of the back passage—a fastidious but determined grimace. The finger slips in.

Once he's in there, though, he's thorough, by God. Not that she isn't grateful for the wonders of modern medicine. It's just that sometimes she feels there are no mysteries left.

He strips off the glove, drops it neatly in the step-on can. He looks quite pleased now. "There don't seem to be any problems with the front and back passages," he says.

Why not check the Northwest Passage? she asks, but not out loud.

Out loud, she says, "That's good."

"Keeping up our breast self-examination, are we?" he asks, and she feels a look of guilt creeping over her face.

He gives her his betrayed saint look. His hands begin to move around her left breast, his fingers warm and capable. If he remembers their first encounter, he gives no sign. Annie, however, remembers it well:

The nurse leads her to an examining room, tells her to undress. She doesn't offer the usual gown or even a folded sheet. Well, Annie thinks, if that's the way they do things here, fine. Annie Ransome is not ashamed of her body.

The doctor saunters in, white jacket and big owl eyes behind snazzy glasses framed in red plastic. Then he sees her. His lab coat quivers. His hands make tiny placating gestures in the air. His eyes, like cornered squirrels, scurry around the room, looking for a safe place to hide. His mouth gapes open for more air than mere nostrils can provide.

It seems he was actually not expecting her to be naked.

He leaps to a cupboard, tears open drawers, yanks out a hospital gown and flings it over her. Face scarlet as a maple leaf in autumn, he vaults from the room. Funny, he didn't look that athletic when he came in.

Some time later he returns. He explains in a strained voice that the nurse forgot to give her a gown. He takes her history, but has trouble concentrating. His hand shakes, he avoids her eyes. He begins the physical exam, uncovering her body in careful measured sections, the way they're taught in medical school.

But it's not working. He's already seen how the parts fit together.

It's time to examine her breasts. He stops to gather courage, takes a deep breath. What he says is, "Have you checked your lumps for breasts lately?"

She's always known her breasts were small, but surely not that small.

There is desperation in his eyes. She forces herself to speak. "No," she tells him, "not lately."

She realizes Larry is talking to her now and forces her mind back to the present.

"I said, how've you been feeling?"

"Not so hot," she says. "I'm real tired all the time."

"When was your last period?"

"I haven't exactly been keeping track."

"Um-hmmn," Larry nods to himself. "I think we'll just do a little test."

She lets that sink in as Larry scrubs his hands.

"I'll send the nurse in, and then we'll just see . . . " And he's out the door.

The nurse, whose name is Kimberly Dawn, gives her a bottle and tells her to go into the washroom and pee in it. Yes, they say "pee" in doctors' offices now. It's taken most of her adult life to learn to say "urinate" without feeling silly, and now they expect her to say "pee," just like that. Never mind, who ever said life was fair?

She pees in the bottle and is amazed to learn that Kimberly Dawn will be right back with the results. Gone is the era of waiting around the house for a couple of days. Yeah, but maybe she's not ready to find out. Never mind, the nurse is going to tell her anyway.

"Great news," she's saying. "It's positive!"

Annie feels a small avalanche roar through her

brain. "You mean I'm . . . ?"

"Pregnant!" says Kimberly Dawn.

It's twenty below and snow is falling again. Christmas is coming. She should go home and get to work, but doesn't really feel like it. Work is typing term papers on a word processor for students at the university, and it's long ceased to be even mildly interesting. She finds herself pulling into a strip mall with a big discount drug store. She'd reminded herself this morning to buy tampons, but apparently she won't be needing them for quite a while. But there's also a small Italian coffee shop in this mall that makes real cappuccino. Before she knows it, she's sitting in a booth sipping a tall glass. She looks at the thick gloppy snow falling outside the window and feels everything sliding away from her.

It's five years since she and Charles stopped using any form of birth control, three years since they had every infertility test known to modern science. Charles has had his sperm counted, no mean feat when you consider that they come not in hundreds or thousands but in millions. She's had pieces of her uterus snipped out and examined under a microscope, dye shot up into her tubes to see if they're clogged up like old drains. She's even had her front passage swabbed after intercourse so the doctors can find out what happens to Charles's sperm as they stroke their way through her slippery inner sea.

Now it seems they've done it. She wonders if she looks different. And then there it is, in the pit of her stomach, the feeling she calls "angel wings," because it reminds her of the way she used to feel lying down and swinging her arms and legs, making angels in fresh snow. She felt it when she got her first period and told all the girls at school that she could have a baby. She feels it again now, a rush of power, as though her body has kicked into some kind of cosmic overdrive, and she can do anything she ever dreamed of. Cosmic, that's the key. Her body, with its usual impeccable timing, has got in touch with the cosmos.

She should have guessed it would come up with something like this. All those years she worked so hard to convince herself everything was all right, that Charles was all right, and nothing happened, not a damn thing. Now that she's ready to toss Charles out on his elbow, why all of a sudden should one of his sperm take?

Maybe they knew this could be their last chance. And they girded up their loins, metaphorically speaking, and ran their best race. They climbed her inner ladders like so many maddened thrashing salmon, because they knew that for them there was no more river. No more Annie Ransome Creek.

She stares at the froth around the rim of her glass, as if this is a crystal ball instead of a glass of cappuccino. What am I going to do about Charles, she wonders. And why is this happening at Christmas?

Christmas brings out the worst in Charles. He believes it's all done with money. His trees have to be silver or gold or pure white, with colour co-ordinated decorations. At their parties he wears suits and ties and spends hours making special punch recipes he finds in gourmet magazines.

His gifts are the worst part. He has a talent for finding the perfect thing that nobody else could find, something small and expensive, and so perfect that it is impossible not to resent it.

If only he'd had a sense of humour. That's one thing she's going to insist on from now on. Really? Does she think it's as simple as shopping for clothes? "Yes, I'll take the hundred per cent cotton shirt, I wear only natural fibres." Men, however, cannot be shopped for in this way.

292

Or can they? Come to think of it, Charles is obviously a rough, wiry, worsted wool, abrasive to the skin. She can't think why she ever bought it. Some days he's grey worsted, sometimes navy blue.

What she really needed was a cotton flannelette man. Red would be nice. Or silk, say a midnight blue silk satin. Or maybe soft cream-coloured linen.

What she has, however, is worsted wool and it's rubbing her the wrong way and has been for a very long time.

If only her cousin Kate were here. By the time Annie gets through describing a problem to Kate, what to do usually sorts itself out. She decides to write her a letter. She pulls a tattered notebook from her purse, and a felt-tip pen. She signals the waiter to bring another cappuccino, and starts right in. With Kate you can skip all the stuff about weather and Merry Christmas and hope this finds you well. All the fat. With Kate you go right to the blood and bone and sinew. And gristle.

Dear Kate, she begins. Guess what? I'm pregnant. All those tests, and temperature charts, and Charles running home in the middle of the afternoon—forget it.

Great, you say, I'm happy for you. But. You knew there'd be a but, right? But I'm not sure I'm staying with Charles. I hate to admit it, and God knows it's taken me long enough, but Charles is really rather dreadful. There, I've said it.

I don't know if you realize it, but Charles wasn't even the only one. There were two dreadful men in my immediate vicinity when I was growing up (dreadful *boys* at the time); it seems beyond belief that I managed to get entangled with both of them. Their very names were a dead giveaway. Lockwood (Locky to his doting mother) and Charles. The names said it all—their parents expected great things for them. Not *from* them, you understand, but for them.

To make it worse, they're cousins. Lockwood is the son of Arnold and Edith Wilkins—the ones in the big house at the end of the block. He tore up all the neighbourhood gardens, wrecked all the birthday parties, and terrorized any kid who went near the riverbank.

Charles is the son of John and Ethel Wilkins, and has been trying to manipulate the entire world since he was born. I even knew this once.

The first hint I had that Locky (yes, I called him Locky for awhile) might have a thing for me was when my high school graduation dance loomed near and I found myself without a date for the big night. When Locky asked me to go with him, I was so amazed that I said yes without thinking. Then I went home and hid in my bedroom closet and screamed for five minutes. Locky Wilkins, for Godsake, he'd pushed me into more mud puddles and brained me with more rock-filled snowballs than I could ever hope to count. Did I really think any date was better than no date?

But I already had the dress, deep rose organza with a satin sash. Mother'd got a discount at the store, but still, it had cost her serious money and she expected me to get some wear out of it.

When he came to pick me up, I couldn't believe my eyes. He wore this white sports jacket, and he'd slicked his hair back like a forties movie star. Really! His hands had never been so clean in the eighteen years I'd known him, and the very insides of his ears shone.

I know, tell me I shouldn't have been flattered. Mother was impressed too, I could see it. She must have remembered the time Locky peed against our fence just to see the look on his mother's face.

He kept it up all through the dance. He might be his normal creepy self again tomorrow, but for one night at least he was capable of sustained charm. Remarkably, he could dance, and not just by the book either; he had perfected the steps to the point where they were forgotten in smooth sweeps of movement. He led me down the same path. I was a tree blowing in the wind. I was light as cottonwood fluff, graceful as grass. No, I told myself, it's not possible. This is Locky. The brain fought on, protesting feebly. The body loved the dancing.

He danced me through the summer and into our first year of university. He danced me through parties and freshman balls, and he danced me into bed. I got pregnant a month before final exams. Just when I knew I had to find the courage to tell mother, I started to bleed. That was the end of taking chances, at least with birth control. It was also the end of our relationship.

It took me two years to get over him, and by then I was sure I'd been innoculated. Charles proved me wrong. Before I knew it, I was noticing how much he'd changed, how much he'd improved. And thinking it was neat to go around with a guy who read the evening news on television.

Annie puts the pen down. She's turning it into a story, trying to shape things she doesn't understand. She always does this, and life always trips her up. Don't go thinking you know anything, life is always telling her, and life is probably right. The cappuccino's gone, only a fleck of cinnamon-sprinkled foam left on the glass.

She sits on the sofa in the dark living-room. She wishes she knew more about heredity. Specifically, she needs to know how much like Charles the baby is going to be.

She imagines herself in about twenty years time advising some young woman not to marry her son. Trying to explain, to someone with no experience of life, what's wrong with him. This is not an idle fantasy. It's what Charles's mother, Ethel, tried to do for her.

They'd sat in Ethel's living room, with the velvet sofa and the oriental rug, as Ethel politely tried to convince Annie that Charles was cold and selfish and power-hungry. Annie'd been shocked and embarrassed. Ethel must think Annie wasn't good enough for him. And yet, what she seemed to be saying was that Charles wasn't good enough for Annie. Of course Annie hadn't believed her.

She flips on the television, with no sound. Charles is reading the six o'clock news. His make-up is perfect, his wavy brown hair beautifully styled. She can almost make out what he's saying. He does special exercises to keep his lips limber. He tells her that's why he kisses so well. She doesn't tell him that he doesn't kiss all that well. His lips keep moving and she starts to giggle. Charles would be mad if he knew she was keeping him silent. Tough toenails, it serves him right for wearing such a perfect grey suit and that paisley silk tie.

Then she begins to feel sorry for him and turns on the sound. He's talking about the economy and how someone very important has said that things are going to get worse before they get better. Charles speaks with what his boss at the station calls "authority." When Charles reads a news item, few people breathing would dare question it. A suit like that could never lie, a paisley tie of that particular shade of muted red could never be anything but reliable.

She's fantasized for months about telling Charles that they're splitting up. She sees herself begin to speak, but he always cuts her off. "Of course we're not splitting up," says the Voice, calm, precise, confident.

She is getting very angry, at the suit, the tie, the Voice, the wavy hair. She wants to turn him off, rip the plug out of the wall. He's nothing but a taker, a manipulator, a talking head who studies how to be a man, who performs being a man and fools thousands daily. But not her, dammit, because she can't be fooled any more.

She can't keep the anger going. It seeps out of her like water, or blood. God, she thinks, he really can't help it.

Charles comes in, looking very subdued. He doesn't notice that she's done nothing about supper.

"Hi," she says. "Saw you on the box."

"I was lousy," he says, surprising her. "I had something on my mind." She recognizes a cue. She hates talking on cue.

"Oh?" she says.

"I may as well tell you, I bid on this job—reporting for network news in Toronto. I didn't get it."

His whole body sags. He has never failed at anything he wanted before, or if he has, he's never told her.

"You never told me," she says.

"I guess I was scared it could go wrong." She doesn't say anything, so he goes on. "They didn't think my reporting skills were strong enough." He almost looks like he's going to cry.

"I'm sorry about that," she says. "But did you think I'd move to Toronto?"

He looks at her, trying to read her mood. It strikes her that everything's changed. She's carrying the beginnings of another person around inside her. If it weren't so common, people would think it bizarre. She feels tired, but also ridiculously strong. The old cosmic overdrive has kicked in again. She finds she has only been inhabiting parts of herself. Other parts have been shut off, waiting to be of use. She feels like a guitar which is suddenly discovered to have six strings, and not just the four she has been playing some not bad tunes on all her life.

"I think you should know," she says, "some things have changed."

"Annie, what are you talking about?"

"From now on, things have to be different."

"Is this one of your so-called jokes?"

"From now on, we're just two people," she says. "You don't know any better than me, and you don't try to pretend you do. You don't bully me, you don't try to get your way every time."

"You're crazy," he says.

"If we disagree," she says, "we negotiate. Nobody gets all the power. I can be funny if I want to. You don't have to. If we can agree—"

"I do not believe this!"

"If we can agree on these things, I'm prepared to stay together."

"Oh, that's big of you! What if I'm not?"

"That would be your decision, of course."

"Annie, what in hell is going on?"

She just looks at him. It unnerves him, because he wants her to explain, the way she always does; to soothe and placate, the way she always does. She wants to tell him about the baby, feels the words on her lips wanting to be spoken, but resists with all her newly discovered strength. He has to decide about the two of them first.

She watches him watching her, trying to understand if she means it. Trying to adjust to the change in her. She looks right into his eyes, wondering if he'll succeed.

RHONA MCADAM

Another Life to Live at the Edge of the Young And Restless Days of Our Lives

I am not going to get maudlin about this
but it seems like everything happens to me
and there's nothing I can do but go along
with it.
      What else can you do, this is life
and if it means you get amnesia or split
personalities or one of those unmentionable
female disorders or your husband gets trapped
in a South American mine shaft and you don't
know if he's alive or dead and you remarry
only this time your man's displaced nobility
who turns out to be your long lost cousin so
the priest says you have to separate and he
disappears in a plane crash but turns up again
years later looking entirely different
and marries your best friend who's told she's
terminally ill so she lies on a *chaise longue*
for many months while around you
both there are things going very wrong
only very slowly so you spend days on the same
conversation changing clothes every time
you leave the room,
              well so be it.

It's not that I'm complaining,
or, heaven help me, having another nervous
breakdown, but I feel sometimes that everything
happens to me.
      I felt it just last month when I was vacationing
in Acapulco and who should check in next door
but my first husband who'd been trapped in a South
American mine shaft and no one knew if he was

alive or dead, and here he is looking somewhat the worse for wear but perfectly okay except that he'd taken up with some bad company and was smuggling cocaine into Florida but later I found out it was against his will because he was being blackmailed by some modern day pirates who'd discovered his real identity after he'd disgraced himself with a mexican barmaid after they'd drugged him and set up a video camera and were threatening to send a tape to the newspaper in our town which would have just ruined his plans of coming back and running for senator not to mention the hurt it would have caused his family, who have quite a good name, really, though there's been just a hint of madness in most of them, including me but they sent me to quite an exclusive little clinic in the mountains for a season and now I'm right as rain, which is something considering I was having an affair with my psychiatrist who turns out to be an old classmate of my husband's, the one who was trapped in the mine shaft in South America at the time though at this stage here he is right next door in the same resort in Acapulco, and he sneaks over at night and confesses what he's been up to for the last six seasons, and I tell him how his son is all grown up and running a model agency right there in the old home town, and we get quite emotional and decide to forgive and forget and so I call the police but before they come the bad guys catch us together and tie me up and leave me in the boat-house with the tide coming in and I look like a goner but my husband, the one from the mine shaft, is able to cut his ropes free with an emery board I slipped him and he knocks out his captors and with the police on his heels he finds me just in time, my hair's hardly wet, and they save me and we get to come back to our old home town and have a lovely

wedding with my best friend as my maid of honour,
though by this time she's pretty weak, and after we
leave on our honeymoon she just fades away, there
on the patio with rose blossoms falling on her head
and my bouquet falling from her hand as the music
swells and the titles come up and the season ends.

MYRNA GARANIS

Black and White

Cosmetics counter
Kerchiefed women
Black-dotted, head to toe
Look long at small black boxes
Perfume under glass
Labels read "That Man"

Hardware aisle
Man emerges
black-booted
                wide, white braces
Calls out sharp
to the women: "Kumsch"
they kum

GLEN SORESTAD

Incident in Thunder Bay

The K-Mart does not permit its cashiers
to give out change for a dollar. This infuriates
me. My wife wants to make a long distance call
and between us we haven't a dollar's change.

In the store rotunda where the pay phones are
I vent my anger, my frustration, wave my dollar bill
like a political manifesto. I am about to launch
my favorite monologue—a rote tirade against
the utter stupidity of bureaucratic chainstores
when . . .
a young woman, leaving, pushing a stroller,
hears my harangue, fears for her child
in the presence of such verbal contamination,
stops, digs in her purse, offers me her change.
She thrusts eighty-five cents at me. I hand
her the dollar. She refuses. But I insist.
Her refusal is even more adamant. A crowd gathers.
Her stubbornness rivals that of Grandfather Sorestad
who built an unenvied reputation for bull-headedness.
(Of course, I don't tell her this.) I try instead
to stuff my dollar bill in her kid's mouth.
But the same streak seems to run in the kid
and the woman's look tells me she is convinced
she's in the presence of a certified lunatic.

In the end, it turns out we didn't need the change.
My wife, by this time realizing the folly
of expecting me to get a dollar's change
without creating a scene, charged the call.
So I am left with a dollar bill in one hand
and eighty-five cents in the other, wondering
what kind of story this good samaritan
will tell her husband when he gets home.

302

BYRNA BARCLAY

After Twenty-Five Years,
Still Working It Out

Oh Baby, he doesn't laugh like that when he's awake.
Curled under the covers, he chuckles in his sleep,
and it's making you crazy. When he slept on his back
and snored you cured him by pinching his nose, and
now you try everything, even pat his bum with a
broom, but you can't stop his snuffling and snorting.
His shoulders shake slightly as if he's sharing a secret
under the sheet the way he did with you when he
could stay awake long enough to romp. You've just
got to know what's so funny. You lie still, hoping he'll
talk in his sleep and give it away, but he never does.

He always told you everything, but every morning he
says he can't remember his dreams. He says he's
happy with you, that's all. But you're sure he dreams
of a four-breasted woman who neighs, one with eight
legs who can fly, or worse: someone you know. The
fluffy secretary who makes up in hair what she lacks
in height. The gas jockey who can't zip up her jacket.
Or the girl with incurable giggles who slaps bums
with the towels she hands out at the Y. You always said
if he ever cheated you would know by the way he
walked down the hall: all the leg action from the
knees down.

You try to tickle him awake to catch him in the act, but
that only makes him chortle louder. He sleeps with
the sheet over his head. You slide out of bed, creep
around to his side, kneel on the floor, carefully oh so
slowly lift the sheet and stick your head under it. Nose
to nose. His twitches. Ears wiggle, bottom lip wobbles,

Adam's apple bobs, chuckle chuckle, chort. He has one grey hair on his chest. And then you know how you can stop him from having such a good time without you.

In his sleep you are laughing.

KIM MORRISSEY

the post-macho man after mating

"I'm so tired of these sensitive louts;
these post-macho men. "   —Wilma Riley

babies are the things he does best
anywhere there's a crowd
and a camera

look at this, he says holding
the tiny head in his hand
lying his child like a piglet
down the length of his arm

As a Daddy . . . . As a Father . . . .
When a Man has a Child . . . .

he uses his baby
to flirt with women in malls
he learns to say "quality time"
      tough love comes later

DONNA CARUSO

His Bowels

She didn't know if choosing Mike would have been so much a better thing than choosing Bertrand. You had to marry somebody, and nobody was without faults. After thirty-four years of marriage, she as likely would have been waiting here in the outpatient's for Mike to have something every bit as indelicate as Bertrand's barium enema; maybe more so. Maybe contagious, given the way he was with the women. Then how would she be feeling, diseased in that way from a man she had to call her husband? At least Bertrand's polyps weren't catching. And even if they turned out to be cancer like the doctors thought they might be, you couldn't catch cancer, especially if you were careful like her, and regular.

But it's a dirty thing, the bowel, especially a clogged one. It made her stomach sick when she thought about things rotting and sprouting inside of Bertrand; and him living with her in her own house and bed.

The bowel wasn't an interesting thing you could talk about, either, like a nice bypass people had nowadays. Who wanted to hear about the awful stink of Bertrand's farts, or how his stool was such a mess and the toilet, too, because of it; and her the one who had to clean it. This wasn't Bertrand's first barium enema either, and it was a disgusting thing as well.

First, they pumped all this stuff from a plastic bag into your rear and you had to hold tight so as not to leak it all over as they took their X-rays. Then they sucked it all out of you, back into the plastic bag. It made you wonder how many times they re-used the stuff and who it had been in before. Sure, they said it was fresh each time, but mistakes happen, everybody knows that. That was part of life. To tell the truth, she wasn't at all surprised at the state of Bertrand's bowels. He had always been one to hang onto things, especially useless things. She could never get him to throw anything out, or change a point of view. It was no wonder that his bowel was a mess as well. He collected messes. His gut was just one more.

Oh, Mike would have been different, yes, always with that twinkle in his eye and those roaming fingers, and that huge bulge there in the front. He wore it proudly, like a peacock. Surely, he had liked her well enough, but no one girl was enough for Mike, whereas one was more than enough for Bertrand.

She wasn't kidding herself, she knew all too well that life with Mike would have been every bit as embarrassing as life with Bertrand; that was plain enough. Once a person got used to all the attention Mike paid, it would have been an embarrassment just like anything else. She figured, you stick with anything for thirty-four years, it's an embarrassment; you know too much about it for it to be anything else. The ones with the stars in their eyes are the blind ones. It was when your eyes were wide open and you could see as plain as day that the embarrassment of it all came clear. Like sex in broad daylight.

She didn't really mind waiting in the outpatient's. Goodness knows she spent little enough time so still as this. She picked up the *Reader's Digest*, thinking she might read the jokes. Not that she ever found them funny. She was one who never knew when to laugh at a joke; she had to watch the others. "He who laughs last probably didn't get the joke," they say, and they're right. But the *Reader's Digest* told you plainly which ones were the jokes, and she figured that it was at the end that you were supposed to laugh. It was good practice for her. Maybe someday she would understand enough about jokes from reading the *Reader's Digest* in the outpatient's that she wouldn't be troubled by them. Now when someone says, "I have a joke," she just about has a seizure, waiting for the punch line. Is that a funny thing? A punch line? It didn't sound funny to her. Jokes were as embarrassing as anything else. But life was full of them and you had to learn to live with them.

The others would think she was a regular fun person, seeing her reading "Humor in Uniform" and the like. They wouldn't see inside her mind and the thoughts she had about the personal things.

She still ran into Mike sometimes in the city. He looked good. Better than Bertrand. He fools around on his wife, of course. Everyone knew that. It would have been a hard life with him and his male needs, watching him turn on the charm to the ladies. He'd tried it with her in fact, expecting her to swoon like a schoolgirl, when here she was as girl-less as she could get. His wife must be embarrassed to have such a husband. But what do you expect from a man with such a big thing? It's like a toy, and the baby has to play. What can you do? Nothing, that's what.

Look at them all, all the men and their problems. And who's to put up with them first-hand? The wives, of course. Like that man, George the plumber, who's on the oxygen, wheezing and spitting all the time. That must be a distraction to live with. And then there's Murray, pissin' his pants after his prostrate operation. Diapers on a grown man! It's the women who have to be strong enough to handle such things. When you're young, you have the sex, the birthing, and the children problems; when you're older, you have the men problems. She wondered if there was a man on earth who didn't fall apart and make an awful mess for his wife in his later years.

Of course, Mike hadn't fallen apart, that was true.

If she had married him, the messes would have been outside her own home. She wouldn't have had to live with them like with Bertrand's messes in the basement, the garage, the spare room, and, of course, the bathroom. And if she had insisted, and she would have, Mike would have worn a rubber on his thing to keep her from getting any of those sex diseases. Yes, in that respect, she would have been better off with Mike, she could see that.

In his younger days, Mike had certainly been one to turn a girl's head, and that was hard to forget. He had the charm, that was for sure. Why, he had had her front buttons undone before nine-thirty on their first date! Lookin' her right in the eye as was his way, and telling her how pretty she was and how special, and how surprised he was that a beauty like her had never shared herself before. She felt like a queen with him squeezing and kissing her chest like he did. It had felt real good, and she had let him every single time. Of course, thirty-four years of that, it would have been embarrassing, too, she knew. He loved it so, he would have needed it every night—at least twenty minutes worth. She could see how it would have worn on her. It had been one thing to do something new on a Saturday night, quite a different kettle of fish when you were married to it every single day for thirty-four long years.

Mind you, she hadn't let Bertrand touch her before their marriage. He didn't seem keen on it anyway. To tell the truth, he had never charmed her like Mike had, not even after their marriage. Never made her want to loosen her clothing and let him inside to explore. But sex with Bertrand had been her first shot at the real thing; you know, with the man's and the woman's things right together. But with Bertrand, it was embarrassment from the very beginning, Bertrand seeming to be embarrassed by his very self. When he saw her naked it was automatic he would just shoot off then turn beet red, as if he were surprised by his own plumbing. She was technically a virgin long after they were married, Bertrand's over-enthusiasm accounting for that. Eventually, he got used to her, and then the real embarrassment started. At least it was over quickly. She couldn't understand at first why it was that sex was so forbidden. It was, she had been told, because of the babies and disease. But experience had taught her it was mostly because of the embarrassment. Better to keep your embarrassment to yourself than to go spreading it around like Mike.

Not that she had ever felt embarrassed with Mike—except when she found out about him and that other girl. But not when he had put his hand right up under her dress on the place between her legs and rubbed till she exploded. Of course, that hadn't been sex like with Bertrand. She wasn't sure what that had been, but she had never had anything like it with Bertrand. It had made her feel good, and pretty, and not embarrassed at all. But Bertrand's thing had been inside hers and *that* was sex. They had had children! Mike had never had sex with her. She was a virgin when she married Bertrand; and afterwards as well, long afterwards.

She didn't know why she was thinking such thoughts. All that was past. The thing to think about now was Bertrand's bowel, not the sex things. That was life, she supposed: a person's focus changes as they age.

It was such a long wait for the barium enema. Bertrand must be having trouble holding onto the stuff inside him. What a mess the nurses would have to clean up, and they not even married to him. She was glad she had never had a career like a nurse or a teacher. Just her own family to look after; only her own children's messes and her husband's.

She put the *Reader's Digest* aside. She hadn't even read it. The clock on the wall was big and slow like Bertrand. She had things to do: carrots and potatoes to peel, floors to mop. Life goes on, she thought; life goes on Bertrand. She didn't have all day. Did she have to wait forever?

BABY, I'M BORED.

RHONA MCADAM

the meaning of my time with you

when i said i'd go for a ride with you
i didn't mean to your ex-wife's place
where i sat in the car while you
went in for coffee & sent the kids out
for a look at me through the car window

when i said i'd go to the bar with you
i didn't mean so i could watch you
get drunk & have you tell me
how much you miss your ex-wife
& how great she was in bed

& when i said i'd cook for you
i didn't mean i wanted your ex-wife's
recipes & tips on homemaking
& you

i didn't mean i wanted to share
what you mean by everything
which includes helping you
pick out christmas gifts for your
ex-wife & kids & then lending you the money

& when i said you should choose
your own gift for me i didn't mean
a bottle of your ex-wife's
favourite perfume & the comment
that it always makes you horny
(said before i'd even worn it)

LOIS SIMMIE

Sweetie Pie

Noreen can't figure out how she got tangled up with Al and Sweetie Pie, God knows she's had enough problems but that never seems to stop her. Them that has gets, they say, meaning rich people and money, but Noreen knows it works the same for her and trouble.

Al is hunched over the wheel, glaring down the highway through his dark glasses as if the heat was sent to torment him and him alone. Thirty-three degrees and going higher, the radio announcer sounds out of his mind with joy, and wet patches are starting to meet on Al's red T-shirt. Noreen winds the window down a fast six inches and up again.

"Shut the goddamn window!" Al yells. "A draft will kill her when she's this hot."

"It was her or me," she says, turning to look at the white cockatoo swaying in the cage on the back seat. Sweetie Pie looks totally pissed off, her head hunched down in her shoulders, her wrinkly grey eyelids closed, horny feet looking like they'll need to be pried off the perch. Her elaborate wooden cage touches the roof of the car.

"Couldn't we just open the window a crack? I'm—"

"Jesus Christ!" Al hits the steering wheel and a drop of sweat flies off his nose. "You never give up, do ya? Even when you've been told and told, ya gotta keep on." He glances at her, two tiny Noreens in his mirrored glasses. "No wonder Eddy did himself in."

Oh. She wraps her arms around her chest, hugging the pain, looks out the window at the crazily melting landscape, damn him, he's made her cry again. God, what is she *doing* with Al, who is meaner

313

than a junk-yard dog, she's beginning to realize. Noreen honestly doesn't know. She just falls into things somehow. She always has.

She wants a beer, dammit, aren't they ever going to get out of this creepy car? It's a Ford Tempo, Al loves it. The dashboard is upholstered in something that looks like human skin—flesh coloured and full of pores. It feels like skin, too, and Noreen freaks out whenever she touches it.

"How much farther to Banff?" she asks.

"A half-hour or more anyway."

"God, we'll all be dead by then."

"Nobody twisted your arm."

He's right, nobody did. But she liked Al better when they planned it and then, what the hell, it was a trip wasn't it? A change of scene. It was so dry at home you couldn't spit.

Men have always wanted to take Noreen places. She honest-to-God doesn't know why—she's not beautiful, her face too thin and foxy, the calves of her legs too big.

"Christ, I need a cigarette," Al says, reaching down and rearranging his crotch. He's always shifting it around and Noreen wonders if he might have prostate trouble. He says he's thirty-seven but she knows he knocked off a few years because of her being only twenty-four. Oh well, we all have our crotches to bear, she thinks philosophically. *Prostrate* trouble is what she's got.

"Al, we've got to stop. I have to pee."

"So cross your legs," says Al, "we can't stop here. Find something on the radio, can't you?" His tone implies it's the least she can do since she can't help drive, she lost her glasses in a bar in Regina a couple of weeks ago. Or in somebody's car. Somewhere. What she'd like to lose now is Al. Noreen sighs and punches a button.

Why did you have to leave me girl, why did you have to leave? Why did you have to leave me girl, why did you have to go?

Oh no, not that. She hits another station.

She only left Eddy that night to get some beer, he needed it, and then she ran into some friends in the bar. Oh, all right, just one, she said, Eddy's real depressed again. And she really was worried about him, that was the worst of it, but then another round appeared and she was having some fun for a change and all at once they were closing the bar.

And while she was laughing it up, Eddy, who couldn't bring himself to kill a deer, had put the shotgun's cold barrel in his mouth and pulled the trigger. She always sees it in a kind of slow motion, will always see it that way—the back of Eddy's head floating up, Eddy drifting forward onto the bed, drifting like a dead leaf onto the pale flowered sheet, the flowers darkening . . . .

"Try to get some news," Al is saying. "If tommorow's this bad, maybe we'll lay over in Banff."

"Oh, that'd be great. We could go for a swim."

"Maybe." The decisions always have to be Al's, or appear to be his.

"It cools off at night in the mountains, doesn't it?"

"Not when you're with me, it don't." Al reaches over and squeezes her leg.

God, is he kidding? He says that about Eddy and then she's supposed to feel horny. There's only lousy music on the radio and some guy with an English accent talking about the mating habits of ostriches. Noreen starts to get interested.

"Turn off that shit," Al says.

Noreen glances at Sweetie Pie. Her beak is open, her knobby grey tongue quivering in her throat. "I think Sweetie's going to kick the bucket," she says. She hopes so, it'd serve him right if she keeled over

315

dead, her horny little toes pointing to Cockatoo Heaven.

"Oh Christ, look at her. We gotta stop. Couldn't you see her water dish was empty?"

Oh sure, her fault.

"There's a picnic ground coming up. I saw a sign back there." Noreen leans forward, fanning her damp tank top away from her back, peering for the turnoff. She can't see shit-all without her glasses. "A cold beer will hit the spot anyway."

"You ain't whistling Dixie," Al says, apparently cheered by the prospect. "How's my Sweetie doing?"

"Still breathing," she reports.

Sweetie Pie opens her eyes and gives Noreen a malevolent look. Her pink head feathers rise and fall, rise and fall. Noreen wishes she could do that with her hair, cool off her head.

"Have a nice day," Sweetie croaks unexpectedly. It's the first thing she's said since they left home.

"You too, Cockatoo," says Noreen.

Sweetie is a beautiful bird if you get off on birds, her creamy white feathers tinged with pink, like peony petals, pink spots like rouge on her cheeks.

She doesn't smell like a peony though. Sweetie and Al were meant for each other—Al thinks deodorant is for sissies. In the morning he picks up his shorts from wherever he's left them, sniffs the crotch, and if that doesn't knock him out he wears them another day. Noreen sniffs her armpit. Not exactly Chanel Number Five anywhere in this zoo cage.

The picnic ground is surrounded by enormous pines, and they park in the shade by a redwood table.

"Don't get out yet." Al rolls the window down a couple of inches. "We need to cool her off gradually." He reaches over and sticks his finger in the cage. "How's my precious Sweetie Pie? Is her not feeling so hot?"

316

"Her problem is she *is* feeling hot," Noreen says.

"Daddy's gonna get his Sweetie a drink right now," Al baby-talks, filling her dish. She dips in her beak and the water disappears. "Holy shit," says Al. "I hope she don't go into shock."

Noreen gets out and stretches, breathes tangy pine-scented air down to her toes. There's crunchy cool gravel under her feet, water trickling somewhere.

Al gets a beer from the cooler. He snaps off the lid and pours it down, swallowing three times and it's gone. He wipes his mouth on his T-shirt, belching into its folds.

"Thanks," says Noreen. "You could've opened me one."

"Big deal." He opens another and flips her the opener. It drops in the gravel. Asshole. On an asshole scale of one to ten Al rates a nine easy. Why didn't she see that right off, that's what's depressing. He came up to her in the bar to tell her he was sorry about Eddy and then starts telling her how his wife just left, just loaded up her boyfriend's half-ton with everything but a cup, a plate, a chair and a pile of old *National Geographics*. Noreen is reading her way through them. Noreen reads all the time. Sometimes she thinks she might even have a good mind but then she rejects the idea—would she be this stupid if she was smart? She carries her beer down the path to the can.

"Don't go far," Al calls after her. "We're not staying long."

"Why the hell not if we're stopping in Banff?"

"I didn't say we were for sure."

"So leave me."

"I will," he says. But he won't. She's not that lucky. Noreen curls her toes into the thick pine needles and leaves on the path. God, it's wonderful here, so green, so many shades of green. When they get to Vancouver she should stay there, she thinks, sitting in the toilet with the door open behind the wooden wall. She sips her beer while a squirrel chitters nearby. Why not? Put it all behind her. Al. Eddy. All the ones before. Make a new start. But this time's gotta be different—she's always turning over new leaves and finding aphids—this time she's got to figure it out, get some direction in her life, some kind of order. Noreen knows she'll need to be alone to do it, for longer than a week or two . . . six months or a year maybe. She's got to stop drifting where the wind blows. Stop lousing things up.

She's starting to feel human again, just one more cold one and she's going to feel just fine. Good, even.

Al has put Sweetie's cage on the roof of the car and is dribbling water into her dish, making smoochy talk. Sunflower seeds spot the roof. Sweetie is excited, she's weaving back and forth on her perch, feet not moving, body undulating like a stripper. "Pretty baby," she says. "Pretty baby. Have a nice day." Al's been trying for weeks to teach her to say "fuck off" but she won't. Suddenly she stops, stretches up to her full height, fans up her crest and gives them her grand slam special—her imitation of a toilet flushing, perfect down to the last gurgle. Then she laughs. She learned it when her cage was outside a pet shop bathroom, and of course, somebody cracked up every time. Noreen thinks it's the funniest thing she's ever heard. Al rewards Sweetie with a pumpkin seed. Even out in the air she has a faint homogenized pet shop smell. Noreen goes to get a beer from the trunk.

"Get me one too will ya?"

She hesitates. "Do you think you should wait till we get to Banff?" They had passed a terrible accident outside Calgary.

"No, I don't think I should wait till we get to Banff. If I want a beer I'll damn well have a beer. I paid for them."

318

He's leaning against the car, his arms crossed and his profile mean. Noreen has read that alcoholics change personality when they drink and she figures Al can't be one because he just gets meaner. She opens the bottle and hands it to him. Sweetie is hanging upside down, gnawing on the rafters of her cage, then she manoeuvres down onto the perch and starts into her stripper act again.

"Well, you have to drive is all I meant," Noreen says.

"Well, you have to drive is all I meant," he mimics her nastily. Pushing away from the car, he heads towards the men's can. "Jesus, you're starting to sound like a wife."

"That'll be the fucking Friday," Noreen mutters.

He stops. "I heard that. Well you can bet your ass you don't need to worry 'cause I won't be asking ya. I got no desire to end up like Eddy." He gives her a long, smug look and starts down the path.

Noreen reaches over and lifts the bar that locks Sweetie's cage. Sweetie hops down off the perch and with a pleased, surprised screech takes off for the trees.

"Hey!" Al's head jerks up in time to see her land in the huge pine. Dark blood rushes to his face. Noreen's heart hammers, oh shit oh shit now you've done it.

"Why'd you have to go and do that?" he says in such a sad, strange voice she's almost sorry.

"Then leave Eddy out of it. You aren't even good enough to talk about him." Now it's done. No turning back.

Sweetie hops down a couple of branches, watching Al. She preens her feathers, making happy noises in her throat. "What are you doing Sweetie Pie?" she says. "Have a good day." Al still looks stunned.

"You can climb up and get her back," Noreen tells

319

him. While he's up the tree she'll run for it. He'd never leave Sweetie behind.

"Yeah. Well I'd *better* get her back."

Al jumps up and catches the lowest branch but he just dangles there, legs bicycling. He's too out of shape.

"Here," says Noreen. "If we carry the table over to stand on, you can reach."

She takes hold of one end of the table. Al drops down and together they struggle towards the tree with it. The benches are attached and it weighs a ton, they must weight it with something to keep people from stealing it. As they stagger along, Al alternates baby-talk in Sweetie's direction—"Stay there Sweetie, Daddy's coming"— with murderous looks and orders at Noreen, "This way more, set it down now, whoa! Hold it! Jesus, that's my foot!" Noreen gets the giggles, she's so nervous. Sweat drips off the end of Al's nose onto the table. Finally they get there and Al starts up the tree. When his dirty white sneakers disappear from sight, Noreen backs into the clearing where she can see.

His head emerges about a foot from Sweetie, who squawks and hops up onto the next branch. "What are you doing Sweetie Pie?" she says, peering down at him with interest. She's having a hell of a good time. Noreen laughs. She should leave now but she wants to see what's going to happen.

"Here Sweetie, come to Daddy now, *bring the goddamn cage willya Noreen?* There darling, nobody's going to hurt you, you'd die out there all on your own."

"Fuck off, fuck off," says Sweetie.

Al's head swivels to give Noreen a proud papa look. "Didja hear what she said? She said—"

"Fuck off," says Sweetie, fluttering several branches higher.

"Oh Jesus." Al's head disappears, then she sees just his arm reaching up slowly, almost touching Sweetie before she backs up the branch towards the trunk. The next time his hand is just ready to close on her legs, a car turns into the clearing, a sporty red job coming fast, the tires spitting gravel. Sweetie lifts off the branch and flies around the clearing, a beautiful pale blur against the dark pines, and lands back on the same branch. When the car engine turns off, Noreen can hear the steady monotone of Al's swearing. She takes the cage over to the picnic table and leaves it there with the door open.

The red car door slams with an expensive chunking sound and a blond guy gets out. Sweetie takes flight again.

"A cockatoo," he says wonderingly. He takes in Noreen and the cage and understanding dawns.

"Gee, that's too bad. Can I help?" He mouths the words and Noreen shakes her head. He looks like Wayne Gretzky but thinner. Nice.

Pine branches are shaking violently, pine cones and needles spattering the table, then Al crashes down the last couple of feet onto the table. He looks fatter than when he went up, maybe because she's been looking at this thin guy. He also looks hot and mad and he's all scratched up. From high up in the tree comes the sound of a toilet flushing and Sweetie's crazy laugh.

"Did you hear that?" says the blond guy.

"Hear what?" Noreen says. "I didn't hear anything." Then she takes pity on him. "It's the bird. That's her super deluxe special."

"You're kidding." He laughs. Nice teeth. "I didn't know cockatoos—"

"Never *mind*." Al gives him a filthy look. "Bring her treats, Noreen."

Noreen shrugs and gets them from the car.

Sweetie is hopping down the branches after Al. He scatters seeds on the picnic table and pretty soon Sweetie is wandering around picking them up from the table top. Then she follows the trail into the cage and Al clicks the door shut. Noreen feels like crying.

Al gets a beer, ignoring the blond guy's friendly comments. Except for one. When he asks how Sweetie got away, Al says, "Ask her," jerking his head at Noreen. The blond guy just raises his eyebrows and wanders away down a shady path.

Al's face is really red. He looks hot enough to explode.

"I gotta rest for a few minutes," he says, and stretches out on the grass under the trees, with the beer on his stomach. It's only half-finished when he falls asleep, the beer tipping over and dribbling into the grass. It would take an earthquake to wake him now. There's no hurry.

Al looks kind of pathetic lying there, like an accident victim, kind of, with all his scratches. His stomach, under the red Miami Mice T-shirt, has fallen around to his sides. Oh well, he'll find somebody else. There's a man shortage out there, not that she's ever noticed. In the cage, Sweetie closes her eyes and turns her head into her shoulder.

Noreen reaches her purse and sunglasses from the front seat, then walks around and hoists her suitcase from the trunk.

"So long, Sweetie," she says. "Don't take any wooden pumpkin seeds."

She's almost at the highway when the red car pulls alongside.

"Need a lift?"

"No."

"You're leaving him, aren't you?"

"Naw. You're imagining it."

She keeps walking, but the red car stays right

beside her.

"Well, look, you'll need a ride, won't you? I mean he's going to be mad as hell when he wakes up, isn't he?"

She stops. He stops. He smiles.

He's right, of course, and it's not like taking a ride with just anybody, she kind of feels like she knows this guy a little bit.

"All right."

She opens the back door, slides the suitcase in. As she buckles her seat belt, the little car glides out onto the highway.

"My name's Darryl," he says, shoving a tape into the tape deck. He leans back and gets comfortable as they drift down the blacktop to Willie's metallic voice telling them he can't wait to get on the road again. The air in the car is so clean and fresh Noreen can smell the faint pet shop aroma that clings to her. Through the sparkling windows she sees sunshine, clouds, mountains, green. Lots and lots of green. She feels her chest expanding.

"Where ya going?" she asks.

"Vancouver." He smiles at her.

"Me, too," she says, leaning back into the red leather seat. "My name's Noreen."

SHELLEY A. LEEDAHL

Gator

I said I'd divorce him if he ever did it again. Picture this. It's Hallowe'en. I'm a respectable Vampirella, even wore the lowest cut sweater I had for the cleavage effect. The black hair doesn't do much for me, but what the heck. It's only for a night. He's a fly. Not *The* Fly, from the movie, but a common household fly. The kind Jimmy Crack Corn creamed. He's made these awful wings, from coat hangers, and a pair of fuzzy shorts from a Salvation Army fur coat. I'm glad he didn't make me sew them. The black pantyhose do nothing for his legs.

He can't sit in the front seat with those wings so I drive the car to the dance while he crouches on all fours in the back seat. Two sheep and Little Red Riding Hood split a gut seeing him crawl out of our car.

We get to this dance, right? Find his friends, two couples dressed like the Munsters. He really knows how to pick 'em. I'm hoping Herman doesn't step on my toes with those clodhoppers of his.

Anyway, I'm thinking this is okay. The costumes are great. The beer is cheap. I've got a few years before I turn thirty. I can still wear short skirts. That one always pops up whenever I count my blessings.

He's twenty-nine and hates it. Thirty is going to be crisis-city. I think I'll send a photo of him to the paper and write something incriminating underneath. Maybe get those pink flamingos and a sign for the front lawn.

He's having a little trouble sitting down. Breathing must be a bitch in that head piece. He sucks beer with a straw through his nose holes. Looks like a real geek, but there's a frog that seems to like him.

The music's good. Rock 'n roll, hard and fast, the way I like it. I do the rounds: Herman, Grandpa. Lily looks a bit pissed off but I happen to know her husband's got a little problem. Actually, it's very little. Don't ask me how I know.

We've been married seven years. We have this unwritten rule: never dance with each other unless we're desperate. Well, the music man is playing "Satisfaction" by the Stones. I like to think of it as my theme song, plus there's no one else around. We dance. His wings had shifted to one side and I notice a long run in the pantyhose. Shit. I was hoping I'd be able to wear them when he was done. Well "Satisfaction" was over and then the DJ plays "Werewolves of London." I kind of like that one too.

After that I spot a tiger I think I recognize. I walk across the room and sure enough, it's Tony. We laugh and dance and I nearly sprain my ankle but it's worth it; Tony spends a long time making it feel better.

Grudgingly, I return to the Munsters. They're turning out to be real bores. The mafia family at the next table, now there's a group with some spunk.

At midnight some long tables are set up and the cold cuts brought out. The music continues, and people dance or eat or whatever.

Me, I'm starved. I join the line up for food and blink a little under the lights. I can feel the white make-up slide right off my face.

He's still out on the dance floor, with the frog. They make a nice couple.

I don't know the people around me so I concentrate on chipping off my black finger nail polish. That's when it happens. I just have to hear the first few notes and I know. They are playing his song, that song, the one someone wrote to torture me with. They are playing "Shout." You probably know it. It's the song that starts fast, then gets slow, fast and slow. It was big during high school. The guys would get down on the floor in the middle of the song, lie on their backs and gator. You know, the convulsion thing.

He did it at the Christmas dance last year. It was bad. I mean, I believe in having fun, but please. There's a difference between having a good laugh and being a good laugh. I guess he hasn't learned that yet. Doesn't he know how stupid it makes him look? Makes me look?

I suppose it represents youth or something. He doesn't want to grow up. I've heard about men and their crises. Did I sympathize? No way. I gave it to him right outside in the parking lot—listen pal, you've just gatored for the last time.

And here it is again. That damn song. I can't look. Not here, not now, not again. I hear laughter erupt behind me and I have to turn around. It's him. Convulsing on the floor like he's being electrocuted. His black fly legs kicking and kicking. His wings bending under him at unnatural angles. Shaking and shaking and a crowd forming around him. I want to die, watching that fly on his back, hearing the hilarious laughter. I'm surprised someone doesn't throw a beer bottle at him, put him out of his misery.

I said I'd divorce him if he ever did it again. He did it again.

BEV ROSS

City in Pain

Nine years we were news at eleven
Nine years, Boy, of scoring with you
Our marriage was made up in heaven
A hockey town's dream had come true
Now you say through your tears you are leavin'
O Wayne, was it something we said?
Your ego, your wife
Or Gainer's big knife
Who blinded those eyes in the back of your head?

        Wayne, O Wayne
        We wanted it all
        The Grey Cup, the Stanley
        West Edmonton Mall
        99 teardrops are all that remain
        We're a shell of a city
        A city in pain

Wayne, she's a pleasure to look at
A sensitive actress to boot
And we do not believe all them stories
That she courted you just for your loot.
Now she says that she did not persuade you
She says that she is not to blame
So said Jezebel
Yoko Ono as well
Is she on the take from the Calgary Flames?

Wayne O Wayne
Is there ice in L.A.?
With their sunglasses on
Can they see how you play?
99 starlets on Rodeo Drive
Will Tinseltown notice
If hockey don't thrive?

Was Peter a good man to work for?
Did he call you a son of his own?
While he tagged you at $42 million
As a pledge on a government loan?
Wayne, did his voice ever falter
As he hugged you and wished you good luck?
It used to be sweet
Now you're so much dead meat
But how can we blame him for making a buck?

Wayne, O Wayne
Guess it's gotta be played
We thought it was love
But it looks like free trade
Business is business
And o what the hell
To Peter, your soul is
An asset to sell

Wayne O Wayne
Is there ice in L.A.?
With their sunglasses on
Can they see how you play?
99 teardrops are all that remain
We're a shell of a city
The sight isn't pretty
A shell of a city
In pain.

PAT KRAUSE

Star Bright

Vickie is waiting for Keith in the listening room. The talking dolls tape is set up on the reel-to-reel Sony ready for him to hear. As usual, Keith is late.

"Vickie loves Keith & Keith loves Vickie," Vickie scribbles on the notes she made for splicing the dialogue of GI Joe and Best Friend Cynthia together.

She puts the red marking pencil in her mouth and inhales. Listening to Best Friend Cynthia has left her feeling spinny, as giddy as a girl in love for the first time. Too bad it isn't that simple, she thinks, she wishes it was. She wishes she had a cigarette to help her think clearly about true love and her media career. She takes the pencil out of her mouth and exhales.

Vickie Ann Seitz, she asks herself, what do you need to be happy, happy?

She draws two stars, prints her name in one, Keith's in the other, connects them with lightning bolts, and sketches a television screen around them.

Smack on focus, she thinks, teamwork with Keith is helping her use radio as a launch pad to stardom on TV. That's what she needs to be happy. John is not in the picture.

How to tell John she wants a divorce has been worrying her thin for weeks. In fact, she has lost fifteen pounds—which is five pounds more than the television cameras add on, and that's great. What she has to do now, tonight, is level with John, get it over with, and not put an ounce of that weight back on again after he's gone out of her life.

Poor John is going to be devastated, she knows it. He still seems to think he can mould her into a replica of her mother, into a sweetness-and-light happy housewife, a household goddess. Lately, he has been offering her boxes of Hostess chips and Belgian chocolates to try and woo her away from her scripts for midnight munchies, and then a little love-making in the master bedroom. Eating in bed just isn't John's thing. John is the kind of man who perches on his side of the bed each night to rub the soles of his bare feet together in case there's any lint on them that might come off in the sheets. She used to think it was cute and sort of sexy, like watching a frog-prince balance on the edge of his ladylove's lilypad to perform a mating dance. Once upon a time it really turned her on.

Not any more. Not since Keith came on the scene as the new announcer-producer of the radio pro-gram that uses her freelance items. Behind the urban cowboy façade Keith adopted to move west from Winnipeg, there's a seasoned media type she can really relate to. As a workmate, Keith has taught her a lot. And as a playmate, he's a boots-on-the-bedspread kind of guy. She smiles.

Keith happens to be staying in the Embassy Ho-tel's newly renovated bridal suite, one of the few rooms the hotel has with a private bathroom, and he claims the fake fur bedspread is one hundred per cent virgin acrylic mink. It covers an under-filled waterbed that would make anyone except lovers on tight deadlines seasick. Nine mirror tiles are on the ceiling over the waterbed and a black velvet painting hangs on the red and gold flocked wallpaper at the foot of it. The painting is of a naked couple, artfully entwined so none of their sexual parts show. They're standing in the beam of a full orange moon under a fluorescent green palm tree that has its fronds dan-gling down around their hot pink flesh like snakes. Keith calls the painting. "Mr. and Mrs. Canuck Stuck Standing-up in Hawaii." Compared to the Wedgwood blue chintz, white walls and watercolour prints of what she'll soon be able to call the "Ms." bedroom at home, it's like travelling to another continent to follow Keith down the street from the radio station to the bridal suite.

Vickie is doodling hearts and flowers when Keith sneaks up behind her and kisses the bump of knowledge on the back of her head.

"Oh! At last!" she says, quickly turning her notes over.

"Apologies, Pardner," Keith growls in the Ben Cartwright voice that makes girls and women write the station for his autographed picture. "Didn't mean to keep the best brains in broadcasting hitched to the listening post this long. Got problems?"

"Nothing I couldn't handle," Vickie says. "GI Joe's voice sounded like grinding gears when I recorded it, but I got Super Tech to filter it. He hasn't been programmed to say much, anyway. I kept pulling his dog tag to see if I'd missed anything, but I hadn't. Best Friend Cynthia's a real chatterbox, of course. Talk about sexist stereotyping! Did I tell you her records are even labelled by topic? 'Get Acquainted' and 'Family' on the flip sides of one disc, 'Outdoor' and 'Indoor' topics on the other one?"

"Yup," Keith says.

"And what little girls have to do to make her talk?"

Keith says, "Nope."

"They have to hike up her dress, pull down her panties, stick a disc into the slot in her stomach, and then press down hard on it, practically make a fist and punch her in the stomach, every time they want the doll to say something. I wish we were doing this for television so my audience could see me expose *that*."

"Radio-vision's what we're after here. Send the sound of a breaking nose out on the airwaves, smack on focus, and folks'll see the fist hit, the bone break, the blood spill. How many times have I chewed that cud of wisdom over with you, Pardner?"

Too many, Vickie thinks, and one of the first things she's going to change about Keith is his phony cowpoke jargon.

"How long's the tape?" Keith helps himself to the stopwatch she has hanging around her neck on a black cord.

It's matter of fact, he doesn't fondle, but dammit, her nipples stand at attention anyway. And she can smell the chocolate scented pipe tobacco Keith uses. Why didn't *he* take the pledge at the Seventh Day Adventist Stop Smoking Clinic at the City Health Centre and report *his* experience trying to quit on-air?

"In Turkey in 1605," Vickie says, "anyone caught smoking a pipe had his nose pierced with its stem and was put on public exhibit. If that didn't stop him, the sultan's death penalty for second offenses was a sure cure, the ultimate cold turkey: he was beheaded."

Keith pats her head. "Tough assignment, eh, Pardner?"

"Listening to B.F. Cindy all those hours without a cigarette? It freaked me out. Gave me a stomach-ache. I almost threw up all over the tape machine listening to her silly chatter without any nicotine to settle my nerves. I haven't done the final timing. It's about one and a half minutes, I think. I was making notes on how to introduce the item and waiting for you to get here so I'd only have to listen to her once more today, not twice."

"Here I am, Pardner." Keith clicks her stopwatch on, off, and resets it at sixty. "Roll the tape."

Vickie turns the switch of the tape machine to the forward arrow and, thanks to her work with a one-sided razor blade and splicing tape—skills Keith taught her—the voices of talking dolls GI Joe and Best Friend Cynthia fill the listening room:

332

I've got a tough assignment for you.

You and I are a lot alike, isn't that groovy?
Do you wear much make-up? I like the natural
look, don't you? Why don't we call your friends?
I'd love to meet them.

This is going to be rough.

I've always wanted to be a doctor or nurse
because I like to help sick people feel better.
Let's listen to some music. Play your favourite
record.

Can you handle it?

I love popcorn. Can we make some? No more
French fries or milkshakes for me for awhile.
I gained two pounds last weekend. What's
your favourite sport?

Follow me.

I'm glad you're my best friend and I can tell
you all my secrets. Will you tell me a secret?

Follow me. We must get there before dark.

Will you vote for me for class president?

Will you help me bake cookies for the bake
sale? Let's exchange phone numbers and you
can call me tonight.

The Adventure Team is needed in Africa.

I can't wait until we're old enough to travel
together. Do you have any pictures of places
you'd like to visit? Don't forget to bring
your camera with us today.

Follow me. Can you handle it?

I really love my family. Do you want to go

horseback riding? Last time I rode the most beautiful palomino.

This is going to be rough.

I'm glad we're so close. I've always wanted my very own horse, haven't you?

Mission accomplished. Good work, men.

Vickie presses Keith's thumb down on the stopwatch.

"One thirty-eight," he says. "Cut 'doctor' and you've got it smack on focus." He bunts her nose with his knuckles. "Gotta hit the trail to do voice-overs on some TV commercials. See you at the Embassy after your Dear John act, Pardner." He hangs the stopwatch around her neck and he's gone.

Vickie waits until the pressure mechanism on the listening room door has sucked it shut. Then she backs up the tape, finds "doctor or . . . "marks it to cut so Best Friend Cynthia will only say she wants to be a nurse, picks up the razor blade, and changes her mind. It stays. She thinks she knows why it's there. A feminist actress in need of money recorded Best Friend Cynthia's voice and managed to slip "doctor" into the script she had to follow so that little girls could squeeze at least one small liberated thought out of their talking doll's gut.

She rewinds the tape, puts it in the box, and labels it: *Talking Dolls Xmas Feature*, Time: 1:38; Opening Cue: "I've got a tough . . . " Closing Cue: " . . . men."

Men! Sometimes she wonders if they're worth all the hassle. She stuffs the tape into her briefcase, which she uses as her purse, cosmetic kit and research file. In it, she has various shades of blush and mascara and moisture-proof lipsticks, FDS and her birth control pills in their wheel-of-fortune dispenser; plus pamphlets and articles and notes on VD symptoms, adult bedwetting cures, a new drug abuse program, instructions on how to knit a uterus (part of a kit for teachers of natural childbirth in rural areas), a booklet on how to obtain a quickie do-it-yourself divorce for a maximum lawyer's fee of seventy-five dollars, and her historical facts about smoking. But there aren't any cigarettes in it. Not even a squashed one at the bottom. Nothing to reward herself for finally getting the damn talking dolls recorded and spliced together in dialogue on one tape. Nothing to relieve her trembly craving so she can think straight and plan a script for breaking the news to John tonight. No, she has to resort to repeating bits of anti-smoking history to herself again.

Vickie leaves the radio station saying to herself: A Russian czar, tah-dah tah-dah, one of the first public health pioneers, had smokers brutally beaten, then banished them to Siberia.

It doesn't dull her craving or make her glad she only has to use will power, but she has an idea. What if she got started on the quickie divorce right away?— like tomorrow? She could quit the damn Stop Smoking Clinic and use her experience ending her marriage to do a new series of "Spotlight on Life" features. Maybe, after he was over the initial shock, John would let her interview him to balance it with a male viewpoint? Why not? She'll talk him into it. And broadcasting her modern divorce would probably increase her ratings on Keith's program. She could lead into each feature with a detail from her old-fashioned wedding to give the series that cigarette ad ambience of *You've come a long way, Baby.*

Three years ago on Boxing Day, she thought being a bride was the only starring role she would ever want.

It was a beautiful, beautiful, traditional marriage ceremony. A High Mass. A choir to sing "The Lord's

Prayer" instead of the Christian Folk Singers doing "This Is Love," an organ instead of guitars. Rice, not confetti, given to the guests by the ushers to shower on them as they left the cathedral. Instead of fake silk flowers, there were bushels and bushels of fresh flowers everywhere; in the bouquets, boutonnieres and corsages, banked on the altar and around the bride's table on the stage of the hotel ballroom, in arrangements at the centre of all the round dinner tables. Five hundred guests had toasted her with champagne. Her mother wept. So did her father, although he tried to pretend his tears were because of what it was costing.

There will be tears when she tells her parents about the divorce, too, she knows it. And what if she had let her parents talk her into taking the money and eloping, like they did? John was all for it. She can thank her lucky stars she wasn't. She wouldn't have such a perfect dramatic contrast to a seventy-five dollar divorce to use on air. She'll have to tell her parents that. But what was it her mother said when she asked her if she'd ever wanted to divorce her father? —"Divorce? Never. Murder, maybe." —and then her parents looked at each other in that secret way they had of communicating that left her totally out. Well, this isn't the era of love and marriage hitched together like a horse and carriage that her parents sing duets about. These days, she'll remind them, you *can* have one without the other, and lots of career women do.

Vickie isn't surprised to find a parking ticket under the windshield wiper of John's car. She'd parked it in front of the Embassy so long ago there could have been half a dozen tickets there. Poor John, she thinks, recalling how eagerly he'd offered her his car keys when her car wouldn't start. In return for him taking the bus, she'd promised to whip right

home from the Stop Smoking Clinic and prepare
him a special home-cooked dinner, have candlelight
and wine, just for the two of them, like she used to do
when they were first married and she wasn't freelanc-
ing. They would have a heart-to-heart, she'd told him.
Actually, Vickie has ordered the divorce dinner from
Homestyle Caterers on Dewdney Avenue and she's
going over there to pick it up now. Another career
choice John wouldn't understand, and Keith would,
she thinks. But she closes the glove compartment and
sticks the parking ticket in her briefcase instead. Five
dollars if she pays it within seven days. A divorce
present. Pay John's parking ticket, she'll add to her
list of the things she still has to do before tomorrow's
program.

Let's see, Vickie thinks as she wheels the car out
of the tight parking space, after John leaves tonight,
she'll have to finish the talking dolls script, come up
with a snappy introduction for a tape that took that
much work, and think of something inspirational
about quitting smoking for her finale to that series.
She wishes she hadn't already used the story about
the woman dying of lung cancer, the one who was so
badly addicted she lit her last cigarette in an oxygen
tent and burnt to death. She wishes she didn't understand how that poor woman felt. She can't even dig
into the ashtray of John's car for a butt. John hasn't
smoked since he was eight years old. Back then, he
thought the men in town smoked to keep their hands
warm, so he and his pal tried smoking dried leaves
rolled in newspaper and made themselves sick. Right
now, Vickie would settle for manure rolled in toilet
paper.

Vickie steps on the gas and says to herself: King
James the First of England proclaimed smoking was
barbarous, beastly, hateful to the nose, a vile and
stinking custom, harmful to the brain.

And she sails through the red light as far as the middle of the intersection before the truck broadsides her.

The impact crushes in the passenger door, pops the empty ashtray out on her lap, and spins John's red Toyota around like a top. As soon as the car comes to a stop, Vickie throws the gear shift into park, hops out, dodges the vehicles careening by her with their horns blaring, and sprints over to the driver's side of the Brown's Auction truck that hit her.

"Oh, I'm so sorry," she says to the ashen-faced driver. "I know it's all my fault for going through a red light but I took the pledge at the Seventh Day Adventist Stop Smoking Clinic at the City Health Centre and I was telling myself what King James the First of England proclaimed to stop my craving for nicotine because I'm telling my husband I want a divorce tonight and the stress makes me sneak puffs of cigarettes whenever I get the chance so I don't know if God got me for that or for cheating on my husband because we had a High Mass when we took our vows and now I'm in love with a cowboy from Winnipeg."

The truck driver's face has turned scarlet. Has she said all that stuff out loud? It feels as if dozens of small fists are punching her in the stomach. "Oh, God," she says. "Have I been babbling worse than Best Friend Cynthia? I just wanted you to know I'm really sorry for going through that red light."

"Hey, lady? Listen, lady, it's okay," the driver says. "As long as you're not hurt. People go through red lights sometimes, eh? Like they just don't see them."

"Oh, but I do, I do," she hears herself say, and wishes she didn't. Her voice sounds squeaky again. She has to pull herself together, quit acting as if she's a talking doll with a record in her stomach. Vickie flops over and does the rag doll exercise to relax herself, lower her voice, like Keith taught her to do before she goes on air. "My profession involves red lights," she says in her radio voice. "They mean I'm in a live studio and—"

"Hey, listen, lady, it's pretty live round here and we're gonna get ourselves killed if we don't get outta the crossfire."

"Please, could you lend me a cigarette?" Vickie asks, hating the whine she can hear has crept back into her voice. She can't stand woman who plead with men. "Please?" she says.

"I don't smoke, lady. Listen, why don't you go get into your car, follow me, and we'll go to the cop shop to report this accident, okay? Can you handle that? Follow me," the driver says.

Vickie nods her head. She's afraid if she speaks she'll tell him he sounds like GI Joe. Bits of plastic and glass and red metal make a trail for her to follow back to John's car. She stops to pick up the chrome door handle.

The truck driver leans on his horn and shouts, "Hey, lady? It's okay, eh? That's not your kitchen floor. You don't have to do that. The city's got a crew comes round to clean up. You're gonna get us both creamed."

It's almost five o'clock. Rush hour. And hordes of people are taking advantage of Thursday night store opening to go Christmas shopping. But Vickie follows the Brown's Auction truck as if John's car was being towed behind it on a short chain. The truck driver keeps blinking the brake lights to signal her to fall back, but she doesn't want to lose him. She wants to march into the police station with him, admit she went through a red light, and show him she isn't just some silly housewife who can't stop talking and doesn't know how to drive.

She is pleased that the driver is standing on the

sidewalk at the rear of his truck when she swoops back into the parallel parking space behind it that isn't an inch longer than John's car. Vickie slips the car in so tight to the curb he steps back from it.

"Hey, not bad, lady," he says, when she gets out. "Couldn't have slid that crushed tin can of yours into there better myself."

"The car belongs to my husband," Vickie says, and she lets the truck driver open the doors into the police station for her.

The policeman behind the counter she marches right up to is smoking. The fists pound her stomach again. She takes a deep breath and says, "Warning! Health and Welfare Canada advises that danger to health increases with amount smoked—avoid inhaling."

"Chief's Clean Air Committee send you to hassle me?" The policeman carefully stubs out his cigarette and tucks the long butt back in his Rothman's pack. "You one of his nicotine narcs?"

"No, no. I'm just another nicotine addict," Vickie says, and smiles at him. Okay, that's the truth, she tells herself, now get to the point and don't tell him anything else personal—no babbling. "I've followed this nice gentleman here to report an accident that's entirely my fault."

"Hah! Who's gonna walk in here and admit that? What's the catch?" The smell of smoke on the policeman's breath makes Vickie lean over the counter closer to him and breathe deeply.

"No catch," the truck driver says. "Hear the lady out, eh?"

"Well, I was on my way to the caterer's. To pick up a special divorce dinner to serve my husband." Vickie is speaking slowly, trying to inhale more than she exhales. "I had a lot of things on my mind. Talking dolls. Do-it-yourself divorce. The pledge I'd taken at

he Seventh Day Adventist Stop Smoking Clinic at the
City Health Centre. And, you know how it is. Going
cold turkey? It isn't easy under pressure. You need a
cigarette."

"Hah!" the policeman says. "Tell me about it."

Vickie smiles, So far, so good. She's enunciating,
moving her lips, speaking softly, but clearly. People
who ought to be a lot less nervous than she is have just
nodded or shaken their heads when she holds a
microphone in front of them during street interviews
to get their opinion on something. They often ask
her if they're going to be on television. She wants to
give the policeman radio-vision, let him see the fist
hit, the bone break, the blood run.

"Well, I guess I had a nicotine fit. I went through
a red light. Or almost through it. This gentleman
couldn't avoid hitting me. With his truck. Dead centre
in the middle of the intersection. May I borrow a
cigarette?"

The policeman takes the pack of Rothman's out
of his shirt pocket, opens it, pulls a cigarette half-way
out, offers it to her, then re-lights his butt.

"Thank you," Vickie says. She puts the cigarette in
the centre of her mouth like a baby's soother. The
policeman holds his lighter under it. "No, no, don't
light it," she says. "I'll keep it for later, for after I tell
my husband I'm in love with an urban cowboy and
want a divorce. Do you mind?"

"It's a gift, not a loan, sweetheart," the policeman
says. "Now then, let's see your drivers' licences and
registrations."

Vickie begins poking through her briefcase.

"No problem," the truck driver says. He pulls his
credentials out of the back pocket of his jeans and
hands them over. "I didn't even get a dent in the
bumper when I hit her, eh? There won't be no
government insurance claim from me or Brown's

341

Auctions." The policeman records some numbers and gives the papers back to him.

"Guess you can handle it okay from here, eh, lady?" The truck driver gives her a light punch on the arm before he goes.

"Keep truckin," Vickie says, and dumps the contents of her briefcase out on the counter. "I don't have the registration," she says to the policeman. "I've got poor John's car today. But my driver's licence is in here somewhere. In my wallet, if we can find that."

"Hah! Looks like you got plenty of problems to solve, sweetheart," the policeman says. "Don't touch a drop of coffee after breakfast's the answer to one of them, I learned." He holds up the pamphlet on adult bedwetting. He sifts through some more of her research, shaking his head, then stops with the mimeographed natural childbirth instructions in front of him. "Bert?" he turns and calls. "Come on out here. Need your help. You're not gonna believe this. Your wife can quit crying about the female surgery she got. Just take her a Xerox of these here instructions on how to knit herself a uterus."

An older policeman with white hair comes out to the counter. He reminds Vickie of her father. "Oh, hi," she says. "We're looking for my licence because I went through a red light and got hit by a Brown's Auction truck and I'm hoping you'll have to arrest me so I don't have to go to the Seventh Day Adventist Stop Smoking Clinic at the City Health Centre and then go home without any dinner to tell my husband I want a divorce." It's those fists again, she thinks, God is turning me into Best Friend Cynthia. She sees her lighter in some VD folders and decides to have a few calming puffs of the cigarette. She lights up, takes one long drag, and stubs the cigarette out in the tin ashtray the first policeman takes out from under the counter and shoves toward her.

The policemen find her driver's licence caught in the wheel-of-fortune card that holds her birth control pills. They take it, and the uterus knitting instructions, and disappear with them into the office behind the counter. She lights up again, takes two long drags this time, and lets the cigarette burn in the ashtray. Men, she thinks, where is my one true love? Why am I always waiting on men to come and go in my life, dammit?

"No charges," the first policeman says when they appear again. "Far as we're concerned, we didn't hear no confession about going through no red light or nothing."

Bert, the one who looks like her father, says, "We think you've got enough troubles already, dear. My advice? Keep yourself busy with something constructive, you know? Otherwise, you get a divorce and you're just going to get screwed, know what I mean? Think you can handle driving yourself home to the one-and-only? It's dark and slippery out there. Want us to call a cruiser to take you?"

"Oh, no thank you," Vickie says. "I'm really a very good driver, but that's very kind of you to offer. I'm glad to find out policemen are so friendly, so, uh, understanding and forgiving. Wait until I tell Keith how nice you both were to me. We'll have to do some really upbeat broadcasts about policemen—interviews that show a policeman can be your best friend—that sort of theme?"

"Will we be on television?" Bert asks, smoothing his hair.

"Radio-vision," Vickie says. "And thanks for the cigarette. I'll finish it after I tell John the news. Merry Christmas!" They both smile at her. They have such nice smiles, she thinks as she hurries to the car.

Her list must be rearranged now. She hasn't got

343

time to go to the Stop Smoking Clinic, pick up the dinner, get wine, candles, or a loaf of French bread to break with John after she tells him what she ha decided to do. And, she almost forgot, she was going to stop at her mom and dad's and break the news to them first, tell them she needs their support, warn them not to go babying John when he runs to them begging to know what else he can do to make her happy, tell her parents she doesn't need any lectures about loyalty to her husband and to her marriage vows. They know she has to follow her own star.

Vickie steps on the gas and thinks about the motto she has on the wall over her desk at the radio station: *Whatever women do, they must do twice as well as men. Fortunately, that's not difficult.*

Unfortunately, sometimes it's damn difficult, she thinks, and telling her parents, telling John she doesn't love him anymore—and about his banged-up car—is going to be one of those times. And then she has those scripts to do, the divorce booklet to research, and Keith expecting her to show up at his passion pit in the Embassy. Men! None of them can ever understand what a tough assignment it is for her to splice together a personal life with a meteoric rise to TV stardom. Maybe a woman with her ambition ought to just stop falling in love.

But Venus shines bright in the clear December sky and Vickie makes her old wish. Star light, star bright, Vickie says to herself, wish I may, wish I might, be with the one I love tonight.

The next thing Vickie knows, she's checking in at the Landmark Motel. The contents of her briefcase are strewn along the reception counter, and the clerk, a pleasant looking older woman who recognized her voice from hearing her on the radio, is helping her look for her Visa.

"Now tell me," the woman says, thumbing

through the divorce booklet without any luck. "Is Keith as handsome as he sounds?"

"Yes, yes, I guess he is," Vickie says. That damn Visa, she thinks, it's got to be in here somewhere.

This Vehicle Stops For All Metaphors.

Saskatchewan
LIT 100
PV!   88

BARBARA MULCAHY

My Muse is a Tramp

My muse has a beehive hairdo; she uses my pencils to scratch her scalp. "This writing," she says, "it's not healthy." She gives me a list of what I need. Red lipstick. Eyeliner. Evening in Paris eau de cologne. "It comes in a blue bottle," she tells me.

I shut the window and the door when my muse visits because she has a loud voice that says, for example, "PEOPLE LIKE SEX" and "DON'T BE DUTIFUL." But when I write down these instructions she acts exasperated.

My muse is a tramp; when a man walks in the room she forgets all about me. Sometimes she walks out with him. "Scritch, scritch" her stockings say and her stiletto heels give her strong stride just the faintest hint of instability.

My muse comes back to me laughing and at ease. She sits on my desk and lassoes me with her smoke rings. Her shiny stockings go "scritch, scritch" when she shifts her hips. I know they're stockings, not pantyhose, because she pulls up her miniskirt and adjusts her garters. She sees me watch her. She looks over at my papers and shakes her head. "Your writing," she says, "suffers from a lack of lingerie."

DAVID ARNASON

A Girl's Story

You've wondered what it would be like to be a character in a story, to sort of slip out of your ordinary self
and into some other character. Well, I'm offering you
the opportunity. I've been trying to think of a heroine for this story, and frankly, it hasn't been going too
well. A writer's life isn't easy, especially if, like me,
he's got a tendency sometimes to drink a little bit too
much. Yesterday, I went for a beer with Dennis and
Ken (they're real-life friends of mine) and we stayed
a little longer than we should have. Then I came
home and quickly mixed a drink and started drinking it so my wife would think the liquor on my breath
came from the drink I was drinking and not from the
drinks I had had earlier. I wasn't going to tell her
about those drinks. Anyway, Wayne dropped over in
the evening and I had some more drinks, and this
morning my head isn't working very well.

   To be absolutely frank about it, I always have
trouble getting characters, even when I'm stone cold
sober. I can think of plots; plots are really easy. If you
can't think of one, you just pick up a book, and sure
enough, there's a plot. You just move a few things
around and nobody knows you stole the idea. Characters are the problem. It doesn't matter how good
the plot is if your characters are dull. You can steal
characters too, and put them into different plots. I've
done that. I stole Eustacia Vye from Hardy and gave
her another name. The problem was that she turned
out a lot sulkier than I remembered and the plot I put
her in was a light comedy. Now nobody wants to
publish the story. I'm still sending it out, though. If
you send a story to enough publishers, no matter how
bad it is, somebody will ultimately publish it.

For this story I need a beautiful girl. You probably don't think you're beautiful enough, but I can fix that. I can do all kinds of retouching once I've got the basic material, and if I miss anything, Karl (he's my editor) will find it. So I'm going to make you fairly tall, about five-foot eight and a quarter in your stocking feet. I'm going to give you long blonde hair because long blonde hair is sexy and virtuous. Black hair can be sexy too, but it doesn't go with virtue. I've got to deal with a whole literary tradition where black-haired women are basically evil. If I were feeling better I might be able to do it in an ironic way, then black hair would be OK, but I don't think I'm up to it this morning. If you're going to use irony, then you've got to be really careful about tone. I could make you a redhead, but redheads have a way of turning out pixie-ish, and that would wreck my plot.

So you've got long blonde hair and you're this tall slender girl with amazingly blue eyes. Your face is narrow and your nose is straight and thin. I could have turned up the nose a little, but that would have made you cute, and I really need a beautiful girl. I'm going to put a tiny black mole on your cheek. It's traditional. If you want your character to be really beautiful there has to be some minor defect.

Now, I'm going to sit you on the bank of a river. I'm not much for setting. I've read so many things where you get great long descriptions of the setting, and mostly it's just boring. When my last book came out, one of the reviewers suggested that the reason I don't do settings is that I'm not very good at them. That's just silly. I'm writing a different kind of story, not that old realist stuff. If you think I can't do setting, just watch.

There's a curl in the river just below the old dam where the water seems to make a broad sweep. That flatness is deceptive, though. Under the innocent sheen of the mirroring surface, the current is treacherous. The water swirls, stabs, takes sharp angles and dangerous vectors. The trees that lean from the bank shimmer with the multi-hued greenness of elm, oak, maple and aspen. The leaves turn in the gentle breeze, showing their paler green undersides. The under- growth, too, is thick and green, hiding the poison ivy, the poison sumac and the thorns. On a patch of grass that slopes gently to the water, the only clear part of the bank on that side of the river, a girl sits, a girl with long blonde hair. She has slipped a ring from her finger and seems to be holding it toward the light.

You see? I could do a lot more of that, but you wouldn't like it. I slipped a lot of details in there and provided all those hints about strange and dangerous things under the surface. That's called foreshadowing. I put in the ring at the end there so that you'd wonder what was going to happen. That's to create suspense. You're supposed to ask yourself what the ring means. Obviously it has something to do with love, rings always do, and since she's taken it off, obviously something has gone wrong in the love relationship. Now I just have to hold off answering that question for as long as I can, and I've got my story. I've got a friend who's also a writer who says never tell the buggers anything until they absolutely have to know.

I'm going to have trouble with the feminists about this story. I can see that already. I've got that river that's calm on the surface and boiling underneath, and I've got those trees that are gentle and beautiful with poisonous and dangerous under growth. Obviously, the girl is going to be like that, calm on the surface but passionate underneath. The feminists are going to say that I'm perpetuating stereotypes, that by giving the impression the girl is full of hidden passion I'm encouraging rapists. That's crazy. I'm just using a literary convention. Most of the world's great books are about the conflict between reason and passion. If you take that away, what's left to write about?

So I've got you sitting on the riverbank, twirling your ring. I forgot the birds. The trees are full of singing birds. There are meadowlarks and vireos and even Blackburnian warblers. I know a lot about birds but I'm not going to put in too many. You've got to be careful not to overdo things. In a minute I'm going to enter your mind and reveal what you're thinking. I'm going to do this in the third person. Using the first person is sometimes more effective, but I'm always afraid to do a female character in the first person. It seems wrong to me, like putting on a woman's dress.

Your name is Linda. I had to be careful not to give you a biblical name like Judith or Rachel. I don't want any symbolism in this story. Symbolism makes me sick, especially biblical symbolism. You always end up with some crazy moral argument that you don't believe and none of the readers believe. Then you lose control of your characters, because they've got to be like the biblical characters. You've got this terrific episode you'd like to use, but you can't because Rachel or Judith or whoever wouldn't do it. I think of stories with a lot of symbolism in them as sticky.

Here goes.

Linda held the ring up toward the light. The diamond flashed rainbow colours. It was a small diamond, and Linda reflected that it was probably a perfect symbol of her relationship with Gregg. Everything Gregg did was on a small scale. He was careful with his money and just as careful with his emotions. In one week they would have a small wedding and then move into a small apartment. She supposed that she ought to be happy. Gregg was very handsome,

352

and she did love him. Why did it seem that she was walking into a trap?

That sounds kind of distant, but it's supposed to be distant. I'm using indirect quotation because the reader has just met Linda, and we don't want to get too intimate right away. Besides, I've got to get a lot of explaining done quickly, and if you can do it with the characters thoughts, then that's best.

Linda twirled the ring again, then with a suddenness that surprised her, she stood up and threw it into the river. She was immediately struck by a feeling of panic. For a moment she almost decided to dive into the river to try to recover it. Then, suddenly, she felt free. It was now impossible to marry Gregg. He would not forgive her for throwing the ring away. Gregg would say he'd had enough of her theatrics for one lifetime. He always accused her of being a romantic. She'd never had the courage to admit that he was correct, and that she intended to continue being a romantic. She was sitting alone by the river in a long blue dress because it was a romantic pose. Anyway, she thought a little wryly, you're only likely to find romance if you look for it in romantic places and dress for the occasion.

Suddenly, she heard a rustling in the bush, the sound of someone coming down the narrow path from the road above.

I had to do that, you see. I'd used up all the potential in the relationship with Gregg, and the plot would have started to flag if I hadn't introduced a new character. The man who is coming down the path is tall and athletic with wavy brown hair. He has dark brown eyes that crinkle when he smiles, and he looks kind. His skin is tanned, as if he spends a lot of time outdoors, and he moves gracefully. He is smoking a pipe. I don't want to give too many details. I'm not absolutely sure what features women find attractive in men these days, but what I've described seems safe enough. I got all of it from stories written by women, and I assume they must know. I could give him a chiselled jaw, but that's about as far as I'll go.

The man stepped into the clearing. He carried an old-fashioned wicker fishing creel and a telescoped fishing rod. Linda remained sitting on the grass, her blue dress spread out around her. The man noticed her and apologized.

"I'm sorry, I always come here to fish on Saturday afternoons and I've never encountered anyone here before." His voice was low with something of an amused tone in it.

"Don't worry," Linda replied. "I'll only be here for a little while. Go ahead and fish. I won't make any noise." In some way she couldn't understand, the man looked familiar to her. She felt she knew him. She thought she might have seen him on television or in a movie, but of course she knew that movie and television stars do not spend every Saturday afternoon fishing on the banks of small, muddy rivers.

"You can make all the noise you want," he told her. "The fish in this river are almost entirely deaf. Besides, I don't care if I catch any. I only like the act of fishing. If I catch them, then I have to take them home and clean them. Then I've got to cook them and eat them. I don't even like fish that much, and the fish you catch here all taste of mud."

"Why do you bother fishing then?" Linda asked him. "Why don't you just come and sit on the riverbank?"

"It's not that easy," he told her. "A beautiful girl in a blue dress may go and sit on a riverbank any time she wants. But a man can only sit on a riverbank if he has a very good reason. Because I fish, I am a man with a hobby. After a hard week of work, I deserve some relaxation. But if I just came and sat on the

354

riverbank, I would be a romantic fool. People would make fun of me. They would think I was irresponsible, and before long I would be a failure." As he spoke, he attached a lure to his line, untelescoped his fishing pole and cast his line into the water.

You may object that this would not have happened in real life, that the conversation would have been awkward, that Linda would have been a bit frightened by the man. Well, why don't you just run out to the grocery store and buy a bottle of milk and a loaf of bread? The grocer will give you your change without even looking at you. That's what happens in real life, and if that's what you're after, why are you reading a book?

I'm sorry. I shouldn't have got upset. But it's not easy you know. Dialogue is about the hardest stuff to write. You've got all those "he saids" and "she saids" and "he replieds." And you've got to remember the quotation marks and whether the comma is inside or outside the quotation marks. Sometimes you can leave out the "he saids" and the "she saids" but then the reader gets confused and can't figure out who's talking. Hemingway is bad for that. Sometimes you can read an entire chapter without figuring out who is on what side.

Anyway, something must have been in the air that afternoon. Linda felt free and open.

Did I mention that it was warm and the sun was shining?

She chattered away, telling the stranger all about her life, what she had done when she was a little girl, the time her dad her taken the whole family to Hawaii and she got such a bad sunburn that she was peeling in February, how she was a better water skier than Gregg and how mad he got when she beat him at tennis. The man, whose name was Michael (you can use biblical names for men as long as you avoid

Joshua or Isaac), told her he was a doctor, but had always wanted to be a cowboy. He told her about the time he skinned his knee when he fell off his bicycle and had to spend two weeks in the hospital because of infection. In short, they did what people who are falling in love al- ways do. They unfolded their brightest and happiest memories and gave them to each other as gifts.

Then Michael took a bottle of wine and a Klik sandwich out of his wicker creel and invited Linda to join him in a picnic. He had forgotten his corkscrew and he had to push the cork down into the bottle with his filletting knife. They drank wine and laughed and spat out little pieces of cork. Michael reeled in his line, and to his amazement discovered a diamond ring on his hook. Linda didn't dare tell him where the ring had come from. Then Michael took Linda's hand, and slipped the ring onto her finger. In a comic solemn voice, he asked her to marry him. With the same kind of comic solemnity, she agreed. Then they kissed, a first gentle kiss with their lips barely brushing and without touching each other.

Now I've got to bring this to some kind of ending. You think writers know how stories end before they write them, but that's not true. We're wracked with confusion and guilt about how things are going to end. And just as you're playing the role of Linda in this story, Michael is my alter ego. He even looks a little like me and he smokes the same kind of pipe. We all want this to end happily. If I were going to be realistic about this, I suppose I'd have to let them make love. Then, shaken with guilt and horror, Linda would go back and marry Gregg, and the doctor would go back to his practice. But I'm not going to do that. In the story from which I stole the plot, Michael turned out not to be a doctor at all, but a returned soldier who had always been in love with

356

Linda. She recognized him as they kissed, because they had kissed as children, and even though they had grown up and changed, she recognized the flavour of wintergreen on his breath. That's no good. It brings in too many unexplained facts at the last minute.

I'm going to end it right here at the moment of the kiss. You can do what you want with the rest of it, except you can't make him a returned soldier, and you can't have them make love then separate forever. I've eliminated those options. In fact, I think I'll eliminate all options. This is where the story ends, at the moment of the kiss. It goes on and on forever while cities burn, nations rise and fall, galaxies are born and die, and the universe snuffs out the stars one by one. It goes on, the story, the brush of a kiss.

RAVI JEYACHANDRAN

Karamazov

Although the Brothers Karamazov
Never threw a single Molotov
They murdered their dad
    And that's just as bad

Writing Romances

A friend came over the other day. She said she'd sat next to a woman on a bus tour who was making thousands of dollars writing pocket book romances. My friend thought I should give it a shot. So I went right down to the library and took out half a dozen, just to get the hang of how to write them.

Well, I found out I had to have a male character whose eyes glittered and if the muscle in his jaw jerked spasmodically I was on my way. And I could see I'd have to give my hero very flexible lips. In just two sentences, in one book, he had to "fasten" them on the heroine's, "ravage" her mouth, "tear" them away, and then "relinquish" them back.

The men in these books all seemed to have a really high body temperature. When one of the women accidentally brushed against his bare skin, the book said "she jerked away as if scalded." Now, I'd heard about spontaneous combustion on CBC's Quirks and Quarks, so I decided, in my story, to watch for any smoke coming from around my hero's collar.

I could see that eyebrows were pretty important. In one paragraph the hero slanted his black brow, then raised only one, then drew them together. The woman, apparently, was really excited by these frenetic eyebrows but "forced herself to relax, one muscle at a time." The whole thing sounded like one of my yoga exercises.

I think, years ago, the writers really had it easy. They got their lovers together in a romantic situation, in which goodness knows what was going to happen next, and then just punched in a line of stars. By the time the reader was allowed back in the room the lovers were showered and dressed and off downtown to get a hamburger.

However, I could see from these books that I'd have to get right in there with them. In this one book, when the man shot out his arm with "snake-like speed" and grabbed this woman's dress, it said the fabric ripped with "a sharp little screech." He then began "caressing each millimetre of her delicate skin." I thought it was very Canadian of him to do it in metric. She kept getting "goosebumps," probably from the "screech" of that dress. I have the same trouble with the sound of chalk on a blackboard, and my daughter can't stand the noise of people brushing their teeth.

I noticed that the men were always tinkering with the engines of their Lincolns while the women fastened diamond necklaces across the top of sequined dresses. Maybe it would be all right if you were that rich but I couldn't afford having someone screeching up my dresses.

And what about the way they talk? I've even tried to talk seductively, like the woman in the book, from "deep within her throat" but my sinuses get in the way. One of the characters made a noise described as "A ragged tearing sound that combines joy, relief and sadness." Just try making one of those and you'll have a lot more respect for those heroines.

MICK BURRS

Insomniacs' Guide to TV Movies

Movie Plot Ratings
*****	Utterly Preposterous
***	Simply Tasteless
*	Quite Revolting
-10	Damned Awful

Bombs over Broadway. A dozen out-of-work drunken actors in Manhattan become toughened men when they train for bombing missions over the Broadway theatres where they once played leading roles. -10

The Bubblegum Follies of 1940. A philandering Chicago chewing gum manufacturer (Fred Astaire) pairs up with a flirting pharmacist from Philadelphia (Ginger Rogers) to take on a squad of Nazi sympathizers at a peaceful Catskills resort, defeating them at shuffleboard, golf, and bingo, with music by Irving Berlin and choreography by Busby Berkeley. *****

Revenge of the Bookworm. A genius with an IQ of 190 barely survives a hydrogen bomb blast near Bikini Island. Unhinged, he stows away on an Hawaian-bound cruise ship, terrorizing a group of vacationing librarians by living off the left side of their brains. (Close-ups of voracious cannibalism intermingle with quiet literary passages and some erotic cha-cha dance scenes.) *

The Transformations of Elsa Malone. Intent upon entering a less stressful profession, Dr. Edward T. Malone, a dissatisfied Toronto heart surgeon, undergoes a self-administered sex change operation. Elsa then becomes a waitress at a Rocky Mountain dude

360

ranch where she unexpectedly falls in love with an unscrupulous movie producer who turns her into a Hollywood star. After a complete nervous breakdown, Elsa is placed in a nursing home where she discovers her true calling as an arts and crafts counsellor for geriatric patients.

***

The Father Callaghan Story. Fired from the Boston police force for taking petty bribes, the future priest responds to his disgrace by descending to stealing bibles from hotel rooms across North America. Then he beholds a vision of a radiant angel during a devastating California earthquake. Instantly converted, he singlehandedly rescues a trapped family of four from beneath the rubble at a seaside resort and restores the sight of their blind French poodle, Mitzi.

-10

ROBERT CURRIE

How I Became a Poet

I'm standing on a platform in James Hall, conducting
the brass section, but my mind is up the hill somewhere, looking across Echo Lake, wisps of cloud
drifting through the sky, their white reflections drifting on the waves. Long, cool waves, but here the air is
hot and still, heavy with the smell of sweating bodies.
As I swing the baton, a drop of sweat runs down my
nose and falls onto the music, a small, wet stain on the
"Earle of Oxford's Marche." Then I miss a beat,
harmony gives way to discord, and I'm back with my
young charges.

Sure, I finally get Horton blowing his trombone
instead of bumping somebody in the head with his
slide, and it's me that messes up. Now he's off again,
bopping the kid in front of him.

"Horton! A wind instrument is not an instrument
of torture. It's meant to be blown through. Now, let's
try it once more—from the top."

I stab the air and the sound comes, louder this
time and more constant, but only a fair approximation of the score that William Bird once wrote. I
wonder when music got to be so mechanical—and
why. Ten minutes later we're done. The kids jam the
double doors, eager to be down the stairs and free for
an afternoon at the beach.

I go out the other way, through the door that's
always open in what's usually a vain attempt to divert
some fresh air into the hall. I sit on the steel fire
escape and light a cigarette, taking a long drag, the
smoke somehow cooler in my lungs than was the air
inside the hall.

In front of me is the old nurses' residence, transformed now to writers' quarters. The only nurse who

lives here these days is the one who passes out aspirin to the kids who get homesick and decide they don't like coming to a summer school. It's been years since this was a tuberculosis sanatorium. Sometimes, I forget it ever was. With the hills on either side of us climbing to the sky, the bandshell out front, the boardwalk running past the pavilions with their long, shaded porches and bright green lawns flowing down to the lake, it seems as if it must always have been a school of the arts.

I stub out my butt on the fire escape and flip it towards the parking lot. There's action down there now, people trooping from the writers' residence, carrying ball gloves and a kit bag with a couple of bats sticking from it, dumping everything in the back of a Chev wagon. Voices float up to me.

"We could maybe play a woman in right field," says a tall guy with a red beard. "Lorie's a better catch than most of us anyway."

"No," says a little guy who looks just a bit like Phil Rizzuto, except he's got a pot belly and is maybe twenty years over the hill. "It's not a mixed tournament. We've got to have at least nine guys."

"Well, Rhonda's kind of flat in the chest. Maybe, we could—"

"No dice! Try Harry. Maybe he's finished his story by now."

The lucky buggers, I think, off to a baseball tournament. Just the kind of thing I'd like to do, get out in the sun, whip the ball around, no music to think about, just legs and lungs working in the clean, country air. You know, I always wanted to be a ball player. Pop used to think it was a good idea too, but I guess it wasn't meant to be.

The writers are milling around the Chev when I see Greg Tilson looking up at me. Greg's from Thomas Gray Collegiate, same as me—only he's an

English teacher. A poet too, writes this modern stuff—you couldn't find a rhyme in it to save your soul. Of course, you can hardly blame a fellow for how he spends his spare time.

"I think I got our problem solved," says Greg, and he's coming up the fire escape two steps at a time. "You finished teaching for the day?"

"Might be—if it gets me playing baseball."

"Softball. There's a sports day up in Lipton. Just for hellery, we entered a team. The Fort San Writers. We're one man short."

"Everybody's a writer?"

"Sure," says Greg. "The little guy in the blue—he's our manager—famous novelist from Toronto."

"Jeez," I say. "He don't look like Pierre Berton."

"Come off it, Fred. You gonna play or not?"

"Sure thing. You got an extra glove?"

So we go down the fire escape and he introduces me to the team, only it sounds more like an introduction to advanced creative writing or something, 'cause what we've got here is four poets, two short story writers, a journalist and a playwright—not to mention the Toronto novelist. Whether there's any fielders, let alone a pitcher or a catcher, is something else again. But I don't really care. I haven't hit a baseball in four years—and then only at the staff barbecue—and I can hardly wait to get a bat in my hands.

I climb into the Chev along with Greg, three other poets, and the Toronto novelist, and we head out of the parking lot, all three cars spraying gravel just like teenagers. I'm even beginning to feel like a teenager again.

Our manager, the Toronto novelist who's sitting in the front seat, cranks his head around and stares at me as if he's trying to recognize me.

"You're not in the poetry class by any chance?"

"Oh."

He turns around and sits there, squirming for maybe sixty seconds, before leaning over to Greg. "We're listed as the Fort San Writers, aren't we?"

"It's okay, Eldon," says Greg. "We paid our fee. They don't care if we're the Fort San Poufs."

"Mmm . . . I suppose so."

"Look," says Greg. "I drove up to the Lipton pub last night with the registration. Soon as I said who we were, the whole bunch in there damn near bust a gut."

"Yeah?"

"Yeah. Five, six years ago, somebody put in a team from Fort San. They got beat twenty-three to zip. In three innings."

Even from behind I can see that Eldon is troubled. "Three innings?" he says.

"Sure. They got a rule that if one team's up by more than seven runs, the game's over after three innings. Speeds up the tournament."

"Well, I suppose that makes sense." Eldon pauses. "I'd sure hate to get knocked out in three innings though."

"Don't sweat it," says Greg. "This is just for laughs."

Eldon nods his head, slowly, as if he doesn't mean it, and slumps back in his seat. Pretty soon, he swivels around for another look at me. "You've never done any kind of writing, eh?

I grin at him. "Sure. Last summer. I wrote a solo for slide trombone."

"Good!" he says. "Good. Welcome aboard." His smile is so relaxed and generous, I decide not to tell him that nobody's ever seen the solo but me.

We've left the lake behind now, climbing out of the Qu'Appelle hills and onto prairie that stretches for miles into the north, so flat and wide you'd think the valley was way behind. Here the land is as smooth as a major league infield. It gets me remembering summers when I was a kid, evenings when Pop and I would lug a bat and a bag of balls over to the school grounds. There was just a softball diamond, but Pop would pace out the sixty feet and pitch to me. He had a bum leg, stiff and shorter than the other—his souvenir from the war, he said—it made his style awkward as a stickman in a wind storm, but after he reared back into this double-jointed wind-up of his and lunged forward with his clumsy kick, that ball was really flying! I'd stand against the backstop and he'd pitch twenty balls, moving them around so that I was hitting high and low, inside and outside. "Hit 'em where they're pitched," he'd say, and, being left-handed at the plate, I'd pull the inside pitches to right field, slapping the outside ones to left. When he'd thrown all the balls, I'd pick up the ones I'd missed and toss them back to him, then hit those too. When they were all gone, the tough part came. With his bad leg, Pop didn't believe in logging any extra yards, so I'd head for the outfield, trotting back and forth till I'd found all the balls. Only once did I come up short. That was one time when Pop gave me his high hard one, and I connected just right, the good feeling surging from bat to wrists and up into my shoulders, the crack of ball on wood carrying, I'll bet, all the way to Main Street. No use looking for that ball. It was just starting to level out when it hit the roof of the school. There was a good, loud whap when it struck; then it bounced out of sight. For all I know, it's up there yet. Pop looked sort of mad at first—like I shouldn't have hit his fast one—then he grinned and said, "Well, son, they ought to write that one up in the papers."

Of course, Mom didn't think much of talk like that. She figured that baseball was just foolishness, that when Pop stepped onto a ballfield he was being silly, stepping back into his childhood. "There's no future there," she used to say. "But you stick with your music, and you'll have a good job some day. It's nice clean work; you can teach and play too."

Pop always used to snort at that. "Look at the papers," he'd say. "Joe DiMaggio. Ted Williams. Stan Musial. But who ever read a headline about a trombone player?" He had her there, I guess.

By this time, ahead and to the left, I can see elevators against the sky. Lipton. And I start to get nervous.

The other two guys in the back seat must be religious or something 'cause they're talking about archetypes and epiphanies. Sure, I think, praying might help, but can anybody pitch?

I ask Eldon and he says, "We're all set. We've got a fellow pitches in a league in Saskatoon."

Greg throws him a worried look. "Who?"

"Cod."

"Cod?" For a second, I think we're going in the ditch. The car swerves to the right, shuddering and fish-tailing in the loose dirt on the shoulder of the road. "Jesus, Eldon, that's a slow-pitch league."

"Slow pitch?"

"They throw so you can hit. They have to loft it like a bloody beach ball.

"Oh," says Eldon.

There's a long pause.

"Well," he says, "I'm sure Cod has a fast one too."

I think I hear him mutter, "He better have," but maybe that's just me, wishing out loud.

Anyway, we turn left off this grid road that's been running straight north, and, just before Lipton, grab a right, bouncing over railway tracks and onto a road which is just two ruts that lead into a field and peter out.

367

This is it, all right. There's a big tent, with the sides rolled up and a Bingo game going full blast, the numbers almost lost in the roar whenever the loud-speakers pick up the wind. There's even a merry-go-round, faded wooden horses bolted to long poles that swing round and round over a series of belts and wheels, turning to music that must've been nice a dozen years ago, but is mostly static now. Still, there's a line of kids laughing and pushing like this is the world's greatest ride.

And there are three ball diamonds. We drive over to number three, which is just pasture grass, the base paths worn deep through years of running, but there's a screen behind home plate, and, behind that, three rows of bleachers. A big guy decked out with umpire's pad and mask lumbers towards us. "You guys the writers?" he says and laughs.

While we lug out the equipment, Eldon is staring at the other team. "My God," he says, "they're wearing uniforms. I thought this tournament was for ama-teurs."

The uniforms are gray, with black pin-stripes. When somebody pops a fly our way, the fellow who lopes over to catch it is an Indian. "Standing Buffalo," it says on his chest.

"They're from the reserve," says our catcher, whose name is Leon. "Probably just play in the odd tournament."

"Sure," says Eldon. "No reason why we can't beat 'em. Hell, even the Pirates beat the Cards once in a while."

I decide not to think about that.

It's almost time for our turn in the field when I see that we're going to have uniforms too. Three of the women writers pile out of a Volkswagen, its door left hanging open, and trot across the field to us. Two of them are carrying Summer School of the Arts

T-shirts, a nice bright orange that will maybe blind the opposing batters. The other one has a box under her arm.

"We whipped into Fort Qu'Appelle for ball caps," she says. And she grins. "They were a bit more than we expected. So we had to settle for these."

When she opens the box, I nearly faint, 'cause what she pulls out is a stack of engineer's caps, the kind they used to wear to drive those old steam locomotives. Casey at the bat all right, but we'll look more like Casey Jones.

I take a good look at our team. Our right fielder is a shrimp with skin so pale he must do all his work at night, and by candlelight at that. Still he seems like an athlete beside our centre fielder, who has a black Afro hairdo and a huge beard which make his head look twice as big as his chest. His eyes look like they're peeking through a thicket. With his engineer's cap perched on all that hair, he looks positively top heavy. I swear, if he tries to run, all that weight is liable to flip him hair over heels in a perfect somersault. He's one of the poets. In fact, when we take the field for warm-ups, I realize our outfield is all poets. Eldon is hoping to keep them out of harm's way, I guess. I wonder if he gave any thought to having three water-boys. The infield better play deep 'cause sure as hell they'll be out there trying to dream up a fancy meta-phor for softball when one goes flying over their heads. Our pitcher is going to be worse off than Charlie Brown.

Eldon is hitting grounders to the infield. The first hit to me is a fast one. I get my glove on it, but it pops right out—like it's made of rubber or something—so I scramble for it and throw too quickly, heaving it a good ten feet over the first baseman's head.

"Some arm," says Eldon. "We better play you at third."

"Just a little rusty," I say. "I'll get the next one down." Which I do. Hitting Wally, the first baseman, in the shins on one bounce. I don't know, but I *used* to play this game pretty well. Still, even making errors, it feels good to play again. My next throw is better, and Wally stretches for it and has it. He's long and lean and quick. We've got a real first baseman, I see—and a catcher too. Leon behind the plate is leaping out of his crouch and, smooth as quicksilver, whipping the ball down to second. Laying it right on the bag.

I'm sort of half-watching Leon when there's another crack of the bat and Eldon knocks one between my legs. I'm slow getting down and just wave goodbye at it.

"Hey there, coach," says an Indian who's leaning against the backstop, his grin so big he could swallow home plate. "You writer fellas wouldn't wanna make a little wager on this game, would you?" And he laughs, the umpire chortling along with him.

Eldon is about to drive another ball, but he turns around real quick. Leon is even quicker. "No," he says, "we're not betting men."

"I think mebbe I see why," says the Indian.

Before Eldon can get a word in, Leon hustles him over to our side of the field. I didn't think poets had reflexes like that, but I guess Leon is the exception that proves the rule.

Eldon is furious, his jaw working away at ninety miles an hour on whatever he's chewing. Gum, probably, though it looks just like chewing tobacco. He's not happy with Leon either, but he keeps his voice down so I can barely hear him. "Look. I don't mind losing a bet, but nobody insults the team. I mean, how'll the guys feel if I won't even bet on them."

I don't hear what Leon says, and I don't care. Eldon may be a writer, but I like the guy. From now

370

on, I decide, no grounders are going through my legs.

A minute later Eldon calls us in for a quick huddle before the game begins. While he's talking, he makes a point of slapping us all on the shoulder or the back. "We've got a good chance," he says. "The way I see it, these reserve guys are over the hill. Look at the bellies on them. Probably train on beer and pretzels."

"Sure," I say, punching my glove. "We can take 'em."

Eldon grins, but nobody says a word. The three outfielders stare at me like I'm part of a line that doesn't quite rhyme. Or, even worse, one that does.

"I almost had some money down on you," Eldon finally says, "but Leon put the kibosh on a good thing. No matter. They get first bats, then we go to work." He claps his hands together, once, good and loud. "Okay. Go get 'em."

We trot onto the field, and Cod takes his warm-up pitches. He's wearing these little, round granny glasses and they suit him perfectly, 'cause he's throwing just like my grandma would—*if* her arthritis were a lot worse. He lofts each pitch into the air almost as if he's trying to knock off the crow that's right now circling the infield, his cawing like an old geezer's laughter. Yeah, and I can see what he's laughing at too.

I nearly break a leg getting over to Cod. "Jeez, Cod," I say, "hadn't you better try your fast one?"

He turns to me with this sheepish look on his face.

"That's it," he says. "I didn't want to tell Eldon. He's taking this pretty serious. I mean, nobody else can pitch at all."

"What're we gonna do?"

"Well," he says, "I could throw my slow ball."

I'm still trying to think of a comeback when I look down at home plate and see the first batter, just itching to get at it. He's about six feet tall and built like a granary. I head back to third and get ready to protect myself.

Cod goes into this screwy little wind-up, curling his left leg over his right and his arm behind his back and then tosses the ball like he's pitching to some girl in grade three. That batter is so eager to clobber that ball, he's all the way around and flat on his ass before the pitch is half-way to the plate.

"Stee-rike one!" says the ump.

"Hey, hey, the ol'sucker ball," I yell, pretending this is how we've got it planned.

When the batter dusts off his pants, he looks mad, glaring first at me and then at Cod. This time he waits before he swings, his left foot striding down toward me at third like he wants to squash me into the dirt. Then crack! and before I can get out of the way, my hand's stinging and there's the ball—caught tight in the pocket. One out, and I don't even have to throw to first. Which may be just as well.

The next guy up is slim and agile, muscles like elastics under his dark skin. Probably got that way bulldogging cows or steers or whatever they do on the reserve. Anyway, he goes after the first three pitches, coming around too soon on each, and that's two down.

He drags his bat back to where his team's sitting on the grass. When he squats down, I hear him say, "You got to wait for it. It's even slower than it looks."

The next batter is strong-looking, but fat, his stomach wobbling as he kicks out a spot beside the plate. He takes a couple of preliminary swings, then settles into a stance that looks comfortable and dangerous. We may be in trouble.

"Time out!"

I see an Indian stand up behind the backstop.

"Time out," he says again. "There's something hanging over the plate."

There's a roar of laughter from his cronies in the bleachers, but the batter just pats his belly and says, "Gonna be hangin' over first base in a minute." Then he eases back into his stance, looking even more relaxed than before.

Relaxed enough to get his timing just right, I guess, 'cause the first pitch comes back about ten times faster than it went in. In fact, it's still picking up speed when it disappears over a bluff of poplars in deep centre field. It'll probably come down about Prince Albert. This Indian is laughing so hard, it takes him nearly three minutes to get around the bases. When he comes past third, he says, "A pitcher like that does wonders for race relations."

I hear Eldon yell, "It's only one, guys, only one."

Then Leon starts in: "Just a little luck, Cod, babee. That's all. Pitch ball, babee, pitch ball, we get 'em, we got 'em."

And the ball comes floating in like another balloon just waiting to be popped, and wham! there it goes again. Except this time somebody's after it, running hell bent for election, and when the force of gravity finally remembers how it's supposed to work and brings the ball down, he's right there to gather it in. One of those poets, if you can believe it. The fellow with the Afro.

We come in for our licks, and Eldon's feeling pretty good. "One run," he says. "We can get that back easy."

I look at their pitcher, and I'm not so sure. Like their big hitter, he's got too much pot hanging over his belt, but I notice it doesn't get in the way of his arm when he whips it around in a windmill that sends the ball slashing across the plate. One of the outfielder poets is looking at him too. He's also beginning to look a little green.

"Don't worry," says Greg. "I can hit him." And he does, blooping the second pitch over the shortstop's head for a single. Well, like I said, he's really a teacher, not a poet. Besides, I seem to remember him hitting the ball pretty good at our staff barbecue. The next batter is the Afro, all that hair balanced crazily between man and cap. I guess he's a real poet 'cause he swings and misses the first three pitches, each one faster than the other, maybe one of them in the strike zone. He trots back to our side, looking relieved that he's escaped with his life.

"I like a fellow who stands up to the plate," says the umpire, who seems to be enjoying himself. While the catcher is gloating over this, Greg steals second. Nobody even notices he's going till he pops up out of a cloud of dust, and there he is. Pretty as a picture. One of these poets could maybe improve on that simile, but I'll bet he couldn't move like Greg.

We've got another of them at the plate, I see. I don't know what it is about these fellows, but they sure like to grow a crop of hair on their faces. Why, this guy's got muttonchops, make him look like he's stumbled out of another century. He isn't taking any chances on getting hit either, 'cause he's right at the edge of the batter's box and leaning back for all he's worth. He's got his bat on his shoulder, and that's exactly where it stays. Still, six pitches and they walk him.

Leon is up next, an athlete at last. He lets the first pitch go by him, maybe wanting to see what this guy has on the ball. When he lines the next one to centre field, Greg is off and running, coming around third like a greyhound after a rabbit. In fact, he's across the plate while the fielder's still bobbling the ball. Ol' muttonchops would've made it too, but he's busy

374

watching the juggling act in centre field and doesn't see Eldon who's waving him on so fast his arm is about ready to whirl out of its socket. Muttonchops finally scuttles down to third after he hears Leon pounding up behind. Leon stops at second and spits in the dirt. I guess he'd rather have a triple.

Next up is Wally, who takes a good cut, fouling three pitches into the backstop, which—I notice now—has more holes than mesh. Every time he fouls one, three rows of bleachers look like a peanut scramble—except everyone's ducking *away* from what's thrown. Wally finally walks, and we've got the bases loaded and only one out. The next batter is another poet; so right away there's two out. At least we've still got the bases loaded.

Enough poets, I think, this has got to stop. And it does. The next one up is me. When I step into the batter's box, I'm not sure this is such a good idea. I mean, the dirt's worn away beside the plate and it's like standing in a hole and trying to hit a ball coming from an arm that's working like a sling. Sheesh, I think, at least with these poets, nobody expects them to hit. The first pitch comes at my head like a tomahawk and I'm so busy protecting my scalp, I sit right back on the seat of my pants.

"Stee-rike!" says the ump. He grins down at me. "Caught the inside corner."

That must be one hell of a curve, I think as I stand up, trying not to feel as foolish as I must look. The pitcher is laughing so hard he almost misses the ball when the catcher lobs it back to him. He is so bloody confident he looks a lot like Lightning Johnson, the best pitcher there ever was in the Moose Jaw Church League. And that's okay too, 'cause back in grade eight, I suddenly remember, I was the only guy on the Trinity Tigers who could always hit Johnson. I used to stand at the plate and grin at him. I never knew whether the grin made him nervous or me brave, but something worked, 'cause against Lightning Johnson I had a batting average of .623.

So I step back into the box and give this pitcher such a grin he maybe wonders what's wrong with my face. His pitch is inside, but it can hit me before I budge even an inch.

"Ball one," says the ump, and the catcher swears once, quietly.

"No swearing," says the ump. "I run a clean game."

Which gives me even more reason to smile.

Yeah, I'm grinning wide now, damn near laughing out loud, and that pitcher is looking a bit worried. Maybe he's got reason. His next pitch is fast and chest high, and I'm a little late with the swing, but the sound and the feel are right when I connect, and the ball takes off down the third base line like Willie Mays just hit it. I've got to admit, it feels so good, I almost forget to run, but a minute later I slide into third.

I'm safe with a triple, and this is as close to heaven as I've been since grade school. The three guys who've just crossed home plate are jumping around like they're nuts, and Eldon is so excited he comes out of the coach's box and hugs me. Right there in front of all those people. "Yessir," he says. "Poetry in motion."

And it's not over yet. A minute later, I'm home, and everybody's hitting. By the time they finally get out number three, the score is seven-one for us.

We're busy laughing and clapping and pounding one another on the shoulders, almost forgetting that we've only played the one inning. Eldon somehow manages to get us all back on the field and in the same positions again, but we're still kind of floating over the grass. What brings us down to earth is the first batter who watches two balls waft by him and then slams the third into the outfield poplars.

Cod looks shaken. He takes off his granny glasses and starts rubbing them on his T-shirt. Anything to postpone his next pitch, I guess, but right away Leon starts up his chatter behind the plate.

"Nemmer mind, Cod babee. We got this one. Pitch ball, babee. Chuck her here. We get him for you, Cod, get him quick, get him slick, get him easy!"

Cod throws one wide pitch, then waves for Leon, who tosses off his mask and trots out to the rubber. They stand there, talking, gesturing with their hands. Then they start to grin.

Eldon sidles towards third and glares at them, his lower lip shoved out like maybe he's Leo Durocher or something. When he can't take it any more, he tugs at the peak on his cap and says, "What the hell is that all about? Go check."

I trot over, and I can hardly believe what I'm hearing.

"For Pete's sake, you guys," I say, "this is a *ball* game."

They just look at me.

"Listen," I say to Cod. "I know you haven't got a fast ball, but can't you put a little spin on it or something?"

"Sure," says Cod, "the old sucker ball."

Leon laughs. "Chucker chatter," he says and walks back to the plate, pounding his fist in his mitt.

Eldon's waiting right there when I get back to third. "Well?" he says.

"Poetry—for Chrissakes!" I shake my head. "Cod's telling Leon he should write a bloody poem. Fulla the things that catchers yell to pitchers." Eldon's face twists up like maybe he thinks everyone but him and me belong in a cuckoo ward. "Yeah," I add, "he's gonna call it 'Chucker Chatter'."

Well, Leon really hits the chatter now, getting

fancy, working on his poem, I guess, the words pouring out like magic.

"Come on babee, come on babee, you and me, babee, shoot it to me now. Groove it, eh? Move it, babee. Blow it by his nose."

Damned if Cod doesn't have that batter swinging like a barn door too. It's just like Leon has him convinced. He gets a little spin on the ball, and a little speed. Strikes him out on four pitches. And Leon is really singing now.

"We get 'em for you, babee. Team'll do it for you. Dream team, babee. On a beam. Shoot here, Cod. Pitch smoke, fella, pitch fire. Now you hot, babee. Burn him, burn him, burn him!"

I wouldn't believe it if I didn't see it. I mean, he must have *them* convinced too, 'cause in the next two innings there are five towering flies to the outfield, and those poets are bounding around like gazelles, dodging gopher holes without even a glance at the ground, snaring every ball that's hit. And that Afro, why, he doesn't look strong enough to catch a ball, let alone run after one, but he chases a fly that looks like it's gone forever. Man, he's out there, dodging poplar branches when he finally makes the catch. It's like Willie Mays in the '54 series, and I'm not ashamed to say it either.

"It's a plot," says one Indian, the only one to get as far as third base. "You knew we were death on fastballs and brought in a specialist."

"Sure," I say, "we had our scouts check things out."

"Injuns send out scouts too—with war parties." He looks mean when he says it, but right away he breaks into a grin. "We musta scouted the wrong teams though. Overlooked you guys." Then he really grins. "Good thing *your* scouts forgot to mention you should bet on this game."

"Buddy," says I, "if we hang on to this lead, I'll buy you a beer."

"Buddy," says he, "if you do, I am gonna need a beer."

Things are going so well that somebody even drives back to Fort San for the school P.R.O. to take some pictures.

Well, I don't mind admitting that I get up to bat once more, with men on second and third this time. After my triple down the third base line, they're all playing me to that side, but I've got my timing now and knock the ball over first, and that's it. We've got an eight run cushion, and the game is over. As I'm taking off for first, I hear the umpire giving Leon the needle: "Should've took that bet, catcher."

And ain't it the truth? Still, we've won, and that's all that matters. Eldon is so worked up he runs right across the field, almost beats me to first base to shake my hand.

"Great!" he says. "Just great!"

We're all milling around now, socking each other, boasting a little, maybe, floating even higher off the ground, when I notice the look of purest joy on Eldon's face. "You know," he says, "even if we lose the next game, we'll still have a better record than the Blue Jays had against the Twins."

Well, we do lose the next game, but that's okay. I mean, nobody can expect more than one miracle a day. Besides, there's something else that happens.

By the end of the summer, half the weeklies in the province end up running the same picture. It's a photo of me slamming the last hit of the game, concentration, co-ordination like a teenage athlete, every muscle tense, a swing like Stan Musial.

Maybe the headline does say, "Poet slams triple," but—what the hell—I guess that's okay too.

DAVE MARGOSHES

Gag!

Know the one about the Polish comedian?

That's me, honest, I'm Poland's greatest comedian. Don't laugh, I haven't done anything yet. So you haven't heard of me, big deal, I'm frequently overshadowed by the Polish national baseball team. And, anyway, who would ever mention a name like Bzykzwlki? But, no, seriously, I am, Poland's greatest comedian. You think Lech Walesa's a good stand-up comic? Sure, these days everybody laughs when Lech cracks a joke. But in the old days, after some of his command performances, he wasn't even a very good *kneel*-up comic. But, hey, seriously, I am, I *really* am Poland's greatest comedian. Go on, ask me what's the secret of my success. Go on, go ahead, don't be shy. Ask.

"What's the secret of . . . "

"Timing."

That's it. Great, eh? I mean, did you get it? *Timing*? Sure, that's one of mine. I've got a million of 'em, like Milton Berle used to say—*Berle*, did I write lines for him? Is the Pope Polish? Whoops, I gotta watch it with the Pope gags, Jesus don't like it, he gimme the evil eye, that pain-and-suffering look he likes so much. "*Kind* jokes, Wally," Jesus says. So forget I said that. But what I was getting at, I wrote so many gags, so many funny lines over the years—almost forty years in the business, stage, clubs, radio and TV—who can keep track? But that one, that one I just did, the Polish comedian, that's still my favourite because, well, it says it all, know what I mean? *Timing*.

People don't realize, the layman, I mean, that being funny is a science. I've known them all, all the

380

really great funnymen of the past, you know, last forty years? Berle, like I said, Benny, Gleason, Hope, Skelton, all those guys, I wrote gags for 'em all—not these punks like Leno and Piscopo call themselves comics these days. But what I mean to say is, some people look at those guys and call 'em artists, *artists*, fer Chris'sake—oops, sorry, Jesus, there I go again—but, you know what I mean? *Artists*, like they was some kinda opera singer or fruity ballet dancer. Shit, what those men are ain't artists, it's *scientists*. I mean, look, they pick a subject, they *study* it, they keep their *eyes* open—empiricism, know what I mean?—and they got their timing down pat, of course, just like Nixon tried, know what I mean? That guy, he saw *Deep Throat* six times, but he still couldn't get it down Pat. *See what I mean?* Slip the old gag in, just like a knife, clean and smooth like the old shiv, it's outta your bod and back in my pocket before you feel any pain, before there's even any blood. You think *any* guy steps on a banana peel and busts his ass, that's funny? *You* try it sometime, see how funny it is. Skelton, he does it, it's funny. *Timing*. Science. Even Jesus recognizes the truth of that. With him, timing is everything. Of course, you gotta have the material, too, or the timing don't amount to diddlysquat, and Jesus, well, his material ain't exactly been the best, which is why (ahem, ahem) he's turned to me. And, I have to admit, I can use the business.

The pickings—until last week, that is, when I got religion, if you'll pardon the expression, and started working steady—have been *lousy*.

The name's Stanhope, by the way, but call me Wally. Wilbur Riley Stanhope. That's the kind of handle you'd expect on maybe the governor of Tennessee, right? Or a book reviewer in the *Times* Sunday section. Guy with a name like that, he went to *Haavaad* and was a commander in the navy during the war, right?

Nope. Grade three, that's me, and the in-fan-tree. The old man, he was Stan Stanhope—can you believe that? No class in that at all—and the Wilbur Riley, well, the old lady, she was a Riley and crazy as all those Cabbagetown Irishers, which sort of explains the Wilbur. That was the name of the first boy she ever had a crush on, back when she was in bloomers and pinafores, or whatever they wore back in those days. So whaddya gonna do?

Wilbur Riley Stanhope. You say it out loud a coupla times, you can see it's got class, real weight to it. Or *schmaltz*, depending on your point of view, as Jesus says. Still, it's a good byline for a literary type, so I never changed it. So maybe what I do ain't in the running for the Nobel, it's writing just the same. I'd stake what I got against Hemingway and those other highbrow cats any day. Me, I write for the people.

That's what Jesus said, the first time we talked. That's what got him innerested, he said. "You've got something I need, Wally," Jesus said. "That common touch."

I'm sitting on the patio at the Pit, at a table made out of skinny little skinned logs, under one of those Cinzano umbrellas, just inhaling a cold draught and scoffing up the free goobers, when I feel these eyes on me, I mean the *real* peepers. I was feeling bad because of something with the waitress, so maybe I was a little slow, but when I looked up, there he was, at the little log bench on the other side of the patio, against the cedar fence, where I *know* he wasn't the last time I looked.

"It really bothers you, doesn't it?" he said.

"Sure," I said—and, I swear, man, it didn't even *occur* to me that I didn't know this cat, that there wasn't any *way* he could have known what I was thinking about, although I guess I had on a sour puss that was telling anyone with eyes *something* was eating me. I just shrugged, like we were old pals and we'd been talking about something and there'd been a lull in the conversation. "No percentage in being mean."

"*Percentage.*" He said it like it was a word he hadn't used for a while and had forgotten how serviceable it could be. "Does everything have to have a percentage for you?"

"Sure. Why not? But it ain't no big deal." All that had happened was, coming through the dining room to get to the patio, a waitress had stopped me, a new girl. "Can I help you?" Maybe it was the rejection slip I'd just picked up in the mail eating me, but it seemed like such a dumb question, I just stared at her, a sweet, dopey little girl no more than seventeen, with sweet little tits hard as apples under her T-shirt, probably on her first day and eager as sweat to please. "Well, I *think* I can manage to walk the rest of the way myself, and what you *could* do for me ain't in your job description, honey." Her face sort of caved in, like the air going out of a balloon all at once, and I went on through the French doors and out onto the patio. I was already feeling lousy by the time I sat down. She sort of looked the other way when she came out to take my order, and when I said "Hey, sorry, kid, I was just kidding around," it just seemed to make it worse.

"You seem to think it is a big deal," this cat says, but, again, it was so natural, I didn't do no double-takes or slap my forehead and shout out, "Hey, this fellow is reading my thoughts."

Instead, I smiled and raised my mug in a barroom salute. "It's an old show biz rule, you know? Why be cruel when you can be kind?"

Jesus didn't have a glass to return the toast with, but he nodded his head, which was hairy, top and bottom, and was topped off with one of those baseball caps everyone's wearing these days. This one was red and had a white badge on the front that said "Case Drilling."

"So you're in show business?"

"Sure." I shrugged. "Well, I *used* to be. Stanhope's the name, gag's the game, but how many stand-ups you see on TV these days? Good ones, I mean." That was the truth, the whole, bloody, painful truth, though I was a little surprised to hear myself blurt it out. "Those turkeys on 'Saturday Night Live' and 'SCTV', they write their *own* material, if you can call it that, though I gotta admit that Martin guy had talent, but he's strictly movies now, and Belushi, his lines were always lousy but he had timing, great timing. But what else *is* there? Everything's sitcoms these days—and you call *those* things funny?—even Johnny Carson's gone, and that Leno, my sister's funnier'n him." I paused for a breath and a swig of beer and to size this cat up. These baseball cap types aren't usually too bright, but he seemed to be with me. "I'm into a lot of magazine work right now, and special projects."

That was no lie. The magazine stuff I've done lately, cartoon gags, ain't exactly James Thurber, and the special projects, they were greeting cards, the lowest of the low—stuff like "Don't give up the ship, there still might be booze aboard. Get well soon"—but it was a living. Sort of. I wouldn't be living out here in the boonies if it was a better one, but you don't hear me weeping in my beer, do ya?

"How would you like to do some work for me?" Jesus said, and all of a sudden I was at attention. One of the waitresses went by, not the one I'd snapped at but another little fluff with an ass tight as a mousetrap, and I didn't even *see* her, let alone take my eyeballs out for some exercise, the way I usually do. *Work* is just one of those magic words, like sex, especially when you haven't had any, of either, for a while.

I took a closer look at the kid. He was wearing jeans with a hole in one knee and a T-shirt that a grease monkey might have used for a hand towel, scruffy workboots and that goofy cap, and was slim built but with powerful arms bulging out of the T-shirt's rolled sleeves, and I guess that's why I'd thought he was young, but behind the beard there was a face that looked like it'd seen a lot of service, with a nose hooked just enough to make it interesting, a wide, friendly-looking mouth and eyes so clear and blue I just knew they had to be contacts. But looks don't mean anything these days—hey, just cast yer peepers at yers truly dooley, fer example—and he coulda been one of those rock stars, easy, or a manager—Christ, he coulda been the bloody Rolling Fucking *Stones*'s manager, for all I knew, or a talent scout from Vegas, even the head of some big label.

"Hey, I'm pretty busy, but, whatcha got? Whaddya need?"

Jesus smiled, that famous smile I've been reading about in the pile of paperbacks he's got over at his place, that can transfix you, the thin, friendly lips curved upward in something closer to apple pie and the eyes—turns out they *aren't* contacts—looking right through you—though I've since discovered it's all a popsicle illusion caused by his nearsightedness, for Chris'sake—*ouch*, sorry, Jesus. "Writing," he said. "I'm looking for a writer."

"Wha, you mean PR? Something for the outfit you work for? I really don't do that kind . . . "

"Gags," Jesus interrupted. "I'm looking for a gag writer."

We looked at each other and it occurred to me suddenly that, even though he was sitting clear across the patio, a good twenty feet away, and was speaking in a soft, almost mumbling voice, I could hear him fine, clear and plain as the pitch on the radio.

"Well, hey, kid, you come to the right man if it's gags you want. Whaddya got, a stand-up routine with one of these rock bands plays around here?" The Pit itself has bands at night, I knew, though I'd never made the long walk down from the cabin except in the afternoon when I liked to get the mail and stoke up on carbos with the peanuts.

"No, I don't do that sort of thing," Jesus said.

"You don't, eh? Just like keeping your buddies rolling in the aisles up there on that high iron, that it?"

"No, that's not it," Jesus said. He dropped his eyelids for a second and looked down, that famous pose, all humility and premonitions of suffering, you know the one I mean, and I sucked up a great big slug of beer into my trap, so fast and hard some of it missed and came dribbling down onto my chin, making me feel like an idiot, though that don't take much, as dear old Pappy used to say.

"That's not it, eh?" I drummed my fingers along one of the logs of the table top.

"No," Jesus said.

"Yeah, well." I let my eyes swing up to take in the rays of sun filtering through the leafy canopy swaying over the patio. "What *do* you do?"

"Don't you know, Wally?" Jesus said, his lips not moving.

Heard the one about Jesus and the farmer's daughter?

No? Well, you won't hear it from me. Never had any qualms before, no taboos, not a sacred moo-moo in a carload, but I'm a changed man now, got religion, you might say.

Working steady, too. Though for little more than beer and peanuts. Jesus is a little short.

And hard? That Jesus, he's a bastard of a paymaster,

won't take more than one out of every ten, maybe twenty lines I come up with—and the ones he *does* like aren't usually the ones I'd've picked. "Standards, Wally," he tells me, "high standards, *quality*, that's the secret of this comeback. We can't just be good, we can't just be *great*, we have to dazzle them. Standards, that's everything."

"No, Jesus,"—we're on a first-name basis, he and I—"No, Jesus," I tell him, "*Timing* is everything."

"I *know* that, Wally." He looks at me pityingly, like a father who's explained a very simple chore to a child dozens of times. "The *timing* is right for *quality*."

Okey dokey, can't argue with that.

Jesus and I and this chick Marylou spend a lot of time together, brainstorming, running things up the flagpole, trying out routines. I come up with the gags and Jesus works them into his patter, I give with the feedback, as all the smart types say these days. His idea, see, is that there's no percentage in the pulpit anymore, that the true church is the TV screen, that the real men of the cloth aren't the stand-ups, so much—he agrees with me they're a dying breed—but the *personalities*, the Carsons and Lettermens and Halls, even the Donahues, and, maybe even more than them, the regulars who come on their shows. That's Jesus's goal: first to make a bit of a name for himself, on the club circuit, then to get onto Oprah, say, where he can really deliver with both barrels, the way Dr. Ruth does. Marylou's role in all this is a *little* fuzzy, to me, at least. She has all the devoted, doting marks of the girlfriend, and she's okay to have around—sweet, cute, though not exactly what I'd call a blood-boiler—but there seems to be something missing in the old chemistry between Jesus and her. Personally, I think she's a prop, in sort of the same category as the pushups and workouts with the iron he's constantly doing to build up the old upper body.

"Image, Wally," he sometimes tells me, "is every-thing," and I gotta admit, he knocks me out with the scope of his mind, that ability he has to see how things fit together, how it's all part of one big thing.

We work in this old cabin Jesus rents for a song on the other side of the river from my sister's place, this really battered old log thing that must have been pretty rickety even when the homesteader who put it up first stood back to admire his handiwork. Some-times we go out back and Marylou and I sit around in these old lawn chairs with chipped green paint, but Jesus, he likes to climb up and sit on a platform he's built along this long snaky limb of a poplar, about eight to ten feet up. He sits there, with his legs dangling over the side, leaning over and smiling down at us, munching on an apple, which is about the only thing he ever eats, his hair puffed over around his ears, never missing a word we say, never having to raise his voice. I guess it makes him feel good being up there, makes him feel like he's closer to heaven or something. Or maybe he's just a big overgrown kid getting his kicks playing Tarzan, I don't know.

It tickles me that we had to come to this out-of-the-way little pocket of lint to bump into each other. Some ways, we're a lot alike, Jesus and me. We're both *wordsmiths*—and ain't *that* a dandy word?—and we both live by our wits. We're both broke, have seen better days and hope to see them again (though in that department I doff my topper to my pal's lofty aspirations). And we're both on the run, though in *this* area I don't think Jesus can hold a candle to me, not with nineteen months of back alimony constantly breathing down my neck. I'm here laying low, trying to keep sober and enjoying the rent-free hospitality of my square sister and her good hubby's summer place and the bounty of their freezer and larder, hoping to keep out of the way of temptation, bad companions, process servers and bad habits. That's a challenge that's easy enough to master, even for me, when the nearest town where you could indulge in those backsliders is thirty-five miles away and Louella left me here with no more transportation than my feet and my thumb, and no more money than will buy me stamps and one cold beer a day at the Pit—*if* I'm careful. Jesus is here getting his shit together, as the youngsters say these days, though "getting his *act* together" is what Marylou says, always careful not to offend. "Preparing myself," is what the boy himself says, giving us one of those faraway gazes he sort of falls into every once in a while, when something someone says sends him spinning back into a memory. But it all amounts to the same thing.

Here's where the differences between us start to show up. Me, I just wanted to cool out for a while, get a toehold on the greeting card racket and stay outa harm's way for the summer, then head back to Tarana for the winter practically a new man. What's on Jesus' mind is the comeback trail, all the way. Unless you were born and raised on Mars, you know his story: guy with a vision, rabblerouser, catches on, over-reaches, comes to a bad end, sets off a movement. It's like the James Dean story, or Marilyn, even bigger in death than they were in life, only *they* don't get a chance to do it over again. That's what Jesus wants. He's not satisfied he's got a third of the people in the world thinking he's some kind of big poohbah, *some* of them even following *some* of the rules he set up. He says the scribes didn't set it all down right. He says there's been a lot of confusion, misinterpretation. He says a lotta people who oughta know better, who oughta *do* better, are full of shit. He says a whole lotta shit's gonna come down if people don't start flying right. Okay, okay, all of this sounds familiar, I know, like a needle stuck in some send-right-away-to-this-address TV pitchman's evangical record album, Billy Graham running off at the mouth on some summer rerun of his Edmonton crusade. The difference here is that Jesus, he's serious. He really wants to run it all over again, his whole act, drastically revised. Beefed up.

"This time, Wally," he tells me, "we're going to get it *right.*"

And to that end he's got me bustin' my chops. Hour on end, at his dump or at my sister's cabin, from as soon as I roll outta the sack in the *ayem* till way past midnight, I'm racking my cork scribbling down those gags, those gems of mirth and humour as my agent used to call them, back in the good old days when I *needed* an agent, even an accountant. And do you think I then sleep the solid, righteous sleep of the just, knowing I earned my daily bread well and truly? Hell, no—I toss and turn, sleeping in fits and waking whenever inspiration shines her sexy little flashlight through my dreams. I keep a pad and pencil by the bedside, and some of my best creations are there when I wake up in the morning. Sometimes, I can't even remember writing them.

Jesus is some tough audience, that's the problem. *No* ethnic jokes—well, gimme a break, willya? I mean, it's been years since I wrote a joke about a black guy or a Jew that makes them look bad, I'm no fool, but Jesus, he won't even stand for a line that makes them look *good*, won't even let one little bitsy Polish joke get by, no Mafia stuff, not even a snigger about Irish and drinking. *No* fag jokes—he's *really* hot about that. No mother-in-law jokes, no politician jokes, no *dirty* jokes—well, gimme *some* credit for brains, eh? But not even the teensiest little double entendre. So what's left? Not much, lemme tell ya. "Nothing that makes fun of anyone, Wally," Jesus says, "nothing that makes *anyone* feel in *any* way diminished."

"But, Jesus," I tell him, "that's what humour's all about, man. I mean, not in a cruel way or anything, but the reason they laugh at the banana peel shtik is because somebody falls down and goes boom. You take away that bang, or the threat of it, solly Cholly, no laugh. I mean, that's what it's all about."

Jesus just looks at me, gives me that famous they-know-not-what-they-do smile. "Solly, Cholly, not this time, Wally," he says. "This time we find a better way."

Hey, listen to this one.

There's this whale, see, swimming around in the North Sea, and he comes into the English Channel and he bumps into an old mate of his, this giant squid.

"Charlie," he says, "'ow's things, mate? *Say*, you're looking a bit peaked."

"Oooh an' I've got this splittin' 'eadache, now, 'aven't I, Guv," says the squid. "I've gotta get over t'the other sida the channel an' I can barely move me arms."

"Well," says the whale, "that's no thicket, mate, just hop on me back and I'll give ya a ride."

So he does, the squid, hops on, and the whale takes off across the channel, to the English side. About halfway there, he runs across this shark he knows, another old mate.

"'ow ya doin', Guv?" asks the shark.

"Tiptop," says the whale. " 'ey, lissen, mate, glad I run into ya. I got that sick squid I owe ya."

She just looks at me blank for a second, eyes big and round as saucers, the colour of strawflowers, her upper lip moving almost imperceptibly, like she's telling herself the punchline over and over, trying to absorb the meaning of it through osmosis. Then her face breaks wide open, like sun suddenly shouldering through the clouds, and her mouth twists into a pickle-biter. "That's *terrible*," she says.

"Terrible? It's terrific."

"Jesus will hate it."

"Oh, yeah, sure. But that one ain't for Jesus. That one was for you."

When I came around this morning, Jesus was gone, packed his knapsack and split to the mountains for a few days, Marylou says. "He needs to do some thinking."

"Thinking? That's what he does all the time around *here*. That's what we all do together."

"That's what he said." She shrugs, her breasts rising under the tanktop like water flowing under ice as her little bare shoulders go up.

"Yeah, well. That boy does too *much* thinking, know what I mean? He didn't say anything to me about going away."

"Well, he didn't say anything to *me*, either." She looks real cute when she pouts, Marylou, her lips puckered like the little curl on the top of a Dairy Queen, just waiting to be licked off. "He just threw a few things together this morning and went off. Said he'd be back in a few days. Said you should just go ahead with what you're doing, whatever *that* is."

"Jesus said that?"

"No, *I* said *that*, silly, he just . . . "

"Okay, okay." I put up a traffic cop's hand and we sort of glared at each other for a coupla seconds. "I guess we got *that* outta our systems, whatever it was. Whaddya say we start all over, eh?"

Since then, we've been like a coupla kids let loose around the house with the folks away, telling jokes, going through skits, scoffing up peanut butter jelly sandwiches, just generally horsing around, *not quite* grab-assing. Not quite, but it looks like we might be working up to it.

392

Jesus and Marylou, I don't know what's with them, but it ain't all there, if you know what I mean. Frankly, I don't think they're having it on, which has gotta make you wonder about Jesus, since he's a healthy enough looking stud, with hair all over his body and all the other signs—except that signs don't mean squat these days—because Marylou, well, she got all the signs too, but in her case they're in neon, the kind of flashing signs that can keep you up nights. She's got tits on her like puppies, squirming around all the time, an ass da Vinci could have painted and skin that's got electric circuits racing back and forth on it. Her face maybe ain't the greatest thing since sliced bread, but it's got those heavenly eyes and that mouth when she pouts, and the kid's body is just a hormone factory where the workers have gone wild. But I don't think those hormones have had much of a chance to do anything but bounce against each other like pinballs, not since she's been hooked up with Jesus, anyway. I got eyes, and I see what I see, know what I mean? I been around—two or three times, to tell the truth.

I was thinking Jesus and me have things in common. Toss Marylou in and we're three regular peas in a pod. She's a runaway, I guess, don't say nothing about where she's from or been, don't say *nuthin'* that has anything to do with anything except here and now. Seventeen, maybe, *couldn't* be more than nineteen, tops, though it's hard to tell from the distance *I'm* looking through. At first, I can't say I thought much about her one way or the other, strictly background music. Now, I'm not so sure. I am, it pains me to admit, six or seven or fourteen times older than her, but I ain't dead yet, I don't have the problem I think maybe Jesus got and I got a few hormones of my own cooking away.

Which reminds me. "Was reading in the paper

the other day, these scientists over in Europe, they figured out a new way to make hormones."

"Oh, yeah?" Marylou says, giving me that blank look.

"Yeah, they get these real big lumberjacks, see, guys with shlongs like this . . . " I hold my hands apart, like a fisherman telling his buddies a story, and I'm starting to crack up, but I got my eyes fixed on Marylou, watching for signs.

"Yeah . . . " she says, this big impatient frown spreading across her pan like she can't figure out why I don't get on with the story, and then, all of a sudden, I got my eyes and my hands full of signs and Marylou's all over me, her mouth, hands, knees all working overtime, her tits rubbing up against my chest like a coupla those electric vibrators they use on football players' legs. It takes all the strength I can will into my arms, but I manage to push her off, clamping my mouth shut and damn near biting my tongue off in the process. "Whoa, girl, whoa. Hold on a minute, willya? Gimme a break, eh?"

Marylou is all cuddly and purring in my lap, like a kitten that's just spilled the milk all over the carpet. "I thought you wanted to play, Wally-lolly."

"Well, maybe I do, maybe I don't. I didn't say I didn't, but just cool off for a minute."

"I don't wanna cool off."

"Just for a minute, damn it, girl. I gotta know about, you know, about you and Jesus."

Marylou gives me a shot of that pout, then lowers her head. Her bare shoulders shiver, just a touch, like a cool breeze had blown in through the chinks in the cabin walls. She looks like a little girl, just like a child, I swear. "That don't have nothin' to do with us."

"Come on, Marylou, I gotta know." I make a motion as if to disengage her from my lap and stand up. "Otherwise, just forget about it, okay?"

394

"*Oh.*" She shrugs, those smooth brown shoulders movings like hard nippleless breasts alongside her face. "Jesus is, well . . . shit, I *love* Jesus, but I'm no goddamn nun. I mean, I'm a grown woman, I'm my own *person*, I got needs, too, you know."

I just stare at her for a minute, my eyes fixed on that trembling lower lip, plump and slick as a puppy's belly. I guess it's that word *nun* that got to me, not that I'm a Catholic or anything, or ever had anything you'd even *remotely* call religion—before I went to work for Jesus, that is. All the gags I ever wrote or heard about nuns flash through my mind, *the nun who gave up smoking because she wanted to quit the habit,* like strips of newsreel spliced together, *this nun and Father O'Malley and Gabriel's horn . . . blowing Gabriel's horn,* and all of a sudden I'm thinking about what they call them, Christ's wives, *Christ's virgin brides,* and I'm thinking about Jesus' eyes and I'm not feeling so hot. It's not the sacrilege, nothing like that, and not guilt, either. I guess I'm thinking about the way I felt when I found out about Rhoda, the used-to-be better half, and that sonuvabitch Danny Roy, who was supposed to be my friend, two or three lifetimes ago.

"Okay, honey, game's been called on accounta rain." I brush her off my lap like she was a cat and stand up quick, before I can change my mind.

"*Hey,*" Marylou squeals. "What's with you?"

"Listen, kid, don't take this personal, okay? I mean, you're a real sweetheart, there's nothing I'd like better, believe me. But I just remembered something I gotta do."

"Fer Chris'sake." She's stomping around the cabin, kicking at things with her bare feet, picking things up and banging them down. "*Fer Chris'sake.*" There's a whine in her voice that ain't exactly music to the ear, but I guess I know what she's feeling like, so I don't say anything more and just quietly fade away.

At the Pit, the same waitress who'd eyeballed me the day I met Jesus for the first time is on duty, but by now we're old pals and she trots off to fetch me a draught before I'm even to the patio door. She's a honey, all right, with nice brown hair that sort of bounces around when she walks and a body that's a lot like Marylou's, just a bit plumper, and I'm letting my tastebuds drown their sorrows in the first coupla swallows of cold beer and thinking about how nice it would be if we two could slip away for a while and make each other happy, when I suddenly feel Jesus' eyes on me, and sure enough, there he is, on that bench across the patio, under the branches of a spruce where a squirrel is chattering away, scolding us for invading his space.

"Jesus, I didn't see you there, man."

"Well, I just got here." He shrugs, his usual gesture. He's not big on explaining things, doing miracles, anything showy.

"Marylou, she said you were gonna be gone a few days."

"I was."

"Oh. Yeah." I take a swig of beer and scrunch up my eyes because the sun is right behind him and it's like looking into a flashlight. "I guess I was thinking it might be more like, you know, forty days or something like that."

Jesus smiles, his solemn smile. "No, Wally, I don't like reruns, you know that. All new this time. Besides, I've already had my temptation. I mean, I'm having it now, it's going on all the time."

"Yeah, I guess I knew that." Another swig of beer, my eyes shifting a little to the squirrel, which makes it easier to bear. "Well, how'd it go? I mean, get any good thinking done?"

At this, Jesus brightens. "Yes, Wally. I did some writing. Gags."

"Gags? No kidding. Let's hear some."

Jesus beams, throws back his head a little. "Okay, here goes. A man arrived late for church, and the minister noticed and remembered this same fellow had been coming in late like that every Sunday for months. So after service, he takes the man aside and asks him, 'Do you always sleep late?' And the man shrugs and says, 'Nope, only in the mornings.' See, it's about not always understanding the thing . . . "

I make myself laugh. "Hey, not bad. I guess I'm gonna be outta the picture soon."

Jesus frowns. "Come on, Wally. Hey, listen to this one. It's long, but I really like it. Maybe you can tell me how to make it shorter."

"Okay, shoot."

He screws up his face, concentrating. "Okay, here goes. There was this mountain climber, see, he was part of a group that went up Everest, oh, back in the early '60s. They didn't actually make it all the way to the top, but almost, and it was a good climb, no accidents, you know? And this man, his name was Peter? He had a marvellous time, it was sort of the highlight of his life up until then. And, as it turned out, later too. Anyway, they had this group of Sherpa guides on the trip, you know? And one of them, a Sherpa mountain climber called Ginsing, owned a restaurant in Katmandu where the climbers liked to go to eat, and the speciality there was this marvellous cherry pie that . . . "

I hold up my hand. "Hey, is this going to be a shaggy dog?"

Jesus looks offended. "*No*. It's more like a . . . a *parable*, I guess.

"Yeah, but is it funny?"

"Oh, sure, it's funny. Wait, you'll see."

"Okay, go ahead."

"Let's see, where was I? Oh, yeah, the cherry pie.

397

It was just marvellous, the best Peter had ever had, and years later in his memory, that pie sort of came to symbolize the whole trip, the climb up Everest, that best, shining part of his life."

"Uh huh." I drain my beer and look around for the waitress but there's just Jesus and me out here on the patio.

"Well, Peter went home, finished university, went to law school and joined a prestigious firm, got married, had a couple of kids, house in the suburbs, the whole thing. Success with a capital S. And it was a good life."

I raise my empty glass, holding it up between us so the light coming from behind Jesus' head diffuses, flying off in a thousand sharp splinters of brightness. "Let me guess—it all falls apart, right?"

Jesus gets that hurt look in his eyes again. "Well, yeah, a few years ago, things seem to start to go sour in his marriage and, well, one thing leads to another and his wife leaves him."

"And he got so depressed he quit his job?"

"Hey, who's telling this story, me or you?"

"You're right, I shouldn't be such a butt-insky, sorry. But just let me guess how this winds up, okay? Peter goes into a funk, right? And he starts thinking about the glories of his youth and he gets a taste to have a piece of that cherry pie again, am I right?" Jesus nods, his face blank, his eyes on me. "So he sells everything and heads for Katmandu, but when he gets there, they're out of cherry pie, so he . . . wait." I hold up my hand when Jesus leans forward, his mouth opening. "No, the café is closed, that's it. Ginsing is retired and he's gone back to his native village, which is at the base of Everest, so Peter treks out there, visions of cherry pie dancing in his head, and when he gets there"—I've got my eyes fixed on Jesus' face, reading it like a book now—"they tell him

398

Ginsing's gone up to the mountain to die, so he hires some Sherpas and sets out after him, right?" Jesus' face is crushed now, the hurt washing over him like a breeze, but I just go on, it don't matter a damn to me. "And there's all kinds of obstacles and hardships, but *finally* he comes on a tent, almost at the summit of the mountain, and inside, there's old Ginsing, good old faithful Ginsing, old and withered and wrinkled but with this big toothless grin on his pan, and he's baking pies, right?"

"*Damn*," Jesus says, "you've *heard* this. I thought I'd just made it up."

"Jesus, *please*," I tell him. "Gimme *some* credit, willya? No, I haven't heard it, I'm a *professional*, like I do this for a *living*? I know how these things go down, and this one, it's like it's made outta glass."

We glare at each other, the way Marylou and I had done just a little while earlier, and that tight knot that had been sticking in my gut is suddenly gone, melted to crumbs like a cookie in a saucer of tea. But a thought has spun into my head, just about the same size.

"So . . . so what happens?" Jesus asks quietly.

"Huh? Oh, so Ginsing's making pies, and Peter says, 'Lemme have some of that cherry, man,' his mouth all watering, and Ginsing says, 'so solly, pal, no chelly today,' and Peter shrugs and says, 'Okay, no sweat, make it apple.'"

"*No.*" Jesus brightens up, a triumphant look flashing into his eyes, which, if I haven't mentioned before, are blue as the sky on the prairies before a summer storm, and I can see the heat lightning in them now, all the way across the patio. "The way *I* thought, he wouldn't even *ask* for the cherry. He'd crawl into the tent, all hot and steamy like a kitchen in winter, with all these wonderful smells, and Ginsing would say, 'What'll it be?' and Peter would

399

think for a minute and then just ask for the apple."

We look at each other. "Not bad. That's a nice twist. I hadn't thought of that."

"See, it's a parable," Jesus says. "I mean . . . "

"That's okay, I get it. It's still a shaggy dog story, and it's too long, but that's a nice twist. I mean, the whole bit, it's not a bad bit. It's too long, and it's got some things that telegraph too much, and your timing is lousy—*timing*, Jesus, I keep telling you, timing is *everything*—but it's got possibilities. We can work on it. Yeah, I like it. We can do something with it."

Jesus smiles, the big beatific smile. "I knew I could count on you, Wally." He gets up and stretches. "You don't mind me calling you Wally, do you?"

"Why not? Everybody else does. *Shitforbrains* is just a tad too clumsy on the tongue, and it beats the hell out of Wilbur. You didn't go away today to do writing or thinking, did you? You wanted me and Marylou to be together, right?"

"Why would I do that, Wally?"

"I don't know. Maybe because *you* did the temptation bit last time around."

Jesus laughs and comes over to the table. He flops down in the chair across from me and stretches out his long legs, his scruffy workboots even muddier and more beat-up looking than usual. "Go easy on her," I say. "She's just a kid, know what I mean?"

"You're nuts, Wally," Jesus says. "Why should I go hard on anyone?" He looks at me, the blue of his eyes darkening half a shade, like maybe that summer storm was coming closer, one of those intense summer storms that drive away the swelter and leave everything cool, and smelling good. "You're nuts, but you're right about one thing. *You're* the gag-writer in this outfit. And I've got to work on my timing, you're right about that, too."

Out of the corner of my eye, I see the waitress pop

her head through the door and I wave her over. "Whaddya say I blow this week's stamp money and buy us a pitcher?"

"Sure," Jesus says, "and bring us some of those nuts, will you, please?"

When the girl brings the beer she gives me a smile that's open as a barn door after the horse gets stolen and I can feel the light in her eyes all the way down to my shoulders. Jesus is chattering away, about this and that, running through some of the gags we've come up with, but I just lean back and let the sun splash over me, let the cool beer trickle down through my throat into my innards like some sweet secret of life, let the happiness I'm feeling swell up inside me and radiate off my skin like heat. In my ear, I can hear Jesus' voice, a soft chattering murmur like the scolding of the squirrel in the spruce tree, but in my mind's eye I can see this cat walking along some street, a sort of Charlie Chaplin guy, baggy pants and a cane, floppy top hat, and here's this banana peel lying on the sidewalk, all yellow and slick and shiny and innocent as a rattlesnake, and you can feel the anticipation as the cat gets closer, the tightening in the throat, and here comes the foot, down and down and down, and it's sliding, the cat is going up in the air, but he isn't slamming down on the pavement, no, he's tumbling through the air, see, over and over past clouds plump as young girls' bums, white as the fleece on baby lambs, spreading his arms like wings, soaring through clear blue air, a smile on his yap as wide as the one on mine, not *falling*, really, but rising, *rising*, through a world where it's just as easy to be kind.

BARBARA MULCAHY

My Muse is Tired of Literature

My muse is tired of being invoked by men who dress her in long white robes. That's why she's in northern Alberta standing by my desk inspiring me. "Cotton—" she snorts. "Ouzo . . . I'm tired of scrubbing out stains."

I write deeply moving prose and my muse inspects my room and complains. She sweeps her hand over my shelves. "Is this all you have?" she demands.

"What kind of literature do you like?" I ask.

"Literature," she says. "Pooh."

I give my muse *Glamour, Mademoiselle,* and the Sears catalogue. She settles down on my bed, peruses shiny fabrics, glittery threads.

I write about humanity and now and then my muse says words aloud—just to hear their sounds. "Revlon Love That Red lipstick," she whispers. "Maybelline Illegal Lengths mascara."

I write with compassion while she flips the pages. When my work's complete, I read it to her. She shakes her head. "You have to put yourself into it," she says. "Like this—" She stands up and recites

The Winter Catalogue

Let me call up the man at Sears
and order me something—a corset
or black brassieres.

Let it be not-on-sale—money well-spent!
that he may know the purity
of my intent.

That though I have–so far–lived by my fears
I now do repent
my careful years.

So let it be lace: easily rent
—because yes!
Life should be spent.

She looks at me knowingly. "Write it down," she
says. "It's good—it comes from the heart."

I shake my head. "Christ," I say.

"It's uneven—it needs a little work," she agrees.
"But it's a start."

"It's not that," I say. "It's just not . . . not what I
had in mind."

"Not what you had in mind?" my muse says.

She lies back down on the bed and opens another
magazine.

"The mind," she says, "is not a good place to
begin."

Acknowledgements

Some pieces in **200% Cracked Wheat** have been previously published or broadcast. **Section I:** "Move Over Lassie" in *The Grande Cache Mountaineer*, July 3, 1990; "A Sliver of Liver" and "How to Tell What You're Eating" in *Jumbo Gumbo* (Coteau Books, 1989); "Mr. Kroski" in *Street of Dreams* (Coteau Books, 1984); "Allowances" in *Places Far From Ellesmere* (Red Deer College Press, 1990); "Unsuitable Suits" in *Yuletide Blues* (Thistledown Press, 1991); "Tricks" in *Yarrow* (Oberon Press, 1980); "Cavitation" in *Grain*, Vol.2, No.2. **Section II:** "Getting Pregnant" in *Inventing the Hawk* (McClelland and Stewart, 1992); "*Heista Kopp* in Love" in *The Salvation of Yasch Siemens* (Turnstone, 1984) and *Liars and Rascals* (University of Waterloo Press, 1989); "Down the Iceroad" in *The Great Northern Limerick Book II* (CBC Mackenzie); "Janvier Makes a Picnic" in *Out of Place* (Coteau Books, 1991); "The First Time" in *The New Quarterly*, Vol. VIII, No. 4; "Call Me" in *The Bridge City Anthology* (Fifth House, 1991); "Man of My Dreams" in *The Malahat Review*, Fall, 1988 and on the compact disc *Brenda Baker*, 1989; "Go Like Sixty" in *After Sixty: Going Home* (Thistledown Press, 1991). **Section III:** "Sex in a Pan" on the cassette *Roberta Nichol*; "News Flash from the Fashion Magazines" in *Grain* and in *Inventing the Hawk* (McClelland and Stewart, 1992); "Turning Forty" on the cassette *Roberta Nichol*; "Bill's Sperm Count" in *Working without a Laugh Track* (Coteau Books, 1990); "Crucial Quiz" on "Afternoon Edition," CBC Radio, June, 1991. **Section IV:** "A City Woman's Guide to the Country Man's Farm" in *Grainews*, April 10, 1989; "Knowing the Game," "Old Jack," and "The Mask" in *Mister Baseball* (The Blue Piano, 1991); "Mother and the Bull" in *Folklore* (Saskatchewan History and Folklore Society, 1990); "In the Beer-Parlour" in *Yarrow* (Oberon Press, 1980); "The Winter of '49" on "Alberta Anthology," CBC Radio, January 21, 1990 and in *Grainews*, January, 1992. **Section VI:** "Cruising" in *The Great Northern Limerick Book II* (CBC Mackenzie); "Standing By" in *The New Quarterly*, Winter/Spring, 1991; "Sunday noon At De Keulse Pot" in *Insight: Canadian Writers View Holland* (Netherlandic Press, 1988) and *Air Canada Owls* (Harbour Publishing, 1990); "the well-equipped carman," "I'm sure the C.P.R. invented spring," and "the interpreter" in *The Secret Life of Railroaders* (Coteau Books, 1982); "Wailing" in *The Great Northern Limerick Book II* (CBC Mackenzie); "Going to Cuba" in *Going to Cuba* (Fifth House, 1990); "visits" in *Rampike*, Vol. 3, No. 3 and *blind zone* (Aya Press, 1985). **Section VII:** "The Rabbit" excerpt from the play *Sins of St. Genesius*; "There Ain't Nobody Here But Us Chickens" in *Way Out West!* (Fifth House, 1989); "Gulls" in *The Blue Machines of Night* (Coteau Books, 1988); "The Land of the Lizards" in *The Eclectic Muse*, Vol. 2, No. 2; "The Prince and the Pelicans" in *Saturday Night*, September, 1987; "The Politics of Moose" in *Another Lost Whole Moose Catalogue*, 1991; "Norris" in *The Bridge Out of Town* (Oberon Press, 1986); "Why Is It That We Do Not See Tyrannosaurus Rex Around Any More?" in MC^2, March, 1992. **Section VIII:** "On the Seventh Day" in *Inventing the Hawk* (McClelland and Stewart, 1992); "A Cotton Flannelette Man" in *South Hill Girls* (Fifth House, 1992); "Another Life to Live at the Edge of the Young and Restless Days of Our Lives" in *Creating the Country* (Thistledown Press, 1989); "Incident in Thunder Bay" in *Air Canada Owls* (Harbour Publishing, 1990); "After Twenty-Five Years, Still Working It Out" in *Snapshots: The New Canadian Fiction* (Black Moss Press, 1992); "His Bowels" in *Grain*, Fall, 1991. **Section IX:** "the meaning of my time with you" in *Life in Glass* (Longspoon Press, 1984); "Gator" in *Harvest*, December, 1990; "Sweetie Pie" in *Sky High* (Coteau Books, 1988); "City in Pain" on "Sunday Morning," CBC Radio, July, 1988; "Star Bright" in *Best Kept Secrets* (Coteau Books, 1988). **Section X:** "My Muse is a Tramp" in *Grain*, Vol. 19, No. 2; "Writing Romances" in *The Saskatoon Sun*, July 14, 1991; "How I Became a Poet" in *Grain*, August, 1988 and *Sky High* (Coteau Books, 1988); "Gag!" in *Matrix*, Fall, 1988, *89: Best Canadian Stories* (Oberon Press, 1989) and *Nine Lives* (Thistledown Press, 1991). Credit for two section titles: Lorine Sweeney.

What reviewers have said about the predecessor of *200% Cracked Wheat—100% Cracked Wheat*:

Alberta Report:
"*100% Cracked Wheat* may be the best thing to come out of Saskatchewan since Gordie Howe."

Quill & Quire:
"*100% Cracked Wheat* is a wonderful book for your cottage, your bedside table, or for any doleful moment requiring a dollop of prairie humour. It contains an astonishing assortment of humorous prose and verse from Saskatchewan, packaged in a bright yellow paperback that purports, with corny exuberance, to be a new breakfast cereal: 'a jest to you each morning!!'. . . . The short stories range from broad farce to understated comedy . . . . The limericks that spice up the pages are particularly delightful—the editors have found a few that would make John Robert Colombo's palms itch."

Canadian Book Review Annual:
"No book reviewer can do this anthology of humour justice. All that the editors claim, that is 'the writers in *100% Cracked Wheat* are witty, pungent, ironic, satiric, droll, whimsical, jocose, farcical, waggish, and hilarious—sometimes at one and the same time' is true. They are also funny, irreverent, periodically a trifle bawdy, and occasionally, philosophical.

Canadian Materials:
"No matter what your taste in humour, you are likely to find something funny in this collection of stories and poems by Saskatchewan authors."